W9-BQT-033

Breaking Silence

Pastoral Approaches for Creating an Ethos of Peace

Rev. Chad R. Abbott and Rev. Everett Mitchell
Editors

Pilgrims Process, Inc.
Longmont, CO

Breaking Silence:
Pastoral Approaches for Creating an Ethos of Peace

Rev. Chad R. Abbott and Rev. Everett Mitchell, editors

Content © 2004 by Rev. Chad R. Abbott and Rev. Everett Mitchell
Book Design © 2004 by Pilgrims Process, Inc.
ISBN: 0-9749597-1-5
Library of Congress Control Number:
2004109385

Printed in the United States of America

0 9 8 7 6 5 4 3 2 1

Dedication

This book is offered in the honor of:

Rev. Dr. Martin Luther King Jr., a man who did not remain silent in the face of war and injustice.

Our cinematic hero and inspiration,
Michael Moore.

All the innocent men, women, and children who have died at the hands of war while the church has remained silent. Forgive us, O God, for we know not what we do in times of war.

"True peace is not merely the absence of tension: it is the presence of justice." —Martin Luther King Jr.

Contents

Acknowledgements

We would like to acknowledge those who have influenced us most on this journey toward breaking our silence. We are profoundly appreciative of Gary White, our publisher at Pilgrims Process, Inc. for seeing and assisting in the realization of our vision of justice and peace. Thank you, Cheryl Byers, for translating our chapter on Passing the Peace by Luis Rivera-Pagán. In addition, we are grateful for all the contributors of this text who have added their voices to this crucial discussion, ensuring that the silence within the church regarding the issue of war is forever broken. We would like to thank those professors at Princeton Theological Seminary who pushed us to live out our theological convictions amid a world of social inequalities and injustices. We therefore thank Dr. Mark L. Taylor, Dr. Peter J. Paris, Dr. Luis N. Rivera-Pagán, and Dr. Brian K. Blount for integrating the realm of politics with the realm of theological discourse. We are honored to present this text in the spirit of your teaching.

Rev. Chad R. Abbott would like to thank my family, Marty, Marilyn, Eric, and Megan Abbott; Joe and Beck Norman; Amy, Bill and Justus Morgan; and all of my extended family for your love and support of my ministry. I am thankful to the Greenville College religion department, Rick McPeak, Brian Hartley, Craig Boyd, and Ruth Huston for all of your encouragement and wisdom. I am also indebted to my hero, friend, and spiritual mentor, Rev. Dr. Jim Reinhard. Thank you to my closest friends who have always believed in me: Ryan Estevan Taylor-Byers, Alicia Taylor-Byers, Dearthrice Dewitt, Jonathan Walton, Erica Smith, Tim Kennedy, Arlene Grace, Matt Nygren, Merrin Mitchell, Litsa Binder and the Northwest New Jersey Peace Fellowship, and Christy Hentz. Thank you to my Greater New Jersey Annual Conference colleagues, Sydney Sadio, Nancy Belsky, Galen Goodwin, Frederick Boyle, Neal Christie, Jack Copas, and the Conference Board of Church and Society. Thank you, Everett Mitchell, for your friendship and strength through making this book a reality and for your continual passion for the poor and oppressed. Most of all, I thank my wife, Shannon Abbott, whose passion for the oppressed, especially the gay community, never ceases to amaze me. Thank you, Shannon, for also assuring me that I would publish a book before I die.

Rev. Everett Mitchell would like to thank my family, my mother Mary Mitchell, Shuntol Mitchell, and Artrai Tatum, as well as my father, Joseph Mason, for their continued support and love as I have ventured out of the nest in order to fulfill God's call upon my life. In addition, I would like to thank all the people who believed in me when I could not believe in myself: Aunt Adrius, Aunt Honey, The Mitchell and McGinty family, Margraet Bell, Zora Gaut, Monica and Dante Quick, Ms. Blue, Little Mama, Mae Boyd, Mrs. Webb, Pastor James Forbes, the First Saint John Church family, and the Zion Hill Church family. Personally, I am grateful for Dr. Aaron L. Parker for his wisdom and challenge for me to remain prophetic regardless of the consequences. I am also appreciative of Overseer K.B. Spears, who demonstrates that God's power extends beyond the church and that it is the Christian's job to seek out and adhere to God's activity in the world. I am indebted to activist Darlene McKnight from Trenton, NJ, who taught me that peace activism is more than words on a page: it is a way of being at peace in the world. I would like to thank Chad and Shannon Abbott for their continual passion for bringing a voice to communities that are forced to the margins within America. Last but never least, I cannot find the perfect words to thank my wife, Merrin Mitchell, for her continual support because she is not only my wife, but also my closest and dearest friend.

A Note from the Editors

This is a book about politics and theology, war and peace, the Church and the ethos in which it lives. Whether it is praying for troops, religious education, or preaching on a weekly basis amid the flurry of images we see daily in the media, pastors are faced with an enormous challenge as leaders of congregations. When the war in Iraq was imminent, many clergy began looking for resources to help them receive a framework for discussion in their churches. If one were to look at the variety of reading material one would find a great deal of individual sermons or small pamphlets on matters of war. But, there simply were no comprehensive books available for congregations and their pastors to engage these issues at the grassroots level. This is how our project on creating an ethos of peace began.

The aim of this book is not to provide absolutes or sure solutions to abolishing war. Our aim is to begin a conversation in local churches. In order to start this conversation, we invited a panel of scholars, pastors, laypeople, and activists to write on war and the Church. The majority of people writing in this volume live, work, and write from the location of the United States. We recognize that such a social location is limiting when it comes to describing war. What war looks like from a United States' perspective may not be what it looks like in the Congo or in Russia. Indeed, there are very similar threads of war that run across all cultures, but without question, living in the only remaining empire in modern history, there is much to engage at the level of a local congregation in the United States. While we believe that world peace is something that is multi-lateral and involves nations and various peoples working together in nonviolence, we are engaging the issue of war for and with United States' religious congregations.

We seek to address matters relevant and present in the local parish, from preaching and scripture to prayer, peace activism, and refugees. Thus, this book can serve as a resource tool and study guide in local congregations. To engage local congregations, we have created a body of questions for discussion that can be found in the appendix. It is our aim that the Church will take seriously these questions, these chapters, and the possibility of creating a world without war.

Rev. Chad R. Abbott and Rev. Everett Mitchell

June 2004

Preface

The Deafening Silence in the Churches
Rev. Robert Moore

As this preface is written (mid-May 2004), the U.S. occupation of Iraq is in a severe downward spiral. More U.S. troops died last month (nearly 200) than any month since the invasion of Iraq in March 2003. There are daily battles in cities that are slipping from the control of U.S. forces. Mistreatment and abuse of prisoners held in U.S. custody have been exposed to the world by photos of Iraqis being sexually and otherwise degraded. Shiite Muslims, the majority of Muslims in Iraq—who had until recently been supportive of the U.S. intervention to oust Sadaam Hussein—are now profoundly alienated from the U.S. and are joining the insurgency.

Yet despite this extreme degradation of the U.S. occupation, bordering on depravity, the voice of the Church is strangely silent. Atheists and agnostics, their humanist conscience being deeply troubled, are asking me, "Why aren't the churches speaking out on this? Isn't this a moral issue of the highest order?" And I must agree with their criticism.

Prior to the invasion of Iraq on March 19, 2003, the situation was somewhat different. In the months leading up to the war, most national religious leaders spoke out and issued statements opposing the option of war. The leaders of virtually every Christian denomination, except Southern Baptists, took an official and public position against war. Some did this on the basis of the long nonviolent Christian tradition going back to Jesus himself. Others did it on the basis that this unilateral preemptive strike didn't meet the criteria for a just war.

But even then, my experience was that there was a deafening silence in the local congregations. At the two small churches I serve as part-time pastor, I brought the issue into many sermons and worship services. But I didn't hear of many other congregations where the issue was raised from the pulpits or in the pews. My sense was that most of the clergy and lay congregational leaders were "playing it safe." They didn't want to rock the boat or generate controversy.

A Presbyterian congregation in central New Jersey gave me one of the few invitations I got at that time to speak at a local congregation. They invited me in frustration because their pastor refused to speak out from the pulpit on the issue. His rationale for refusing was that the sermon was a "monologue." I wondered what Jesus would have refused to preach based on this limitation. We ended up having a great discussion at their adult class—with a number of honest questions and concerns that were respectfully heard and answered—without any divisiveness resulting.

I've been organizing full-time for peace long enough (26 years as of this writing), that I know things need not be this way. I was one of the early co-initiators of the Nuclear Weapons Freeze Campaign in 1979. From the beginning, that Campaign had strong participation from churches—both denominational staff at the national level, and, more importantly, numerous clergy who preached, taught, and interacted with their lay people at the congregational, grass-roots level on this great issue of the time: stopping the nuclear arms race. Excellent educational materials were disseminated widely, many of them biblically based. Courses were taught at seminaries and in local congregations. Forums were held at church gatherings. The church's response to Iraq now is in sharp contrast to that strong involvement.

More importantly, by failing to speak and act for peace in the current context, I fear the Church is losing its soul and its sense of faithfulness to the Gospel of Jesus Christ, the Prince of Peace. How can we proclaim the vision of the Kingdom of God, a kingdom of peace and justice—in Hebrew *shalom*, best translated as "wholeness"—and remain silent in the face of such immoral and violent policies? How can we remain silent as thousands die and a country's future is decimated?

I am certainly not suggesting there aren't gray areas, sometimes very difficult to sort out morally and theologically. But the invasion and occupation of Iraq presents a stark choice between right and wrong, between peace and war, between truth and deception. And the Church is basically a sleeping giant, a potentially huge force for peace that instead sits on its hands at this critical juncture of history. Some might excuse this by bureaucratic needs to fund the structures of the Church, to maintain unity and not create division. But we need to remember that Jesus didn't hesitate to confront the religious establishment of his time, to create controversy, to speak truth to power. He didn't worry if it would hurt his fundraising. As a result he was silenced in the way the establishment thought would work—by crucifixion. But God validated and exalted his ministry and courageous witness with the Resurrection!

It is time for the Church to find its voice—its voice for peace and justice. It is time to stop playing it safe, and instead to be faithful—and I might add, relevant. This book is a tool intended to present a vision for doing that and to offer some practical tools for moving forward on that great challenge at the level where we experience Christian community most closely and regularly: in our local congregations.

May 20, 2004

Welcome

"A War-Like People"

The Ethos of War in Pastoral Context

Rev. Chad R. Abbott

On April 4, 1967, exactly one year prior to his assassination, the Rev. Dr. Martin Luther King Jr. spoke out against the war in Vietnam at a gathering of concerned clergy and laity at Riverside Church in New York City. His speech for the day was titled "A Time to Break Silence," in which he spoke of the connections between the unjustifiable war in Vietnam and its profound impact on the issues of civil rights in the United States. King suggested that what was at work in America was a great sickness and if we did not seriously deal with this reality, this sickness, that we would, indeed, pass on our sins to the next generations. In this famous speech he prophetically spoke:

The war in Vietnam is but a symptom of a far deeper sickness within the American spirit, and if we ignore this sobering reality we will find ourselves organizing clergy and laymen-concerned committees for the next generation. They will be concerned about Guatemala and Peru. They will be concerned about Thailand and Cambodia. They will be concerned about Mozambique and South Africa. We will be marching for these and a dozen other names and attending rallies without end unless there is a significant and profound change in American life and policy. Such thoughts take us beyond Vietnam, but not beyond our calling as sons [daughters] of the living God.[1]

The sickness of the American spirit has, without question, continued to the next generation. Little did King know that in the decades to follow that the U.S. would invade the many countries and murder the millions that we have. Little did he know that thirty years after he delivered his speech at Riverside Church, a conservative think tank consisting of the likes of Donald Rumsfeld, Paul Wolfowitz, Jeb Bush, and Dick Cheney would be devising a construct for U.S. global dominance and leadership with the aim of stifling any rival superpower in the world. In June of 1997 the components of this think tank, making up what is known as "The Project of The New American Century," created a document of its core principles stating its aim to "make the case and rally support for American global leadership." It went on to state,

> If we shirk our responsibilities, we invite challenges to our fundamental interests. The history of the twentieth century should have taught us that it is important to shape circumstances before crises emerge, and to meet threats before they become dire. The history of this century should have taught us to embrace the cause of American leadership . . . We need to accept responsibility for America's unique role in preserving and extending an international order friendly to our security, our prosperity, and our principles.[2]

So here we stand at the beginning of a new century, a generation after King and the Civil Rights movement, and we are concerned over Iraq and Afghanistan, Israel and Palestine, Iran and North Korea, Cuba and Colombia. In short, we live and breathe the sick reality of war, whether it is in our politics, in the media, in our schools, or in our churches. In the words of writer Chris Hedges, "War Is a Force That Gives Us Meaning."[3] But war in fact goes even deeper than merely giving a sense of meaning or purpose. It seeps into our most destructive human desire—the thirst for ultimate power.

In a "black-coffee" briefing on the Iraq war on March 25, 2003, Michael Ledeen, a scholar from the conservative American Enterprise Institute for Public Policy Research spoke of our thirst for war. When confronted with the issue of the legitimacy of war in light of human casualties he remarked, "I think the level of casualties is secondary. I mean, it may sound like an odd thing to say, but all the great scholars who have studied American character have come to the conclusion that we are a warlike people and that we love war. . . . What we hate is not casualties but losing."[4] We have, indeed, ignored the sobering reality of our sickness that King so aptly pointed out to us a generation ago and, in turn, we have continued to create an ethos of war, or what historian Charles A. Beard and essayist Gore Vidal have called a "perpetual war for perpetual peace."[5]

Pastors and their congregations have all too often ignored the social, political, and theological complexities present in the ethos of war. Many of us in the United States are still confused about how to lead congregations in discussions around matters of war, especially when there are those in the congregation who have daughters, sons, or relatives overseas. We do not want the waves of controversy to begin crashing. We are also confused, or scared, because many of us do not understand the systemic and powerful influence of political structures that drive us to war. Of course, we are assuming here that churches even discuss the issue of war at all.

We, as the Church, remain apathetic in our silence in that we do not possess, or even care to possess, the proper tools or language to fully understand how or why war, and its consequences, may or may not be an adequate means to an end. How do we pray without being militaristic or believing that somehow God is *only* on the side of the United States? How do we do pastoral care with those who have sons or daughters in wars? How do we preach and teach? What do we say to our youth? How do we disagree gracefully? How do we stand up for justice? These are all complex social, political, and theological questions that, when it comes down to it, we are not adequately equipped to answer.

The aim of this book is to help pastors and their congregations come to grips with the complexities evident within the ethos of war. Ultimately, we will argue, like King, that the drive to war is in part symptomatic of a larger systemic problem of power and control within our culture, one that the Church must respond to in her liturgical and communal life. In this introduction, I will begin by outlining our theological foundation and assumptions for approaching the issue of war from a pastoral perspective. Having our theological foundation in place, I will define the theological and practical task of pastoral ministry in the Church and in engaging the political world. In engaging the political, we must take up the task of responding to matters of war. I will, then, depict the ethos of war in its systemic nature of control by drawing on its *power, ideology,* and *tools.* With these pieces in place, it will be the task of the remainder of this book to address how the Church can break her silence and find her voice while so many die at the hands of war.

Theological Foundations

The foundational theological centerpiece of this book is the belief that the truth of God, or truth in general, is found in community. While it is certainly possible for individuals to comprehend or ascertain truth on their own, it is our belief that whatever truth individuals gleam in solitude has its origins in human community. A community consists of human exchange and interaction, a place where ideas and questions are explored and debated openly. Community is the drawing together of human experience to reflect upon the world and to seek answers to life's most complex questions. It is the coming together of minds so that we can learn what it means for us to live together as different people but in the same polis. A community consists of a relationship, such as two or more. Community can most aptly be seen as a nation, a racial or ethnic group, a church, school, workplace, family, friends, the environment, or even the world.

In the Church, we are concerned with two kinds of relationships, vertical and horizontal. The vertical relationship of community is our connection with God. The interaction we have both individually and communally with God is crucial to our existence and our way of see-ing, believing, and living in the world. The horizontal relationship of community is our connection to God's creation, most specifically how human beings live in relationship with one another. No Christian can ever be Christian in isolation from community. This has been the case from the very beginning. The story of creation in Genesis begins with God creating community. God created the heavens and the earth, sun and moon, light and dark, human beings and animals, all of which are interdependent upon each other. Community implies interdependen-cy. Thus, to be Christian means to live and find our source of mean-ing, structure, and purpose by living together in community with one another, God, and God's creation.

In the field of Christian theology, theologians such as Karl Barth, Paul Tillich, James Cone, John Wesley, and others have claimed this give and flow of community between vertical and horizontal to be a dialectical theological orientation, an orientation that combines the theological and the political. The Wesleyan tradition even suggests that human experience plays a role in how we interpret the scriptures, how we interpret the world, and how we interpret our political communi-ties. The use of human experience in the life of theology is not only crucial in the Wesleyan tradition, but it has been pronounced even stronger in the current liberation theologies throughout the world. The theme of liberation constitutes the locus of salvation in the liberation of human communities, which is imbedded in how God and humanity interact in the face of injustice. It is in bringing the social, political, and spiritual experiences of all human beings to the table of community that we find a window into truth. When we exclude others from the table, the fullness of truth is not present. Truth is dominated, then, by the experiences and interests of a few, rather than the common good of all. Truth is found in community and community is accounting for the humanity of all and struggling in the give and flow of debate, and love and compassion and empathy for the lives of others.

War, therefore, is a break in community. It is the creation of a dualistic world that places people, both individuals and groups, into the category of enemy or the demonized "other." Indeed, there are cir-cumstances when participation in war comes at a time when evil dic-tatorships rule over a people in need of liberation, and military force may or may not be the appropriate way to bring about liberation. But even if this is the case, such conflict still exists as a result of the dualistic creation of a demonized "other." The world God created is one of interdependency upon creation. The machinery of war disrupts this interdependency. It destroys life, and its aim is to force upon the "other" a set of circumstances that control and manipulate. Community does not exist where fear, control, and manipulation rule the day. Community exists where love, mutual freedom, and equality exist. Community exists when we see one another as friend and not enemy. The community of God is one that holds together mercy and justice.

The aim of this book is to address the need for the Church to confront how war is a break in community. Regarding the most recent war in Iraq and the so-called global war on terrorism, the Church has been silent. The U.S. government sent us to war in Iraq based upon deception. There are no weapons of mass destruction, no connections between Sadaam Hussein and Osama Bin Laden, and with the U.N. Security Council and the whole world watching its every move, Iraq was and remains no threat to the security of the United States. Yet the United States has lost nearly 1000 troops in just over a year, and over 10,000 Iraqi citizens have been killed. We continue to see growing violence and insurgencies all over Iraq, while Halliburton continues its business unmoved by the contradiction of its presence in a so-called "free" Iraq. This war is unconscionable, and statements of opposition from denominational leadership or from a few courageous pastors will not suffice. The Church must break her silence.

The most amazing power present within the Church is that it is local; it is at the grassroots level. We have the potential to mobilize millions of people towards the cause of peace and justice. This brings us back to community. Resistance to war and empire begin and end in community. It is in the meeting of the minds, the give and flow of relationships that consider all people's social, political, and spiritual existence to be of sacred worth, that we will find truth. But our churches are not talking about war and not struggling with Jesus' moral imperative to love our enemies while others seeks revenge. How can the Church speak "truth" to power if we do not have a voice? In order for us to find that voice we must first engage in defining the task of pastoral ministry and the role of local congregations.

Describing the Pastoral Context

What does a pastor do? Indeed, there is much debate over what exactly qualifies as "pastoral." Much of the debate is mundane and irrelevant. However, it is crucial for us to seek to define the pastoral role here for the sake of those whose lives are damaged and impacted by the effects of war. The *American Heritage Dictionary of the English Language* defines the word "pastor" as "a Christian minister or priest having spiritual charge over a congregation or other group."[6] The word pastor has its roots in the word "pasture." It is not surprising, then, that many have referred to pastors has "shepherds" of a flock. In the case of a shepherd it is evident that it is her or his responsibility "to tend" to the sheep and their surroundings. Do they have enough food? Are they safe? What are the potential dangers of the environment? In order to be a good shepherd, a person would need "to tend" to the entire context of the herd.

Pastoral ministry is no different. Pastors must "tend" to the entire context of those under their care. While this may seem like an outsider looking in, pastors, however, remain a part of the communities they serve. William Willimon writes in his book *Pastor* that, "The ordained ministry is a species of a broader genus called *Christian*. The pastoral ministry is always a function of what needs to happen in the church in order for the church to be faithful to its vocation."[7] A pastor is one who aids the Church in the living out of its mission and life. In this sense, pastors are "servants of the servants of God."[8] But serving God's people implies action. What, then, are the actions pastors must "tend" to in the life of the Church?

Perhaps it is most fitting to begin with the most obvious pastoral activities. The three main areas in the life of pastors are worship and preaching, pastoral care, and administration. Pastors are those who preach, teach, and lead worship. They are responsible for interpreting the scriptures in ways that are relevant to the congregation and current events, and yet are faithful to the texts themselves. After interpreting the community and the texts, pastors speak in public about those texts in worship, in study, and in small groups. What is more, the worship context must be as such that it challenges the hearts and lives of those attending. Pastors also engage in pastoral care. This is the creation of a safe space for congregants to come and share their lives, feelings, struggles, and dreams with the pastor. It is a setting of confidentiality and boundaries that allows the congregants to feel safe in sharing their minds. It is often a place of counseling and a place of healing. Finally, pastors share in the duties of administration. This involves giving time and energy to the committee and polity structure of the church. It is in this environment that matters of finances, buildings, and the organization of the church are addressed.

Pastor and professor Eugene Peterson makes the pastoral role even more specific than the above categories in his book *The Contemplative Pastor*. In this book he suggests that the name "pastor" is in need of redefinition because of the different ways people have come to understand and distort the term. "Pastor," he suggests, is a noun and therefore sterile of meaning. In order to recover a more vibrant definition of pastor he suggests adding three different adjectives to the noun: *unbusy, subversive, and apocalyptic*.[9]

The *unbusy* pastor, Peterson suggests, is one who is not all consumed by the calendar book. He calls the "busy" pastor one who betrays the flock and does not care for her or his own well being, let alone those in the congregation. Time is sacred and it is the *unbusy* pastor who is most effective because she or he balances time appropriately. The *subversive* pastor, according to Peterson, is one whose ministry points to a greater Kingdom among us. The "real world" we live in is one that is being replaced by the work of God through the Spirit. Thus, the language and work of the *subversive* pastor points to that greater reality in a roundabout way and without full disclosure. Peterson remarks, "Words are the real work of the world—prayer words with God, parable words with men and women. The behind-the-scenes work of creativity by word and sacrament, by parable and prayer, subverts the seduced world."[10] Finally, the *apocalyptic* pastor is one who points to an impending reality. Peterson reminds us that the word "apocalyptic" is a word of danger and elusiveness, while the word "pastor" is comforting and familiar. Indeed, it seems a bit strange to combine the two, but he suggests that a world that has gone mad and out of control, such as the United States, is exactly in need of pastors who speak to that reality. Apocalyptic points to a revelation, a vision, a reality of the current world and the pastor is called upon to give voice and vision to these realities, no matter how harsh.

There are many adjectives we could combine with the word pastor. The three chosen by Peterson certainly raise some very challenging ways for us to engage the Church as pastor. However, in light of our theological foundation and the fact that this book is directed toward issues of war, it is fitting to add one more adjective to Peterson's assessment of a *contemplative* pastor. As Peterson lays out these very helpful definitions of a pastor, his text begs the question of the *prophetic* pastor.

It is clear from Peterson that the apocalyptic pastor is one who examines the cultural context of her or his congregation. An apocalyptic vision is one that sees a culture for what it is and names it as such. A pastor is called to speak and preach to her or his congregation on matters of culture and society that may come into conflict with the vision of God. However, Peterson's notion of apocalypticism does not assume that we are called to acts of justice as pastors. Prophets are not merely people who speak to the reality of injustice in the world and name it for what it is. The prophet is one who names the reality of injustice and calls the people of God to acts of justice. The prophet calls for a new world, a new way of living, a new way of acting. The prophet demands action of the people. The *prophetic* pastor certainly draws upon apocalypticism, but she or he takes it to the level of action.

Pastors may envelope many things, but the key phrase in our definition of pastoral ministry is that a pastor is one who "tends." A pastor tends to the contextualities of the community she or he is serving. This means that the pastor must engage the realities of the culture, its values, its inequalities, its ways of controlling those they serve. The pastor must engage the life circumstances of congregants. She or he must care for their entire beings, including death, illness, marriage, divorce, depression, love, failure, success, disease, tragedy, and mission. Pastors must preach with each of these things in mind, but never without the full context of the congregation in mind. If pastors tend to all of these things in the lives of congregants and fail to tend to matters of social justice and inequality, then they have failed to tend to the entire context of those they serve. There is no church that has ever existed that was not somehow imbedded in the cultural ethos of its context. Therefore, a pastor is one who tends to the spiritual and political, the communal and the individual, life and death, liberation and salvation, for in so doing she or he embraces the fullness of those whom they serve.

Since we have established that pastors must tend to the full context or ethos of congregations, we now turn to that ethos, one that is filled with war.

Defining the Ethos of War

The author of Ecclesiastes writes, "There is nothing new under the sun"(Ecclesiastes 1:9). Accordingly, war has always existed and yet it always seems to find new ways of remaking itself. It is ancient and yet new. The only difference between the old and new is the tools used to enact war. Instead of stones, fists, or knives, we use biological warfare, nuclear bombs, or combat machine guns. Otherwise, the idea of war is nothing new. The *American Heritage Dictionary of the English Language* defines war as, "A state of open, armed, often prolonged conflict carried on between nations, states, or parties."[11] The root of the word "war" stems from the French word *werre* or the German word *Werra*, both of which are defined as "confusion" or "conflict." To call it conflict, in our current day of weaponry and nuclear threat, would be putting it mildly. While it is impossible in this current volume to describe all that war entails, we will draw upon three major foci entailing a working definition of war: *power, ideology,* and *tools*.

Power is the competitive force that dominates a nation or group and its cultural system for the sake of controlling the circumstances of conflict or politics as they manifest themselves in a given society. *Ideology* is the system of communication and control of opinion by which those in power manipulate the people to their wishes. Ideology is also the central intellectual argumentation for a nation's foreign policy agenda. Finally, *tools* are the machinery a nation or group uses in times of war to combat or destroy the so-called "enemy." In the end, war is an ethos, a culture of fear propagated by those in power for the sake of their own interests. It is a sickness that values greed, control, power, and aggression towards others over mercy, compassion, justice, or love. It is a sickness that threatens our very survival.

Power

Power involves leadership. Leadership in a democracy involves those in governmental leadership and those at the grassroots level, the people. The concept of power is a double-edged sword in an ethos of war. The power of the people and their general opinion of the state of affairs in the world have enormous influence on how policy is enacted at the level of government. However, power can also be manipulated to control the people vis-à-vis persuasion or propaganda by the government. How we live out the dynamics of power in community ultimately dictates what decisions are made on matters of war. The history of the United States has been consistently characterized by a power system of white, heterosexual, middle to upper class, male leadership and domination. This system of power is a controlling force, and although we have become much more diverse in our politics in the U.S., it is clear that this kind of leadership uniquely shapes our discourse regarding war.

Essayist Ralph Bourne argues that power is a controlling double-edged sword in his most famous statement, "War is the health of the state."[12] Bourne suggests there is a distinct difference between the concept of a people as a "country or nation" and "The State." A people as a "country" is a place where we share in mutual advancement, admiration of diversity, and the embracing of our living together. A "country" is the joining together in a noncompetitive interaction between cultural experiences to create and embrace a common narrative of peace. Bourne accounts for this embrace of peace as "our own people merely living on the earth's surface along with other groups, pleasant or objectionable as they may be, but fundamentally as sharing the earth with them." Bourne continues, "Country is a concept of peace, of tolerance, of living and let live."[13] Theologically, a country, then, is one part of God's whole body (the world) working with other parts of the body so that the body maintains its health. When we function as a country we take into consideration peace and love, interdependency, and the courage to live together in spite of our differences.

The virtues of country are admirable and even ideal, but they are not realistic when a people act as "The State." Bourne suggests that when we function as The State, the ideals of country are disregarded for the sake of political gain over another. He writes that the "State is essentially a concept of power, of competition: it signifies a group in its aggressive aspects."[14] While the people as a country are essentially non-competitive, the essential nature of a people living under the control of The State are by definition competitive. The State is the gathering of a political few to assume responsibility for grounding a people in social control. Bourne writes, "The State is the country acting as a political unit, it is the group acting as a repository of force, determiner of law, arbiter of justice."[15] Thus, he suggests, that war takes place when a country acts as The State and seeks aggression against another State. War derives its origins from the elite people in power and comes as a shock to the people because the rest of the people are often never consulted.

The shock of war on behalf of the people provides the government, which supposedly acts on behalf of the people, with the power to act in times of war. Bourne powerfully remarks that The State comes into its own when war is enacted. He proclaims, "The Government, with no mandate from the people, without consultation of the people, conducts all the negotiations, the backing and filling, the menaces and explanations, which slowly bring it into collision with some other Government, and gently and irresistibly slides the country into war."[16] Power, in an ethos of war, is therefore a competitive force that dominates a nation or group and its cultural system for the sake of controlling the circumstances of conflict or politics as they manifest themselves in a given society. But if power is a system of control, there must be a prevailing ideology driving the system.

Ideology

The drive to war is never a function taken upon by The State without a logical system of communicating its purpose and without drawing upon the ideals and supposed character of the people. A system of communication designs a rationale for war coming from the top (the power elite) down to the people. It is rarely dialectic between the government and the people, and is, therefore, in most cases, propaganda to be sold to the people. Author Chris Hedges suggests that this form of communication drums up the case for "mythic war." He writes that mythic war imbues "events with meanings they do not have. We demonize the enemy so that our opponent is no longer human. We view ourselves, our people, as the embodiment of absolute goodness."[17] The ideology of war, then, is to destroy the interdependency of human and world community, and to prop oneself up as the bearer of ultimate and unilateral righteousness in the earth.

The ideology of unilateral righteousness, or what Noam Chomsky calls global "hegemony," is the prop of war. It is a call for people to recognize their nation as superior and, therefore, worthy of sacrifice. As a result, uncritical patriotism rules the day and demands that all citizens respect others who are willing to sacrifice their lives for the ideals of the nation. In a contemporary setting, the United States ideology is the so-called cause of freedom and democracy. It has created the demonized other in "the terrorists," or in the words of George W. Bush, "thugs" and "evil-doers." Through the ability to create such a dualism, anything that seems in opposition to this system of communication is seen as siding with the so-called "axis of evil." Having the ideology of United States' global leadership intact, the drive to war is made possible. The rationale given to the people of the United States for going to war with Iraq, for example, was that Sadaam Hussein possessed weapons of mass destruction and was, therefore, a threat to the United States.

While the citizens of the United States were very divided on the issue of the war in Iraq—and continue to be so—the ideology of the day was embraced by many of the media outlets. The media, often funded by large corporations of political influence, gave voice to the government system of communication regarding the war.[18] Regardless of dissent among many peace activists, the ideology continued to live on with many added complexities and nuances. Ralph Bourne suggests that this is a form of control taken upon by The State in times of war, a form of control often accepted by the people. He notes that this is what is known in many psychological circles as the "herd mentality." People merely follow the crowd instead of critically examining all the data available. In fact, what is most disturbing about this reality is that most people would be unwilling to buckle under the same kind of pressure if it were any other human or religious ideal. Bourne writes,

> Not for any religious impulse could the American nation have been expected to show such devotion en masse, such sacrifice and labor. Certainly not for any secular good, such as universal education or subjugation of nature, would it have poured forth its treasure and its life, or would it have permitted such stern coercive measures to be taken against it, such as conscripting its money and its men. But for the sake of a war of offensive self-defense, undertaken to support a difficult cause to the slogan of "democracy," it would reach the highest level ever known to collective effort.[19]

In the end, the system of communication present in the ethos of war feeds us with the sick belief that one nation is superior to others and therefore is justified in all of its endeavors with other nations, especially when it comes to war. It is a false justification for the killing of people whom God has created and called good. Indeed, war is a force that not only provides us with a sense of purpose and meaning in the world, it is also a force that creates a world of mythology and power with the aim of controlling a people. Hedges powerfully states, "The potency of myth [ideology] is that it allows us to make sense of mayhem and violent death. It allows us to believe we have achieved our place in human society because of a long chain of heroic endeavors, rather than accept the sad reality that we stumble along a dimly lit corridor of disasters."[20] Under this rubric, ideology is the system of communication and control of opinion by which those in power manipulate the people to their wishes, and it is the central intellectual argumentation for a nation's foreign policy agenda. This agenda, however, is carried out not with ideology alone, but also with the tools made available within the ethos of war.

Tools

The aim of war is to overcome whatever opponent stands in the way of a group's progress or realization of ideals. If war is a "conflict" it is then assumed that war must have weapons, ways of enforcing and accomplishing the goals of conflict. Power is the system of control that pushes a group towards war; ideology is its rationale and ideals; and tools represent the machinery or weaponry as the means toward the end goals of warfare. It is clear that the contemporary use of tools and machinery far exceeds that of previous generations. With the capacity of planes, the technology of Star Wars, nuclear bombs, biological and chemical weapons, and other assault rifles, it is no wonder that Noam Chomsky writes that the challenge of the twenty-first century is between "hegemony or survival."[21]

Understanding the tools of war must begin with the people who use them. In fact, it is easily argued that the people who serve in any military capacity are used themselves by the government as "tools" of war. The people who live out the harsh realities of war are a part of an establishment, a tool used for political gain. Bourne suggests, "War cannot exist without a military establishment, and a military establishment cannot exist without a State organization . . . No one will deny that war is a vast complex of life-destroying and life-crippling forces. If the State's chief function is war, then it is chiefly concerned with co-ordinating and developing the powers and techniques which make for destruction."[22] The destruction is performed by warriors of the State, but the destruction comes as a result of the use of their machinery or tools.

The design of a structured use of force and destruction is organized by the State with the assistance of weapons of destruction, some of which are weapons of mass destruction. These weapons range from threatening small numbers of people with a pistol or knife, to the atomic or nuclear bomb, which threatens the lives of millions. These tools are ultimately effective, however, if there is a proper set of circumstances created by the use of vehicles or occupation of land. The use of planes, boats, submarines, tanks, utility vehicles, and other means of travel provide mobility that diverts opposing threat and allows for removal from hostile environments. The use of spy technology, Star Wars satellites, or radars also creates a level of intelligence attempting to provide visual and geographical locations for targets of enemy combatants. The use of these materials targeting other nations is the creation of an ethos which embraces force and aggression as a means toward an end. The tools of war represent the enabling or actual force of war.

The actuality of war, however, is never created in a vacuum. Besides the necessity of a convincing ideology, there are the tools found in the world of finance. It is usually the case that most nations possessing military might and power over others are wealthier than those being dominated. Most of the fallout, for example, between the Russians and the United States during the Cold War was the incapacity of Russia to financially maintain its military in order to keep up with the United States and its allies. Money itself, however, is also not found in a vacuum. It is through taxation of the people that we raise millions and billions of dollars to fund either homeland security or the military already active in battle. After September 11, 2001, the United States spent more than $399 billion on military engagement, while the so-called "axis of evil" spent only a combined $7 billion. Incongruously, our federal domestic spending on matters of health care was only $41 billion, and funding for reducing our dependency on foreign oil was kept to the small amount of $2 billion.[23] Indeed, money is the political dominance for creating an ethos of war and the use of weaponry.

Weapons, whether they are minimal or whether they are weapons of mass destruction, create a culture of fear. Fear perpetuates the culture of domineering social control given to us vis-à-vis the ideology of those in the power elite. Weapons create a continual cycle of violence, and their influence threatens nation after nation with the prospects of war and intimidation. Therefore, tools are the machinery a nation or group uses in times of war to combat or destroy the so-called enemy. In the end, the three foci entailing a working definition of war, power, ideology, and tools, help create an ethos of violence that must be met with resistance.

Breaking Our Silence

The central foundation of this work is that truth is found in community. Community involves the dynamics of dialogue, debate, and the mutual embrace of social and political differences. War is a break in community. In most cases, war defies diplomacy and the dynamics of debate. As a result, war creates the dualistic demonization of the other and sets up an ethos of violence, an ethos of "us" versus "them." How do we respond to or repair this break in community? It is the contention of this book that it is in breaking our silence in the Church and living out the long-standing tradition of nonviolence that the reconciliation of broken community may be realized. Faith communities around the world cannot sit idly by while thousands die each month at the hands of war. Pastors and their churches in the United States can no longer remain silent from the pulpit, the pew, the classroom, in the public square, or in their view of mission. We must take up the role of the *prophetic* pastor and call for acts of justice. We must respond. We must act. We must break our silence.

The remainder of this book provides resources for local congregations and their pastors so that they may come to grips with how to respond to an ethos of war. Because the central tenant of this text is that truth is found in community, we believe that it is at the grassroots level that this discussion must take place. The most well-attended communal gathering of most local congregations is Sunday worship. In this light, we have organized this text in the form of a worship service, in the assumption that discussions of war are not exempt from worship or from the community. In fact, it is in these venues that engaging war is most appropriate. Therefore, we have gathered together essays from a wide range of clergy, laypeople, intellectuals, and peace activists to give voice to areas within the parish where the ethos of war can and should be discussed. Indeed, those involved in the communal act of writing this text are not all of one mind when it comes to whether or not war is justified in all cases. We are not all pacifists, but we each share a genuine concern that the social, political, theological, and moral complexities of war remain at the forefront of our educational and liturgical lives in the Church.

The worship service organized in this text begins with a "Call to Worship," written by Rev. Robert Moore, who addresses the Church's call to peace activism. Our "Scripture Lesson" is shared by Christopher Hays, who confronts the issue of scripture and war through the lens of the Third Commandment, "You shall not take the name of the Lord your God in vain." We "Pass the Peace" with all of God's creation when Dr. Luis Rivera-Pagán speaks to the world community concerning how religion plays a role in the world peace movement. A moment of "Celebrating Our Youth" is embraced as Eric Anderson explores how we speak to our youth concerning matters of war and peace. We hear the "Testimonies" of God's people when Rev. Stacy Martin, Rev. Everett Mitchell, Rev. Jackson Day, Rev. Gregory Guice, and Ajit Prasadam engage us in the contextualities of refugees, African Americans, military chaplaincy, and Mahatma Gandhi. The "Special Selection" is offered by Darren Burris as he helps us to understand how the media provides images for a congregational praxis in times of war. The preaching of God's word, "The Sermon," comes to us from Rev. Dr. Dave Davis who shares how sermons reflect the dialectical process of engagement between the congregation and the world in which we live. Dr. Kathleen McVey helps us respond to the preached word through the "Statement of Faith," in which she provides a comprehensive historical look at how Christians throughout time have responded to war. Our time of "Prayer" is led by Rev. Frederick Boyle and Rev. Neal Christie as they help us to see the interlacing of global peace and inner peace, of spirituality, of prayer, and social activism within the Church. The "Benediction" is given by Jim Winkler, who sends us forth into the world to actively break our silence and confront an ethos of war with an ethos of peace. Finally, Rev. Chad Abbott and Rev. Everett Mitchell provide the "Postlude" of closing words on how the Church can create an ethos of peace.

Creating an ethos of war did not happen over night; neither will creating an ethos of peace. An ethos of peace begins and ends with faithful people, clergy and laypeople, relentlessly working towards that place where peace is the rule and not the exception. Will the Church reclaim its moral authority? Will the Church embrace the long-standing tradition of nonviolence? Will the Church resist those who attempt to conquer and seek empire? Will the Church live, move, and have her being with the poor and oppressed? Will the Church stand up for justice? May this volume serve as a tool for peace and justice. May the voices spoken in these pages serve to create a new ethos, a new world, a new way of living, a way of peace. Now, more than ever, is a time to break silence.

Endnotes

[1] Martin Luther King Jr., "A Time to Break Silence," in *A Testament of Hope: The Essential Writings and Speeches of Martin Luther King Jr.*, ed. James Melvin Washington (San Francisco: Harper San Francisco, 1986), 240.

[2] See www.newamericancentury.org. "Statement of Principles," June 3, 1997.

[3] Chris Hedges, *War Is a Force That Gives Us Meaning* (New York: Anchor Books, 2002).

[4] See www.aei.org. "Iraq: What Lies Ahead," transcript from Tuesday, March 25, 2003, for the American Enterprise Institute for Public Policy Research.

[5] Gore Vidal, *Perpetual War for Perpetual Peace: How We Got To Be So Hated* (New York: Thunder's Mouth Press, 2002).

[6] See *The American Heritage Dictionary of the English Language*, Fourth Edition (New York: Houghton Mifflin Co., 2000).

[7] William H. Willimon, *Pastor: The Theology and Practice of Ordained Ministry* (Nashville: Abingdon Press, 2002), 17.

[8] *Ibid.*, 50.

[9] Eugene H. Peterson, *The Contemplative Pastor: Returning to the Art of Spiritual Direction* (Grand Rapids, Michigan: Eerdmans Publishing Co., 1993), 16.

[10] *Ibid.*, 37.

[11] See *The American Heritage Dictionary of the English Language, op. cit.*

[12] Ralph Bourne, "The State: War is the Health of the State," 1. See www.antiwar.com. This essay was left unfinished at the time of Bourne's death. It was collected by those who began The Ralph Bourne Institute and was posted on the website of the Institute, but also with its affiliate, www.antiwar.com.

[13] *Ibid.*, 3.

[14] *Ibid.*, 3.

[15] *Ibid.*, 3.

[16] *Ibid.*, 1.

[17] Hedges, 21. The idea of "Mythic War" stems from LeShan, Lawrence, *The Psychology of War* (New York: Helios, 1992).

[18] For further guidance on how the media plays the drums of war for the ideology of government see, Amy Goodman and David Goodman, *The Exception to the Rulers: Exposing Oily Politicians, War Profiteers, and the Media That Love Them* (New York: Hyperion, 2004).

[19] Bourne, 6.

[20] Hedges, 23.

[21] Noam Chomsky, *Hegemony or Survival: America's Quest for Global Dominance* (New York: Metropolitan Books, 2003).

[22] Bourne, 12.

[23] See www.truemajority.org on global military spending and federal domestic spending. This extreme amount of over-funding to U.S. military endeavors has cost us an enormous budget deficit and the cutting of social programming taking us back decades of reform and progress.

Call to Worship

Rise up, O Church! A "Call to Worship" is a call to prayer and action before God. In this opening chapter, Rev. Robert Moore shouts out a call to the Church and all religious communities to live out their faith through activism for peace and justice. He explains why engaging in such activism is important and provides religious congregations with practical ways of engaging in peace activism. Rev. Moore's challenge will continue throughout this book as we see how the Church in very specific ways can engage matters of peace and justice.

Peacemaking Rooted in Local Religious Congregations

Rev. Robert Moore

In the autumn of 1979 a concern arose in the Princeton Clergy Association, a group that included the clergy of the Protestant, Catholic, and Jewish congregations in the communities of Princeton, New Jersey. The concern was the escalation of the nuclear arms race and the threat that presented to the entirety of God's creation. Presidential Directive 59, signed by then-President Jimmy Carter, had codified a wide range of situations in which nuclear weapons might be used and be used *first*.

President Carter's Directive included instructions for the military to begin developing nuclear weapons that might be used in such contingencies. Nuclear warheads, such as the infamous neutron bomb (which would focus on killing through radiation, rather than blast, and thereby allow the attacked area to be quickly re-inhabited) were being proposed.

The clergy planned a two-day Conference and Interfaith Service for September 1980. It started on a Saturday night (after sundown, in respect for the Jewish Sabbath) and continued all day Sunday. The Sunday program included the Interfaith Service for Peace at 11 A.M. at Princeton University Chapel. The overall event was entitled "Can We Reverse the Nuclear Arms Race?" Some top speakers were secured, including Prof. Harvey Cox of Harvard Divinity School, Dr. Richard Barnet of the Institute for Policy Studies, Ambassador Paul Warnke, and Dr. Helen Caldicott, then President of Physicians for Social Responsibility. The clergy didn't know what kind of response to expect. They were overwhelmed when 2,000 people came.

Virtually every speaker responded to the question in the title, "Can we reverse the nuclear arms race?" by answering, "Yes, but the involvement of average citizens like you is what it will take." More than 6,000 government meetings on disarmament had taken place to that point without stopping a single nuclear weapon. Clearly something more was needed: the advocacy of millions of average citizens. In response to that challenge, a follow-up meeting was called a short time later, and 400 people came. This gave birth to what was initially the Coalition to Reverse the Nuclear Arms Race, now called the Coalition for Peace Action.

The first year, the group was entirely volunteer and formed committees that carried out activities such as a Peace Sabbath pulpit exchange, a commemoration of the atomic bombings of Hiroshima and Nagasaki, and planning for a second Conference and Interfaith Service in the fall of 1981. I was hired as the first full-time staff person and began working on September 8, 1981, just prior to the second annual conference at the end of that month.

As this chapter is written, the Coalition for Peace Action has become a year-round regional organization with four paid staff and three paid consultants. The heart of its support base has continued to be congregations and religious groups, especially in central and southern New Jersey. The first conference was co-sponsored by seventeen congregations. The twenty-fourth annual conference in November 2003 was co-sponsored by 103. The range of faiths represented in the congregations involved has expanded as well, now including Muslim, Buddhist, and Sikh.

Grounded in twenty-five years of organizing experience by the Coalition for Peace Action, this chapter explores three questions:

1. Why should religious congregations be involved in peacemaking?
2. How can we foster personal transformation toward peace?
3. How can we organize to get faith communities involved in peace and justice?

Our experience in New Jersey suggests that if we address these questions well, it can lead to a strong and sustained effort for peace at the grassroots level. For the local congregation, this is where the rubber really hits the road—reaching local religious leaders and the diverse lay people in their congregations. In this sense, it is my contention that peace activism has its roots and most powerful impact when religious congregations and other peace activist organizations or individuals create a synergy, a peace-giving force, which recreates our world, a world steeped in the ethos of war.

Why Organize for Peace in Religious Congregations?

Before discussing how we can be most effective and faithful at organizing for peace in religious congregations, I think it is important to consider why we should seek involvement and support for peace and justice efforts from them. I will discuss three reasons.

First, religious congregations are mainstream institutions that are a way to reach millions of people that peace organizers could not otherwise reach. While attendance at religious services in the U.S. has been in decline, a large majority of Americans are still associated in some way with a house of worship. The grass roots of the religious community is of course the local congregation. In my experience, there is almost always a diversity of perspectives and priorities among the members of the local congregation—reflecting the diversity of the broader society. Nonetheless, there are often key points of contact—clergy, social ministry, peacemaking, or mission committees—where one can often find support for peace and justice initiatives.

Often, that part of the congregation may only be a minority within it—sometimes just a handful of people, a faithful remnant, a prophetic minority. But they can still in one way or another take action within their congregations—organizing adult forums, taking mission or peacemaking offerings, or sponsoring letter-writing tables in support of upcoming peace legislation during coffee hours. They can also participate in local or regional peacemaking activities in the broader interfaith community and thereby join with other faithful remnants to create a real critical mass with significant visibility and powerful witness.

In fact, it is precisely by joining together on an interfaith basis that we synergize the strongest expressions for peace and get the most positive responses from the larger community. Any one congregation or faith group alone doesn't generate such a synergy, but working together to affirm the centrality of "peace on earth" as a vision of all the great faith traditions makes the most powerful, unified witness and has the greatest impact.

I have organized a number of faith-based speak-outs, for example, on issues such as the war and occupation of Iraq. I have had as many as twelve faith leaders from a variety of faith communities give brief statements or prayers: Protestant, Catholic, Jewish, Muslim, Sikh, and others. Even though these faith leaders aren't necessarily speaking for all or even the majority of their congregations, they have moral authority and affirm a common faith-based vision of peace and justice. The response, both from those attending and from the press, has been highly positive.

Second, as institutions, religious congregations not only offer a way to communicate with a wide swath of mainstream Americans, but they also can provide resources such as free meeting space and contributions. The organization for which I have served as executive director for the past twenty-three years, the Coalition for Peace Action, has most of its meetings in religious congregations. When chairing a New-York-based committee to organize a rally during the Nuclear Non-Proliferation Treaty (NPT) extension conference in 1994-95, I was surprised to discover that it was often hard for the New-York-based peace groups to find free meeting space. We have been blessed with nearly carte-blanche approval to use space in religious congregations in the

Princeton area since the group was founded by—and has maintained strong ties with—the religious community.

As an institution, the religious community also has access to significant financial resources. Annually, the Coalition for Peace Action receives donations from over ninety religious entities. Some of these are a donation (suggested $100) to co-sponsor our annual Conference and Interfaith Service for Peace. Others are substantial donations from the annual budget of the congregation (last year, two gave us $1,500; another $1,000).

Third and finally, faith communities offer credibility and a compelling moral vision that commands respect from a broad spectrum of people throughout the world. When the Roman Catholic bishops of the United States endorsed the U.S.-U.S.S.R. Nuclear Weapons Freeze in their Pastoral Letter on Peace in 1982, it made headlines across the U.S. A Gallup poll done after the letter was covered in the mass media and read from many Catholic pulpits in the U.S. showed that it actually made a difference in the views of the "people in the pews" of Roman Catholic parishes; they become more peace-oriented and pro-Freeze. At least partly as result of this upsurge of support in the religious community, the majority of the House of Representatives passed a resolution supporting the Nuclear Freeze in 1983.

One final note for any peace leaders who may not routinely organize with the religious community: Don't be afraid to incorporate faith perspectives and people of faith in your peacemaking efforts. Some of the most positive responses we get are to interfaith events we do. As long as a wide spectrum of faith groups are included and none appear to be excluded, you are tapping into a very positive and highly respected resource. We've even had very positive responses from atheists who care about our issues, since they realize the faith community is a group of major importance to involve in peace and justice organizing.

We are organizing our twenty-fifth annual Interfaith Service for Peace as this chapter is written. In the early years, there were fewer than twenty local congregations, all Christian and Jewish, who co-sponsored the first events. Only Christian and Jewish faith leaders were part of the liturgy. Last year, we surpassed 100 congregations and religious groups that co-sponsored, and we have expanded to include Muslim, Sikh, and Buddhist faith leaders. The response was highly favorable: nearly

1,000 people attended, and they were almost universally positive. In addition, they contributed over $2,000 for the offering taken during the service, which was designated to benefit our organization.

A Story of Personal Transformation toward Peace

For the past twenty-six years (1978-2004) I have worked full time as a professional organizer for peace and justice. For nine years prior to that, I had been involved primarily as a volunteer. So all together, I've organized for peace for thirty-five years.

During most of that time, I have worked in and with religious congregations and communities as the locus for my work on peace and justice issues. This locus emerged for two primary reasons: first, because it was through the church that I experienced transformation and initially became involved; and second, because the religious community has a God-given vision and mission to work toward peace and justice (known in Hebrew as *shalom*), and I felt called to help that community move in that direction. I share this not because I want to impress you with my longevity in working in this field. Rather, I share this background to demonstrate what can be an important clue as to what might motivate others to become involved for the long haul: i.e., examining what leads people to become involved and then to stay involved.

For me, the journey began during my freshman year at Purdue. Being the son of a career Navy enlisted man, I entered college as a hawk on Vietnam. I had a very simplistic view of the world and thought that U.S. involvement in Vietnam was a matter of stopping the evil Communists from taking over the world. The horrors of Stalin and of the Communist take-over in China were well known. Certainly, we had to stop these "godless" communists from going further.

By then, the Vietnam War was coming to the national forefront, especially after the demonstrations at the Democratic National Convention in Chicago in the summer of 1968. When Dow Chemical, the maker of napalm, came to recruit and interview seniors at Purdue in the fall of 1968, there was a protest by students who held giant blown-up photos of napalmed children in Vietnam. This really made me stop and question the simplistic view I had held and to look more deeply at not only my world view but also at the moral issues involved.

The place I turned to sort out these issues was the campus ministry. Based on a life-long involvement, I perceived the church as an institution that I could trust and that could help me sort out difficult issues. We had an outstanding campus minister who was a World War II veteran but subsequently became very much opposed to war. He helped to connect me with the campus ministry community and to see that Christ's primary message and calling in regards to violence was one of peacemaking and nonviolence. From my Sunday School training and my confirmation classes, even from sermons I had heard as a regular churchgoer throughout my youth, I had no idea of the deep theological foundations for such a calling and journey.

The first place I began to see what a profound change in my life's direction this would have was in a campus ministry trip during the semester break of my freshman year. Led by the Quaker campus minister, we went to Hominy, Oklahoma, to work on an Osage Indian reservation to re-roof a Quaker church. The deep community and joy of serving together for those ten days was something I had never experienced before. The many spontaneous conversations with fellow students, campus ministers, and others helped start me on a journey of Christian nonviolence that has continued to this day. Nobody scolded or attacked me for having the "wrong" position on Vietnam; rather, they helped me examine my many questions and seek answers from Scripture, from contemporary theology, and from secular sources and reason.

It seemed only right and natural that I should continue this peacemaking journey within the church. And while I have certainly had my share of butting heads with and feeling rejected by the church and its leaders, I have also felt supported and nurtured and in community with enough of it that I have maintained that as my primary base. As I sensed a prophetic call toward peace and justice, the church was the locus where I felt called to exercise and grow that ministry. I have remained grounded in the religious community in my various peacemaking endeavors ever since.

From my experience, we get a glimpse of the transforming power of the religious community and of the faith grounded within it to move any person into peacemaking—even if that involves dramatic reversals. As the son of a Navy officer who, as a senior in high school applied to get into Navy ROTC (I wasn't accepted due to poor eyesight), as a hawk on the Vietnam War, and now as a person who has devoted twenty-six years of full-time ministry to peacemaking, I have come to see the transforming power of working to create an ethos of peace. I know of no other institution in society that offers nurture and support to that kind of dramatic transformation.

How to Organize in Local Religious Congregations

Now that I have discussed the reasons for being grounded in religious congregations while working for peace and have illustrated the transformative power of such a context, I will outline how to organize in and with local congregations. I have learned a number of "dos and don'ts" about working with religious congregations through my thirty-five years of working within and among them for peace with justice. What follows are fourteen suggestions for organizing in these communities of faith.

First, don't expect to get significant results from form letters or emails. This is the standard outreach for seeking to involve religious (as well as secular groups) in peacemaking. I can testify from personal experience that clergy get loads of such letters and emails every day. There simply isn't time to deal with most of them. Therefore, this kind of approach can be quite ineffective and disappointing.

I recall that in the first parish I served in Washington, D.C., we housed a group called the Community for Creative Non-Violence (CCNV) in one of the row houses the church owned. The winter before I came to D.C., eight homeless people had frozen to death in the capitol of the wealthiest nation on earth. CCNV decided to send a form letter asking all 1,400 congregations in the DC area to open their doors to house people the next winter to prevent such a tragedy from re-occurring. Just one congregation responded favorably. That is a pretty low response rate, typical of the results from the "form letter" approach.

Second, use personal letters with follow-up phone calls and meetings. For the past twenty-four years, we in the Coalition have sent hand-addressed letters to our religious contacts asking them to co-sponsor the annual Conference and Interfaith Service for Peace. Of the approximately 200 groups solicited, about 25-30 respond to the letter. Another 70 respond only after the follow-up calls and/or face-to-face meetings, particularly if the contact is from someone they know. It is through personal contact that you become noticed and taken seriously by the religious leader and congregation. It is through the process of conversation and dialogue that this engagement can lead to initial and, perhaps, ongoing involvement. The majority of congregations that co-sponsor our annual event repeat annually. But some drop out, for whatever reason, while others respond favorably to an initial approach. Out of a total of 275 organizational contacts we approached last year, 103 agreed to co-sponsor.

Third, be specific and persistent in making your request. We've had good results asking for co-sponsorship of an educational event with an interfaith component. We delineated to the prospective congregation exactly what we are asking for: their name for publicity, to help spread the word to their constituency, and a suggested (not required) financial contribution. (Sample letters requesting co-sponsorship are available to the reader on request.) We have also had some success asking for support to distribute non-partisan voter education materials in congregations.

Some time ago, I compared notes with a friend who was involved with an interfaith peace coalition that had formed in Louisville, Kentucky. It started with excellent and diverse response from a range of religious communities in the metropolitan area. But over time, nobody reached out on a one-to-one basis to the religious leaders and communities involved to ask for their continued support. As a result, it atrophied. When my friend heard about our annual specific request to the religious congregations in our region, with persistent follow-up, he concluded that such intentional, regularized contact was what helped us maintain our involvement from the religious congregations in our region.

Fourth, be respectful and open in your contacts. If we try to harangue folks into doing what we think they should do, we are unlikely to succeed. The overture should be invitational, flexible, and open. If the religious leader or congregation to whom you are making an overture has a specific issue or concern with the request, try to understand fully and then work from there to see if there is a way to arrive at some positive response.

When I was younger, many of my overtures to religious groups were self-righteous and left little room for dialogue or for any response except complete agreement with whatever I was advocating. I had the attitude that I was absolutely right and anyone who disagreed—even a little—must be on the wrong side of the issue. I tended to pigeonhole people and groups as totally pro-war or completely pro-peace.

What I have learned as I have matured and, hopefully, grown in my understanding and my faith, is that there is almost always more than one aspect to "the truth," and that nobody has a corner on the whole truth. If we are open, we can learn from those who disagree with us and come closer to the "truth-force" that Mohandas Gandhi characterized as his focus of nonviolence. Support can sometimes come from the least-expected quarters if we are open to it. For example, two of the groups with whom we are now working closely in opposing the war and occupation of Iraq are Veterans for Peace and Military Families Speak Out. The latter is a group of family members of U.S. troops deployed in Iraq, some of whom have lost loved ones there, who strongly oppose current U.S. policy in Iraq. At first blush, both of these groups could easily have been pigeonholed as "pro-war." But by being open to their input, we discovered the pro-troops perspective they bring is very much in harmony with our anti-war advocacy.

Another example of this need for flexibility is that on more than a few occasions a congregation has declined to respond favorably to the particular request we have made but has expressed an openness to another possibility. Sometimes this has led to us sending a representative to lead their adult forum, give a sermon, or give a "minute for mission" at their worship service. Other times, it has led to financial support we hadn't anticipated. One congregation said it wanted to devote its monthly communion offering to us; this amounted to over $500, far more than the $100 we had requested for co-sponsoring our conference. Other congregations didn't respond favorably by our deadline but sent in their co-sponsorship after the annual conference was over; they just could not finish the decision-making process sooner.

In making the contact with and request to a congregation's leader, always use proper titles (Rabbi, Reverend, Imam, etc.) unless and until the individual says you can be less formal. Understand and be tolerant of the very real limits religious communities encounter: a variety of political persuasions, the need for enough advance time to make decisions and give an answer, inability to endorse candidates *for* office, easier to support educational activities than advocacy—to name only a few. By being flexible and understanding, we can sometimes achieve the beginning of a productive and positive relationship with a group that really wants to support peace but with its own integrity.

I recall giving a series of talks on the Nuclear Freeze to the adult forum of a congregation I was part of in the mid-1980s. Two members who were present were Republicans and were skeptical of the Nuclear Freeze. They kept saying that the problem wasn't the hardware, i.e., the nuclear weapons themselves, but rather the hostile U.S.-Soviet relationship. I finally suggested that we extend the series to hear their views in more detail. We did so and I discovered that they indeed had an important additional truth that I needed to hear and incorporate into my thinking and organizing. We began to work on citizen initiatives toward improving the U.S.-Soviet relationship, known as "citizen diplomacy," and found that such initiatives unleashed a great deal of new positive energy in our organizing in the region.

Fifth, build relationships. This is ultimately what all good outreach is about. It also means that any overture should be approached with sensitivity and grace, not high-handedness and self-righteousness. I recall years ago being very impressed with a fellow organizer who had amazing results in persuading religious leaders to sign interfaith pastoral letters on key peace issues. When I investigated how he managed to do this, it became apparent that it was the result of respectful relationships he had built over many years with the bishops and other leaders he approached.

The relationship with a local congregation should be developed with the clergyperson and also with the leader(s) of the social ministry committee if at all possible. Often, lay heads of committees have more freedom to advocate support for specific peace initiatives than clergy.

It is especially effective if there is contact with both so they can be encouraged to work together in support of peace. It is also important to have ongoing contact—through emails, letters, attending meetings, participating in events they are part of, etc.—so the overture is not written off as a one-shot deal or a flash-in-the-pan effort. Relationships require sustained contact.

Sixth, use denominational networks. Almost all religious groups have a social ministry division at the regional and/or national levels. They can be very helpful in offering direct support, as well as in helping mobilize the grassroots congregations. After an initial burst of involvement with the Nuclear Freeze Campaign in the early 1980s, I began to feel somewhat distanced from my own denomination's (the United Church of Christ) social ministry arm, known as the Office for Church in Society (OCIS). They worked on a lot of other peace and justice issues, mostly defined by various regions of the world (Africa, Latin America, Asia, etc.) but seemingly not on nuclear disarmament.

About five years ago I heard from a new young staff person the Office had hired, a recent seminary graduate. She came and met with me to re-establish a sense of connection. She then sent out a notice of our upcoming annual Conference and Interfaith Service for Peace, over her signature, to every UCC congregation in the New Jersey Association. She also got the OCIS to be a co-sponsor. Subsequently, when I was invited to join a Peace Advisory group for the denomination, I was delighted to accept. A sense of covenant (relationship) and connection was re-established.

Seventh, be a presence in the congregation's life. It is particularly effective to do a "minute for mission" presentation during worship, then be available afterwards for respectful listening and dialogue. It is also effective to have adult forums and sermon talk-backs (if the preacher is persuaded and moved to preach a pro-peace sermon). It is by going to the congregation at the center of their communal life— worship, education, fellowship, etc.—that we have the best chance of engaging people.

One of the strongest responses I've had to peace overtures in one of the congregations I've now served for fifteen years is when we sent "empty shoes" to Washington in the early 1990s to represent the 40,000 victims of gun violence per year. As part of the offering that day, we placed the empty shoes being offered by members of the congregation in front of the communion table and prayed for God's blessing on them. Even though I was the only one who actually attended the March of the Empty Shoes on the Mall in front of the U.S. Capitol, I felt I was representing the entire congregation.

When "special programs on peace" are offered on a weeknight or at a time when the congregation isn't normally gathered, it is hard to get more than a small handful of attendees. But when witness and dialogue are offered at the time the congregation gathers for the center of its life together—worship, religious education, etc.—there is a "captive audience." While this can run the risk of alienating some congregants (e.g., they may ask why are we are bringing controversy or "politics" into the congregation), if it is handled with grace and openness to dialogue and sharing, it can be powerful and reach a significant portion of the gathered community.

Eighth, appeal to the best of the community's tradition. We don't want to come across as bringing in "politics" or something alien to the faith community's vision and priorities; nothing could be more likely to generate opposition and a backlash. The Bible has many passages that call for a vision of "peace on earth," as does the Koran and other holy books. Do your homework and lift those passages up as the ultimate values that we share with that community.

My talks and writings aimed at the faith community almost always begin with a Scripture quote or reading. One that I've used repeatedly in recent years is the place in the Sermon on the Mount where Jesus says to "... first take the log out of our own eye, then we can see to take the speck out of our neighbor's eye" (Matthew 7:5). This goes to the heart of the self-righteous "do as we say, not as we do" way U.S. foreign policy is justifiably perceived by much of the world.

As this chapter is being written, the Bush Administration is proposing funding for two new kinds of U.S. nuclear weapons while at the same time calling on other nations (North Korea, Iran, etc.) and terrorists to not obtain them. The Sermon on the Mount has a strong injunction against such hypocrisy. With over 10,000 nuclear warheads, the U.S. is the one with the nuclear log in its eye, and that is where we need to start if we are to make real progress in stopping their spread. This is also a cornerstone of the Nuclear Non-Proliferation Treaty in

Article 6, which commits the nuclear "haves," including the U.S., to negotiate the elimination of their nuclear weapons if the non-nuclear signatories agree not to seek to obtain or build such weapons.

Ninth, organize on an interfaith basis. I've related to local clergy associations (that usually meet once a month), as well as to the NJ Council of Churches, for many years with great response. As stated at the beginning of this chapter, the Coalition for Peace Action grew out of concern and initiatives coming out of the Princeton Clergy Association. Councils of Churches, interfaith alliances, and other such organizations are all good venues for establishing a presence and building relationships.

Again, we need to have a broad vision and look at more than just the Protestant, Christian, or Jewish congregations. The United States is rapidly diversifying, ethnically and religiously. Some of the fastest growing faith communities are "non-traditional," such as Muslim, Buddhist, and Sikh. Moreover, don't forget those congregations that often are not included in the "Christian" family, even though they grew out of it, such as Religious Society of Friends (Quakers) and Unitarian Universalists. Such congregations have been among our strongest supporters since our inception.

Tenth, use the religious leaders you recruit to relate to other religious leaders. We've had great results when our chairperson and often other volunteer leaders are religious leaders. They tend to get a better response in reaching out to other religious leaders as their colleagues. For instance, each year after we send out our appeal to co-sponsor our annual Conference and Interfaith Service for Peace, we have volunteers do the first round of follow-up calls. That normally gets the number of co-sponsors up to around fifty to sixty. But the last forty to fifty only agreed to co-sponsor when they get a personal call from me, as a clergyperson and colleague. There is something about being asked by a colleague—especially one they know—that gets better results.

Eleventh, use religious leaders to speak at public events. As mentioned earlier, clergy have moral credibility and can appeal to a compelling vision for peace and justice. In addition, they have a lot of practice at public speaking. There is also an element of helping the religious leaders feel connected and to feel some ownership of a peace activity. If they are speaking at an upcoming peace event, they are more likely to feel some ownership and responsibility to announce it to their congregation (in verbal announcement, sermon, newsletter, etc.), inviting the congregants to join them in supporting it.

Of course, using religious leaders does not need to be exclusive. Our most successful public events have a diverse spectrum of speakers: scientists, trade unionists, women's groups, civic leaders, as well as religious leaders. This conveys the image we want: that support for peace is diverse and broad. However, in using multiple speakers, the organizers need to be clear and firm on time limits for each speaker. To overload or bore a supportive crowd with too many speeches, or ones that are too long, can be counterproductive and de-energize our supporters. At the event mentioned earlier with twelve religious leaders, veterans, trade unionists, etc., we limited each speaker to two to three minutes. However, this also made it easier for each speaker to accept our invitation, since they knew they wouldn't have to do a lot of preparation.

The other primary caution I would give is to be sure the religious leaders understand they are talking to a mixed group and they should frame their message to not alienate those of other faiths or of no faith, i.e., to have broad appeal. We had a fairly embarrassing situation at our annual Interfaith Service for Peace one year when the speaker, a prominent Catholic, repeatedly invoked Jesus Christ in a Christian sectarian sense. We salvaged the situation by apologizing to the non-Christian faith leaders present. Since then we have been more intentional about avoiding any such sectarian statements.

Twelfth, have public events include a faith perspective. In addition to our annual Interfaith Service for Peace, we have occasional vigils and interfaith gatherings to promote peaceful initiatives. In 2001 and in 2003 we had interfaith commemorations of 9/11. In 2003 we lifted up the vision of September 11 Families for Peaceful Tomorrows and used many of their materials. We had faith leaders from Presbyterian, Roman Catholic, Unitarian Universalist, Sikh, Episcopal, United Church of Christ, Jewish, and Muslim traditions (the latter was by two youth). It was extremely well received. We did a candlelight vigil at the end in which some Muslim women lit the candles for us. It got front-page photos and stories in three local papers. One photo was so striking (Muslim women wearing burkas honoring the dead of 9/11) that a local paper printed the photo again in its year-end round up.

Thirteenth, don't be afraid to speak out from your own personal faith convictions. Sometimes we can be intimidated from speaking out of our own religious conscience, afraid that it will make us unpopular or even make us ostracized or isolated in taking a public stand. Yet in my experience people are almost always respectful of such expression as long as it is theologically based, sincere, and not high-handed or closed to dialogue. In fact, my sense is that people, including the "un-churched," are often looking for someone to say a clear prophetic word and will be attracted to that. If we allow ourselves to be intimidated into "going along so we can get along" and not rocking the boat, we may well be inviting that gnawing feeling of being untrue to our integrity and our conscience.

I recall that during buildup to the first Gulf War in 1990, I began speaking out against the option of war during my sermons. I articulated this perspective from a clear biblical and theological grounding. A number of people who hadn't attended church in years began attending, and a number of un-churched people began attending for the first time. I remember two sisters who started coming after they met me on the bus to a peace march in Washington, D.C.; they both subsequently joined the church and became active in it.

Moreover, I had one of the proudest moments in being the pastor of that small congregation I've been serving part time for the past fifteen years during this time. I began announcing upcoming meetings of the statewide NJ Coalition Against War in the Middle East. First one member started to come. Later, one Sunday afternoon, a meeting of this coalition took place in the next town over from the church. Of the forty people in attendance, eight were from my little church (about half our active membership at the time!).

Fourteenth and finally, be patient and tenacious. We can labor in the fields for many years without seeing much of a harvest. But if we keep putting our message out in a respectful and courteous way, congregations and other supporters may slowly, eventually respond. As mentioned earlier, we reached our highest number of co-sponsoring organizations for our annual Conference and Interfaith Service in 2003. Some of that was undoubtedly because we succeeded in getting two religious leaders of great renown to speak: The Most Reverend George Carey, the just-retired Archbishop of Canterbury; and Dr. Cornel West, author and Princeton University Professor of Religion and African American Studies. But some of it was also because we were tenacious and didn't give up on congregations that hadn't previously agreed to co-sponsor.

On a more organizational level, we have experienced surges of increased involvement in our efforts, especially as the U.S. hovered on the verge of war. Last year, we had a one-third increase in our membership. Much of this increase was due to the high visibility we had in organizing against the Iraq war. Some of it was due to the careful follow-up calls we made to those who participated in our events, inviting them to support our ongoing efforts by joining the Coalition for Peace Action. Had we not been patient and tenacious, there might not have been an infrastructure in which these new supporters could become active.

Remaining Persistent

Religious congregations and people who organize within and between them must remain persistent in their pursuit of peace and justice. In the early 1980s, we had a huge upsurge in involvement, membership, visibility, etc., as we fought against the escalation of the nuclear arms race when President Reagan was first elected. We succeeded in getting the Nuclear Freeze passed in a statewide referendum by 66% of New Jersey's voters, while nine other states and sixty municipalities also voted favorably by a national average of 60%.

By 1983, the Freeze passed as a resolution in the U.S. House of Representatives, but it never passed in the Senate. After a short time, participation began to drop precipitously, and many of the 200 Nuclear Freeze town committees we had across the state of New Jersey began to fade out of existence. Americans tend to expect instant results, (perhaps due to our television culture), and when success didn't come quickly many new activists dropped out.

But because we were rooted in a faith vision and grounded in the institutions of the religious community, we were able to sustain ourselves. For effectiveness, we re-focused our admittedly reduced person-power on the decision-makers in Washington, D.C., i.e., with grassroots lobbying for peace. By having this "staying power," we were eventually able to be part of creating enough pressure to achieve, and also to celebrate, the first nuclear reduction treaty in history, the Intermediate Nuclear Forces (INF) Treaty. Signed by Presidents Reagan and Gorbachev in 1987, this Treaty was the first to actually reduce the numbers of nuclear weapons and to eliminate an entire class of nuclear weapons (medium-range). By the time the Berlin Wall came down and the Cold War ended, that and subsequent nuclear reduction treaties reduced the world's nuclear arsenals by 50%, from 70,000 to about 35,000. While that is still immense overkill, it nonetheless represents real progress.

I recall a fellow faith-community organizer talking to me early in my peacemaking career. We were lamenting how many peace organizers were burning out, doing such work for a few years while young and then getting exhausted or demoralized. She prophetically said she thought that would not happen to me for two reasons: I had a supportive family and I had a strong faith. Now, twenty-five years later, I would add a third reason: that the religious community has been able to offer a sustained base of support and active participation in this mission of peacemaking to which we are called in all of the great faith traditions. Without these religious communities as a base of support and nurture, burnout and cynicism would have been inevitable. However, the ethos of war is never inevitable. The hope and vision of "peace on earth" is rooted in a living God of history, a God still at work today. We live in hope of a new world. Rise up, O Church!

Scripture Lesson

Scripture is one of the primary points of entry for people of faith when it comes to speaking about matters of war. In this essay, Christopher Hays engages the interpretation of the Third Commandment in light of issues of war. He uses the events of September 11, 2001, to examine how scripture intertwines with public events. In the end, this chapter suggests that one of the primary tasks of congregations is to tell the truth in times of war and conflict. What is the truth that the church must speak in this hour?

Trauma, Truth, and the Third Commandment

Were Christian Responses to 9/11 Biblical?

Christopher B. Hays

לֹא תִשָּׂא אֶת־שֵׁם־יְהוָה אֱלֹהֶיךָ לַשָּׁוְא

כִּי לֹא יְנַקֶּה יְהוָה אֵת אֲשֶׁר־יִשָּׂא אֶת־שְׁמוֹ לַשָּׁוְא

You shall not lift up the name of the LORD your God in vain,

for the LORD will not acquit anyone who lifts up his name in vain.

—Exo. 20:7

How do we speak the truth in God's name in a time of war? Do we dare at all, when new facts are being reported daily that change our view of the world? Studying the Bible teaches humility—the richness and diversity of the vast historical stream of interpretation makes one realize that the view of any time on another is limited. This is all the more true of our understanding of our own times—there is so much that will be better understood by later generations. As if interpreting the Word and the will of God were not hard enough, the horrific events of the twentieth century—especially world war and Holocaust—have only complicated the answers Christians thought they had. But neither can we refuse to be a part of God's ministry of reconciliation that was begun in Christ.

In post-disestablishment America, church leaders do not hold the reins of the warhorses, and this chapter does not anticipate an audience of national politicians. It is offered to Christian laypeople, clergy, and professors. Our individual decision-making power is limited by our representative government, so this chapter is not an attempt to assess the biblical arguments for or against war, although these demand attention.[1] Instead, it is about doing what all of us can and must: speaking truthfully in the name of God. And it is about doing so when the stakes are the highest and the times seem least propitious for telling hard truths, when our symbolic world is uprooted and overturned, and old certainties are shaken. This chapter tries to strike a balance between our own limited knowledge and the historical "rooted-ness" of ethical speech about war by looking backward at a historical moment and the ways in which religious leaders spoke about it to their audiences: September 11, 2001, when thousands of Americans died in terrorist attacks.

In a lecture shortly after the attacks, Bruce McCormack of Princeton Theological Seminary said, "It was as though the sheer godlessness of the world had been exposed; the abyss of hell had yawned open. . . . Doing theology in the shadow of the opening of the abyss is not easy. . . . I just want to listen and to do theology as one who is learning it all over again, as if for the first time."[2] Remarks like that emphasize the magnitude of the shock. It was difficult at that moment to check our preconceived notions about God and the world against the sources of revelation that God has given us, and harder still to speak the truth that they hold for us. In the troubled waters of history, where navigation is difficult, one *must* begin with true speech. Our culture is a consumer society, so we begin to take it for granted that everything is marketing—the political word is "spin"—but we must not allow decisions about war to be compared with those about what food to eat or what car to drive.

This emphasis on truth is also necessary because truth has been distinctly lacking from the national conversation about war, especially from the rhetoric of the Bush administration. A recent study at the University of Illinois enumerates twenty-three different rationales for the war in Iraq that have been employed by the administration.[3] Some of the most important reasons the country was given for the necessity of war have proven to be false, notably the presence of weapons of mass destruction that posed an imminent threat to the safety of Western nations.[4] One commentator in *The Washington Post* concluded that "the Bush administration has been even more willing than its predecessors to spin, prevaricate and, if necessary, coldly lie for its own advantage," and that, "with honorable exceptions, the American news media have not lived up to their reputation for hard-nosed skepticism when it comes to challenging the administration's claims."[5] In other words, while there is a long tradition of lying in politics, the twenty-first century may see the breaking of new ground. If the political culture descends, the Church must try to do better.

A biblical theology of truth telling begins with the Third Commandment, which warns all who speak in the name of God to speak truthfully. Despite the prominence of the commandments, it seems to have been overlooked a bit, or taken too narrowly, as if it applied exclusively to oath taking. There is some warrant for this interpretation in the Bible itself—one can cite numerous related examples from Pentateuch law that specifically forbid false oaths in God's name,[6] and even Jesus picks up on these secondary traditions in the Sermon the Mount (Mt. 5:33-37). The later tradition, in short, "continued to apply the commandment in its narrower function."[7] But the narrower statements in Lev. 19:12, Deut., 6:13, 10:20 (all with *šbʿ*, "to swear," rather than *nsʾ*, "to lift up") should only draw further attention to the broad possibilities of the commandment as it comes to us. Historically, that has not happened. The rabbis, from the Targums to the medieval period, were mostly satisfied with this interpretation.[8] Even reformers John Calvin and Martin Luther have little more to say about the commandment, perhaps because they were challenged in their day by radical reformers who did not believe in swearing oaths in God's name at all.[9] That debate is now largely a historical curiosity, but the Third

Commandment should still speak forcefully to us today because it has significantly wider implications.

There are signs within the wording of the commandment itself suggesting we should look a little longer, a little harder: Its curse formula is striking: "*the* LORD *will not acquit anyone who misuses his name.*" Those are strong words, arguably the strongest in the Decalogue. Although our commandment is placed alongside prohibitions of murder, adultery, and theft, it is the misuse of the divine name that is specially marked as unforgivable. Furthermore, if it were to refer only to oaths, then the Ninth Commandment would seem somewhat redundant.[10]

In this essay, I first want to examine the exact language of the text (which is the same in Ex. 20:7 and Deut. 5:11), and argue that its intention is first to protect God's name from disrepute. The glory of the name was God's concern and purpose throughout Exodus (e.g., 9:16)—God alone protects and glorifies it as far as Sinai but now he enlists his people in that task. Above all else, the commandment enjoins us to tell the world the truth about God. After immersing us in the text, I want to consider how various other Old Testament texts shed light on what it means to tell the truth about God. And I want to hold these up alongside various sermons, lectures and statements issued shortly after September 11, when it was harder than usual to know and speak the truth about God.

The Language of the Commandment

"The Name of the LORD"

The construction "lift up the name" does not appear elsewhere in the Old Testament.[11] The theological freight of God's name, however, is extensive. A survey of the use of the name throughout the Bible shows what an important theme it is.

The Old Testament claims that the worship of the name of the LORD is "the primeval religion of mankind in general,"[12] since it begins to be called upon (Gen. 4:26) before the LORD is self-revealed to Abraham. The divine name is strongly tied to "God's keeping of promises and making of covenant"[13]—Abraham and Isaac invoke it immediately after receiving promises from God (Gen. 12:8, 26:25), and God reveals it definitively to Moses (Ex. 6) before he leads the people out of Egypt. God also promises to Moses that he will "proclaim before you the name, 'The LORD'" (Ex. 33:19). When the people enter the Promised Land, that name goes before them and becomes a source of power: "All the peoples of the earth shall see that you are called by the name of the LORD, and they shall be afraid of you" (Deut. 28:10; cf. Ps. 102:15) as the reports of God's mighty redemptive work become known throughout the world (Josh. 9:9). In the monarchy, too, the name of the LORD is an expression of the pride and might of Israel. Says David to Goliath, "You come to me with sword and spear and javelin; but I come to you in the name of the LORD of hosts, the God of the armies of Israel, whom you have defied" (1 Sam 17:45; cf. Ps. 20:7).

The name of the LORD is not only mighty, it is holy. The law codes expand on the Decalogue, protecting the name further: "One who blasphemes the name of the LORD shall be put to death; the whole congregation shall stone the blasphemer" (Lev 24:16). Eventually vows are made in the name of the LORD: "Jonathan said to David, 'Go in peace, since both of us have sworn in the name of the LORD'" (1 Sam. 20:42).

Solomon finally builds "a house for the name of the LORD" (1 Ki. 8:20, etc.), and its renown spreads further. The Queen of Sheba is drawn to Israel by "fame due to the name of the LORD" (1 Ki. 10:1). The temple, and all the theology that goes with it, continue to be associated specifically with the name, so that Isaiah foretells of the nations streaming to "Mount Zion, the place of the name of the LORD of hosts" (Is. 30:27). It could be argued that the characteristics of power and inviolability that come to be associated with Zion initially are properties of the divine name.

All of the foregoing threads are taken up again in the psalms, where of course the name is also an object of effusive praise. Therefore the name of the LORD is spoken of by Israel as all the things that God is: shield (Gen. 15), strength and song (Ex. 15). Allan Harman writes, "In Hebrew usage, the name did not just mean the vocable by which someone or something was known. Rather it was a term that often included the ideas of existence, character, and reputation. This was especially so in relation to the Lord."[14]

The divine name, in its holiness and power, became the standard by which not only oaths but also prophecy and theology were judged.

In a well-known passage from Deuteronomy 18, Moses reports to the community God's promise to raise up a prophet to speak in God's name. The name of God confers power, but it also holds a prophet accountable to speak the truth:

> "Any prophet who speaks in the name of other gods, or who presumes to speak in my name a word that I have not commanded the prophet to speak—that prophet shall die." (18:20)

Just this threat is used by Ahab to extract a true prophecy from Micaiah ben Imlah in 1 Kings 22. After Micaiah initially gives a positive prophecy for the upcoming battle, Ahab says, "How many times must I make you swear to tell me nothing but the truth in the name of the LORD?" (22:16). Micaiah then changes his tune and correctly predicts defeat.

God's name continues to be a source of power in the New Testament. "The seventy returned with joy, saying, 'Lord, in your name even the demons submit to us!'" (Lk. 10:17). It is still a holy name set aside for invocation in prayer (Mt. 6:9 and pars.); it is a call to discipleship (Mt. 19:29), and a mark of Lordship (Mt. 28:19, Rev. 14:4). As Old Testament figures sought help in the name of the Lord, so "everyone who calls on the name of the Lord shall be saved" (Acts 2:21, Rom. 10:13). And the name of the LORD spreads further (Acts 9:15, 15:17), so that new prophets can appeal to their churches "by the name of our Lord Jesus Christ" (1 Cor. 1:10, etc.). This is indeed one of Paul's strongest pleas.

"In Vain"

The precise phrasing of the Third Commandment is "You shall not lift up the name of the Lord your God לַשָּׁוְא (*lashav*)" What exactly does לַשָּׁוְא mean? It is not a common idiom, although Jeremiah likes it, accounting for five of its nine biblical occurrences:

> Go up to Gilead, and take balm,
> O virgin daughter Egypt!
> In vain (לַשָּׁוְא) you have used many medicines;
> there is no healing for you. —(Jer 46:11)

"In vain" is a fine translation, although it is difficult to pin down the precise semantic range of שָׁוְא by itself, as the variety of translations by the NRSV committee demonstrates: falsehood, futility, destruction, delusion, emptiness, vanity, worthlessness. In any case, it is always a powerfully negative word, very often signifying a false or empty theological claim. Its use in the phrase "הַבְלֵי־שָׁוְא" (Jon. 2:8, Ps. 31:6), usually translated "vain/worthless idols," emphasizes its religious undertones.

The Septuagint translates שָׁוְא as μάταιος, a term that continues to be contrasted with God's truth in the New Testament: "We bring you good news, that you should turn from these worthless things (ματαίων) to the living God" (Acts 14:15, cf. 1 Cor 3:20, Eph. 4:17). Throughout the biblical witness, then, although the semantic range of לַשָּׁוְא is wide, it has an essentially *theological* connotation: it is not merely falsehood or emptiness that is usually forbidden, but falsehood and emptiness with respect to God.

"He Will Not Acquit"
Finally, what does it mean that God "will not acquit" (לֹא יְנַקֶּה)? The verb ties this commandment to the classic formulation of God's character in Exodus 34:17: "forgiving iniquity and transgression and sin, yet by no means clearing (נַקֵּה לֹא יְנַקֶּה) the guilty." Yet this does not specify any other transgressions that will not be forgiven. Proverbs, however, does: he who sleeps with his neighbor's wife (6:29); the arrogant (16:5); those who are glad at calamity (17:5); false witnesses and the liars (19:5, 9); and those in a hurry to be rich (28:20). Widening the inquiry to include forms of נשׂא,[15] one also notes Joshua 24:19-20, which adds idolatry to the list of unforgivable sins. This is a very serious list, but the Decalogue again seems to emphasize theological truth; there, the only other law that comes with a threat is the commandment against idolatry (Ex. 20:5).

In the New Testament, the primary unforgivable sin appears to be the refusal to forgive: "For if you forgive others their trespasses, your heavenly Father will also forgive you; but if you do not forgive others, neither will your Father forgive your trespasses" (Matt 6:14-15). This may be because in Christ it is revealed more clearly than ever that God is a God who forgives, and thus for the community of believers not to witness to God's character amounts to a theological lie.

In the foregoing analysis it is clear that the Third Commandment has in view first and foremost *theological* lies—lies told about God, at the expense of God, or in the name of God. In the Deuteronomic Decalogue, the Ninth Commandment shares the same word for "false witness" as is translated "wrongful use" in Exodus 20:7 (שָׁוְא). The Third Commandment is the vertical version of the ninth. We might paraphrase it: "You shall not bear false witness concerning God." The phrasing of the commandment is purposely broad and purposely slanted toward the theological.

Telling the Truth about God: 9/11 and the Old Testament

Let us now turn to some examples of post-9/11 theology, bringing them into conversation with Old Testament texts that speak to the problem of false witness in the name of God.

Hannaniah: The Charlatan Prophet

Jeremiah 27-28 tells the story of the conflicting prophecies of Jeremiah and Hannaniah. In Ch. 27, the word of God comes to Jeremiah, telling him that Jerusalem must submit to Babylon or be destroyed. Jeremiah dons a wooden yoke, symbolizing the yoke that Judah must bear, and he brings this word to the priests and the people. There is no record of their response, but soon afterward they get a very different word from Hannaniah: "Thus says the LORD of hosts, the God of Israel: I have broken the yoke of the king of Babylon." Jeremiah says, essentially: "We'll see," an implicit invocation of Deuteronomy 18's prophecy test. But Hannaniah, who is every bit the showman that Jeremiah is, takes the yoke from his neck and breaks it—a neat piece of symbolic street-theater.

False prophets often are also master marketers. In lieu of the power of the truth, they have learned how to package and promote their lies effectively. The religious opinion that received the most coverage in the wake of the World Trade Center attacks was that of Jerry Falwell. It seems that Falwell has always had a knack for getting himself in the news. I can remember his outbursts from my childhood; he has always been there in the national consciousness. In an appearance on the 700

Club just two days after the attack, Falwell had this exchange with Pat Robertson:

> **Jerry Falwell:** And I agree totally with you that the Lord has protected us so wonderfully these 225 years. And since 1812, this is the first time that we've been attacked on our soil and by far the worst results.[16] And I fear, as Donald Rumsfeld, the Secretary of Defense, said yesterday, that this is only the beginning. And with biological warfare available to these monsters—the Husseins, the Bin Ladens, the Arafats—what we saw on Tuesday, as terrible as it is, could be miniscule if, in fact—if, in fact—God continues to lift the curtain and allow the enemies of America to give us probably what we deserve.

It sounds as if Falwell is incriminating himself for what has happened. But he doesn't. He continues:

> **Falwell:** The ACLU's got to take a lot of blame for this.

> **Robertson:** Well, yes.

> **Falwell:** And, I know that I'll hear from them for this. But, throwing God out successfully with the help of the federal court system, throwing God out of the public square, out of the schools. The abortionists have got to bear some burden for this because God will not be mocked. And when we destroy 40 million little innocent babies, we make God mad. I really believe that the pagans, and the abortionists, and the feminists, and the gays and the lesbians who are actively trying to make that an alternative lifestyle, the ACLU, People For the American Way—all of them who have tried to secularize America—I point the finger in their face and say "you helped this happen."[17]

> **Robertson:** I totally concur.

The next day, America's headlines screamed "Falwell blames WTC attack on abortionists, feminists, gays." It was immediately clear to anyone who could read and think that these claims were false. Terrorists did not attack the World Trade towers in New York because they were situated in a permissive and libertine city. The attack on the Pentagon showed that much—surely there are few institutions in the country that are less permissive and libertine than the military. The attack was aimed not at a specific lifestyle within the United States, but at the way America treats the world—policies that they perceived to be underwritten by a financial nerve center in New York and protected by a military capitol in Arlington, VA. It was an attack on our policy decisions that affect the whole world. Least of all do Muslim terrorists care if Christian values are upheld in our courts and schools.

Would that Falwell's claims were only false! Instead they are damaging to every other Christian in the country. If I may be allowed a couple of personal anecdotes: I have found myself, through my academic affiliations, involved in an Internet bulletin board over the past few years, a board where everything from public policy to sports to religion is discussed. It is a civil forum, yet because of the board's broad national readership, it draws people with a wide array of perspectives. In my opinion, the anonymity of the Internet leads to a certain frankness that one would not get at a cocktail party. What is striking about the religious discussions that take place there is the extent to which some Americans' negative opinions about religion are based on figures like Falwell. And this accords with my own experience. Although I grew up in a household with a theologian and in an extended family rife with ministers, there was a long portion of my teenage years when the effect of the culture's image of Christianity was stronger than the truer one being modeled in my own home, and I left the church. Like the people I encounter now on the Internet, I wanted no part of hypocrisy. Terence Fretheim writes: "The name of God is so commonly associated with empty phrases or easy religion or the latest ideology of a social or political sort. . . . As people hear it so used, they may come to associate [it] with a cause they wish to avoid or reject. . . . At the deepest level, use of God's name is a matter of mission."[18]

Falwell's indiscriminate excesses in denouncing sin also rob the church of its public credibility in witnessing against real sin. For example, it's easy to oppose freedom of prayer in schools if it appears that only the Jerry Falwells of the world want it. So as Hannaniah's false prophecy endangered Judah, so Falwell's remarks endanger the Church.

Jeremiah gets the last word in his story. He says to Hannaniah: "You have broken wooden bars only to forge iron bars in place of them!

The LORD has not sent you, and you made this people trust in a lie." It is to the credit of many ministers of God's word that they stood up in the days following Falwell's remarks and publicly disowned them.[19] Disputing false prophecy is itself an act of prophecy.

Samuel: No Time for the Truth

Not every form of false prophecy is as public or as dangerous as Falwell's, but it must still be recognized as false. The story of God's renunciation of Saul is a fascinating and subtle one; in fact, the central issue is lost in most translations. In 1 Samuel 15, after Saul fails to execute the ban and destroy all of the Amalekites and their property, God says to Samuel, "נִחַמְתִּי כִּי־הִמְלַכְתִּי אֶת־שָׁאוּל"—literally, "I repent[20] that I made Saul king." Samuel's response? He "was angry; and he cried out to the LORD all night." This may seem strange to a reader who does not have the whole story in mind. In context, however, it makes perfect sense. Samuel may have been the best religious leader around, but he was hardly a perfect one. As he grows old, he first sets his own sons over the people, but they are corrupt. Then the people cry out for a king, and Samuel takes it as a personal attack. He may be right, but God sees the heart of the thing: "They have not rejected you, but they have rejected me" (8:7). Samuel rails so bitterly to the people about the evils of a king that God has to tell him twice to acquiesce to their demand (8:9, 22)—and even then, Samuel's way of agreeing is sullenly to send the Israelites home. In his old age, Samuel is so comfortable with the way things have always been that he is no longer as responsive to the word of God as he was in his childhood, when he said, "Speak, for your servant is listening" (3:12).

So when God tells Samuel he has repented of making Saul king, Samuel again seems to think only of himself: perhaps he dreads the embarrassment and hassle of choosing a new king. Therefore when he speaks to Saul, who needs to hear the truth, he makes the message simple and final—by lying. "The Glory of Israel will not recant or repent (יְנָחֵם); for he is not a mortal, that he should repent (לְהִנָּחֵם)" (15:29). Yet that's just what God did! Most translations render נחם as "change his mind" here (although even the venerable King James translation picks up the echo). The repetition of the root seems calculated to make the reader think about Samuel's claim—may God not repent? The question is the subject of an entire monograph;[21] suffice it to say for now that there is significant reason to think that we may speak in that way of God (cf. Gen 6:6-7, Jonah 3:9-10). Therefore Samuel's word to Saul, while perhaps not harmful to Israel, is false.

A slightly different response to the 9/11 attacks was drafted by a group of conservative evangelical leaders including James Dobson, and sent to pastors across the United States. It is entitled, "A Biblical Response to America's Emergency."[22] Based loosely on Isaiah 30, it begins promisingly: "It is time to reflect and repent. It is time to rend our hearts and not our garments. . . . Our goal is not to make others look bad in order to make ourselves look good. In many ways, the church is as guilty as our society at large." The tone and perspective of the document are indeed different from Falwell's incendiary accusations. Yet the sin of which it calls the church to repent is essentially complicity in the same moral failings that Falwell identified: restricting prayer in schools, "unimaginable perversion" in the media, and abortion. Furthermore, the document says that the church's ministry of prayer should be to the United States' government and its people, with no mention of anyone outside our borders. The nationalism and the polemic are brought together in this rather odd formulation: "We are thankful for the Statue of Liberty in New York City's harbor, but we also need a Statue of Responsibility in San Francisco's harbor." The drafters' hope is to "spark a national revival"—whether this ambiguous phrase refers to church or state seems beside the point in a document that does not distinguish between the two.

Although the statement was distributed within religious channels and thus did not appear on the national radar, it was as misleading to those who heard or read it as Falwell's statement. One could only hope that those who heard it in their churches would ignore it and turn to God more truly, just as Saul repented and prayed to God.

Job: The Wisdom of Silence
A third approach to false theology appears in Job 13. Job is a book devoted to the mystery and transcendence of God. Job suffers for no reason except divine caprice, and the only answer he ever gets ("Where were you when I laid the foundation of the earth? . . . Shall a faultfinder contend with the Almighty?"[38:4, 40:2]) is so unsatisfying theologically that some interpreters take Job's final response to God as still bitter and stubborn.[23] God is finally rather inexplicable, but that does not stop Job's friends from trying to explain. Much of the book consists of

their windy monologues to Job about why he is suffering. Job quickly gets fed up with their theological arguments. He knows some theology himself (13:2), and he knows that their reasoning crumbles under the actual, inexplicable weight of his suffering:

> As for you, you whitewash with lies;
>> all of you are worthless physicians.
>
> If you would only keep silent,
>> that would be your wisdom!
>
> Hear now my reasoning,
>> and listen to the pleadings of my lips.
>
> Will you speak falsely for God,
>> and speak deceitfully for him? —(Job 13:4-7)

"If you would only keep silent, that would be your wisdom!" That was another response to the 9/11 attacks and, as Job says, a wiser one than false accusations. On Sept. 19, 2001, John Piper preached a sermon entitled, "Why I Do Not Say, 'God Did Not Cause the Calamity, But He Can Use It for Good.'"

"Many Christians are speaking this way," Piper says, but he argues that a God whose providence selectively excludes our suffering is neither the God revealed in scripture nor a God who could be trusted to bring about good. In a sermon in which he references Job often, Piper says,

> How God governs all events in the universe without sinning, and without removing responsibility from man, and with compassionate outcomes is mysterious indeed. . . . [T]he Bible teaches that he could have restrained this evil (Genesis 20:6). "The LORD nullifies the counsel of the nations; He frustrates the plans of the peoples" (Psalm 33:10). But it was not in his plan to do it. Let us beware. We spare God the burden of his sovereignty and lose our only hope.

Piper is, in fact, right. The magnificent and terrible claim of the Bible is that God is in control of human history. Faced with the most awful events of that history, however, we often cannot and should not offer justifications. Piper did not (at least in this sermon) go on to offer reasons for the attacks, but it takes a certain sort of courage just to stand up and say, "This means *something*. Think about it." Beyond that, it may be that, like Job's friends, we are better off keeping our mouths shut. "It is good . . . to sit alone in silence when the Lord has imposed it" (Lam. 3:28).

McCormack came to that same conclusion in his lecture: "Where the unspeakable happens, the best thing to do is to stop speaking; to enter into a holy silence, to cover our mouths and listen for what God would have to teach us."[24]

Jeremiah: A Way Forward

On the other hand, believers in the God of Israel and of Jesus Christ cannot always be silent. As Mordecai says to Esther, "If you keep silence at such a time as this, relief and deliverance will rise for the Jews from another quarter, but you and your father's family will perish. Who knows? Perhaps you have come to royal dignity for just such a time as this" (Esther 4:14). The burden of speaking is especially heavy when keeping silence would be tantamount to denying our faith. That was the conclusion of Karl Barth and the signers of the Barmen Declaration: "We may and must speak with one voice in this matter today . . . we may not keep silent, since we believe that we have been given a common message to utter in a time of common need and temptation."[25]

The hardest word of all to speak does not promote false prophecy, nor does it merely silence it. At a time of tragedy, the constructive task—knowing what we *should* say, rather than just what we shouldn't—is always the hardest. When Luther finished his preaching against the wrongful use of God's name, he said, "You must also know how to use the name of God aright."[26] And even as he advocated silence, McCormack said, "I am not saying that we should keep our silence permanently" but only until we know "what God would have to teach us." There, the Bible is our textbook. Understood rightly by the power of the Spirit, the name and word of God show a way forward.

> How can you say, "We are wise,
>   and the law of the LORD is with us,"
>   when, in fact, the false pen of the scribes
>   has made it into a lie?

The wise shall be put to shame,
>   they shall be dismayed and taken;
>   since they have rejected the word of the LORD,
>   what wisdom is in them?

Therefore I will give their wives to others
>   and their fields to conquerors,
>   because from the least to the greatest
>   everyone is greedy for unjust gain;
>   from prophet to priest
>   everyone deals falsely.

They have treated the wound of my people carelessly,
>   saying, "Peace, peace,"
>   when there is no peace. —(Jer. 8:8-12)

Even in Jeremiah's condemnation is a call. He does not simply shout down the false prophets and priests; he diagnoses their sin, and a diagnosis is the first step toward a cure. The religious leaders are guilty of the same sin as everyone else: "from the least to the greatest," they are "greedy for unjust gain" and "deal falsely." This is the repeated word of the prophets to a nation in decline: The people have forgotten that their God is a God who cares for the poor, the widow, the orphan, and the sojourner. Very few preachers were willing to deliver such a word in the wake of a national tragedy. Richard Crocker, then pastor of Central Presbyterian Church of Montclair, N.J., came face to face with Jeremiah 4 in the lectionary that week and was at least pushed in that direction:

> God is not punishing the people who died and their families; God did not fly the airplane into the buildings. People did that—people who were caught up in a desperate, raging, hateful cruelty that is the opposite of God. But that does not mean that there are not lessons to be learned. Instead of reacting with unthinking desire for revenge—as understandable as that is—it would be better if we asked: have we been too concerned about amassing our own power and wealth, and too little concerned about the well-being of others? Have we contributed—knowingly or unknowingly—to the hatred that has erupted?[27]

Crocker let the question rest there for the time being—probably a fair decision in a commuter community that had lost a number of its citizens in the tragedy.

The most prophetic voice I heard in the days after 9/11 was that of a rabbi, Michael Lerner of Beyt Tikkun Synagogue in San Francisco, in an article entitled "A World Out of Touch With Itself":

> We may tell ourselves that the current violence has "nothing to do" with the way that we've learned to close our ears when told that one out of every three people on this planet does not have enough food, and that one billion are literally starving. We may reassure ourselves that the hoarding of the world's resources by the richest society in world history, and our frantic attempts to accelerate globalization with its attendant inequalities of wealth, has nothing to do with the resentment that others feel toward us. ... The same inability to feel the pain of others is the pathology that shapes the minds of these terrorists.[28]

There were certainly Christians saying similar things, but it just so happens that a Jew gave especially artful expression to Matthew 7:1-5's insight about specks and logs: Rather than taking up our cross with Christ (Mark 8:34-35) as Christ took judgment upon himself, we have rushed to judge others. It may be hard to hear that the world is not as simple as "the righteous us" versus "the evil ones," as George W. Bush would have us think.[29] But Lerner's response calls us to remember that we are heirs not only of Adam (and thus sinners) but also of Abraham (and thus called to be a blessing to all the families of the earth). And Lerner's call accords precisely with the word of the prophets. Like Jeremiah's Israel, we grind the poor under our heel. The primary difference between them and us is that our greed touches and harms the entire world.

This is not to equate any individual American with the terrorists, only to say, as Miroslav Volf does in *Exclusion and Embrace*, that true reconciliation cannot come through vilification of the other and claims of righteousness for oneself. Rather, the Christian way is the way of the cross, the way of repentance. Vengeance belongs to God (Rom. 12:17-21).

Balaam: Not for Sale

Those of us in the churches and "the Academy" must not be tempted by self-righteousness, tempted to forget that our salaries and our educations are largely paid for by the same corporate dollars that Lerner condemns. We must consider more carefully than anyone the ways in which the wealth that surrounds us and buoys us affects the things we write and speak, and even the way we think. We might look to an unlikely biblical hero: the prophet Balaam.

As Israel approaches the Promised Land, Balak, the king of Moab, fearfully summons the prophet. Balaam at first refuses to go at all, because God appears to him and warns him not to, but eventually God sends him. Still, even once Balaam is under the hire of Moab, he can speak only "the word God puts in my mouth" (Num. 22:38). Balak gathers an impressive cultic and financial outlay for the occasion of cursing Israel, setting up seven altars and sacrificing a bull and ram on each. "Come," he says to Balaam, "curse Jacob for me; Come, denounce Israel!" (23:7) Then at the moment when all is in readiness, when the state of Moab has planned everything perfectly to suit its own ends, *God's* purposes interpose themselves, thanks to a prophet who will not be bought and will not lie in the name of the LORD. "How can I curse whom God has not cursed?" Balaam asks. "How can I denounce those whom the LORD has not denounced?" (23:8)

Balak reacts in much the same way one would expect George W. Bush to do if James Dobson, Billy Graham, and the establishment of the Christian Right were to suddenly turn their backs on him: "What have you done to me?" (23:11) It is the politician's cry of dereliction, when the order of things he thought he knew no longer functions—and to be realistic, it is not common. But it does happen. Any church can apply itself to the cause of justice, and popular sentiment can stop wars and end oppression. It is a slower tool than military force but a more precise one. Still, in the end, the powers and principalities are likely not to want voices in their midst that they cannot control. Balak says to Balaam, "Do not curse them at all, and do not bless them at all" (23:25). In other words, "Shut up and go away."

Conclusion

The story of Balaam illustrates for us the essential questions raised by the Third Commandment: Who are we? and Whose are we? In a time of war these are especially pertinent questions for congregations to be asking themselves. Will we be bought and sold by the powers of the world, or will we belong to God? In the context of the first tablet, it should have always been clear to interpreters that oath taking was too limited a sphere for this word. It follows right after who God is, and it marks off God's people in order to keep them holy; thus it leads us naturally into the commandment that sets apart God's day.

It has been pointed out that Numbers 6:27 offers an interpretive key to the Third Commandment. After the Aaronic blessing, God says to Moses, "So they shall put my name on the Israelites, and I will bless them." This idea of having God's name stamped on God's people extends right to the end of the Bible, right to the eschaton: "[God's] servants will worship him; they will see his face, and his name will be on their foreheads" (Rev. 22:4).

To bear God's name means to be God's "treasured possession" (Ex. 19:5). But that is a blessing that comes with responsibilities. When we take up God's name and go forth into the world bearing the name "Christians," we have the potential to honor it or dishonor it. When we are faced with the reality of war and the responsibility of responding to a calamity such as September 11, what will be the words of truth that the Church will speak? Mercifully, we are not without help in our struggle to speak the truth: the Spirit helps us in our weakness. To take up the name of God also means to take up the armor of God and be made "ready to proclaim the gospel of peace" (Eph. 6:15).

Endnotes

[1] For a Christian approach to pacifism, the reader may find useful John Howard Yoder's *The Politics of Jesus* (Grand Rapids, Michigan: Eerdmans, 1994) or *Nevertheless: The Varieties and Shortcomings of Religious Pacifism* (Scottdale, PA: Herald Press, 1999). For a Christian approaches to just-war theory, Paul Ramsey's *The Just War: Force and Political Responsibility* (Landham, MD: Rowman & Littlefield, 2002) is a representative modern example. One important recent book on the ethics of peacemaking that also ought to be noted is Miroslav Volf's *Exclusion and Embrace* (Nashville, TN: Abingdon Press, 1996).

[2] Bruce McCormack, unpublished, untitled lecture delivered September 2001 at Princeton Theological Seminary.

[3] Devon M. Largio, "Uncovering the Rationales for the War on Iraq: The Words of the Bush Administration," *Congress and the Media* from September 12, 2001, to October 11, 2002.

[4] David Kay, then the CIA's chief weapons inspector, testified to Congress in February: "It turns out we were all wrong. ... I think there were no large stockpiles of WMD." (*U.S. News & World Report*, 136 (5) [February 9, 2004]: 24)

[5] Godfrey Hodgson, "Trust Buster," *The Washington Post*, December 18, 2003, C03.

[6] Ex. 23:12, Lev. 19:12, Deut. 5:20, 6:13, 23:21-23, etc.

[7] Brevard Childs, *The Book of Exodus* (Louisville: The Westminster Press, 1974), 412.

[8] Allan Harman, "The Interpretation of the Third Commandment" (*The Reformed Theological Review* 47.1 [1988]) 1; cf. Rashi, *The Metsudah Chumash/Rashi* (tr. Davis, Hoboken, N.J.: KTAV Publishing House, 1996), 260.

[9] Notably, Article VII of the Schleitheim Articles reads: "Christ, who teaches the perfection of the law, forbids His [followers] all swearing, whether true or false."

[10] Indeed, some reflections on the Ninth Commandment, including the second half of Walter Brueggemann's "Truth-Telling as Subversive Obedience" *Journal for Preachers*, Lent 1997, seem more relevant to the Third, by my interpretation.

[11] However, note Ps. 24:4, which says God will bless those "who do not lift up their souls to what is false. "What is false" translates the same Hebrew term rendered "in vain" in the third commandment.

[12] Gerhard von Rad, *Old Testament Theology*, vol. 1 (Louisville: Westminster John Knox Press, 2001), 113.

[13] Bruce C. Birch et al., *A Theological Introduction to the Old Testament* (Nashville: Abingdon Press, 1999), 114.

[14] Harman, "The Interpretation of the Third Commandment," 3.

[15] The common verb חלס appears most often to occur positively, with reference to grace.

[16] Falwell here seems to ignore the attack on Pearl Harbor. Perhaps he meant the first time our mainland has been attacked in that span.

[17] A nearly full text may be found on the Internet at http://www.truthorfiction.com/rumors/f/falwell-robertson-wtc.htm. Excerpts may be found at http://www.cnn.com/2001/US/09/14/Falwell.apology and http://www.washingtonpost.com/ac2/wp-dyn?pagename=article&node=&contentId=A28620-2001Sep14&notFound=true.

[18] Fretheim 228.

[19] Falwell and Robertson offered partial apologies in the days that followed.

[20] Or "I regret."

[21] Joachim Jeremias, *Die Reue Gottes: Aspekte des alttestamentalischer Gottesvorstellung*, Neukirchen, 1997.

[22] Full text available on the Internet at http://pe.ag.org/pentecostal-evangel/Articles2001/4564_davis.cfm

[23] Jack Miles, among a few others, argues that instead of "I despise myself and repent in dust and ashes," 42:6 should be translated "I shudder with sorrow for mortal clay," because now Job knows that God is unjust (Miles 322ff.). The most interesting implication of this debate for the theology of the book in general may be that the verse is ambiguous enough that one cannot be sure. Carol Newsom picks up on this ambiguity in *The Book of Job: A Contest of Moral Imaginations* (Oxford ; New York : Oxford University Press, 2003).

[24] Bruce McCormack, unpublished, untitled lecture delivered September 2001 at Princeton Theological Seminary.

[25] *The Book of Confessions (PC-USA)* (Louisville: Office of the General Assembly, 1999) 248-249.

[26] Martin Luther, *The Book of Concord* (Decatur, Ill.: Johann Gerhard Institute, 1996), 373.

[27] Richard R. Crocker, "The Reason for Hope," preached September 16, 2001, at Central Presbyterian Church of Montclair, N.J.

[28] Text available at http://www.peterussell.com/WTC/Lerner.html.

[29] A search of the George W. Bush speech archive at www.whitehouse.gov turned up fifty-nine hits for speeches including "evil ones," and forty for "evildoers."

Passing the Peace

Dr. Luis N. Rivera-Pagán speaks in this chapter on the global significance of war in the twentieth century. Discussing issues prevalent from Latin America to the Hutus and Tutsis of Rwanda, he declares that amidst the terror of war there is hope if we will begin to see one another in a different light. Perhaps it is in our diversity and mutual engagement of culture and religion that we will create an ethos of peace throughout the world. This chapter was a lecture given on March 10, 2004. It was sponsored by the University of Puerto Rico UNESCO Chair for Peace Education.

Between Terror and Hope

Reflections about Religion, War, and Peace

Dr. Luis N. Rivera-Pagán
Translated from the Spanish by Cheryl Byers

> I do not offer you peace, dear brother
> because peace is not a medal:
> peace is an enslaved land
> And we need to liberate it . . .
> May the bloodied temples toll
> Hurling us to love is enough. —Jorge Debravo

The Warrior Century

On the occasion of the first centennial of the Nobel Peace Prize in December, 2001, in Oslo, Norway, the British historian Eric Hobsbawm gave a lecture titled "War and Peace in the 20th Century." [1] From his observations, we can arrive at the following conclusions:

1. The wars of the twentieth century have been the deadliest in human history. Directly or indirectly they were the cause of approximately 187 million deaths. Impressive advances in military technology multiplied geometrically the fatal consequences of the many wars that proliferated.

2. The distinction between combatants and civilians, fundamental for the classic doctrines of just war, was eroded. War ceased to be a conflict between armies and became a confrontation between nations. From Guernica to Hiroshima there is a fatal and tragic logical continuity that goes on to the bombardments against Belgrade and Baghdad. If the calculations of civilian casualties were approximately 5 percent in the First World War, these elevated to 66 percent in the Second World War. Today it is estimated that 80 to 90 percent of those affected seriously by attacks are civilians. The city, core of social life, loses its immunity and becomes a privileged target of bombardment, a labyrinth of bellicose terror, a metaphor of hell. Guernica, Dresden, Tokyo, Hiroshima, and Nagasaki are horrendous parabolas of Dante's Hades.

3. Despite intense efforts to establish a system of international structures capable of resolving political conflicts through multilateral processes of negotiation, at the end of the twentieth century, war persisted as a privileged resource to continue, as Clausewitz would say, politics by other means. The Kellogg-Briand treaty proclaimed in 1928 the end of wars. Soon it would be more worthless than the paper it was printed on. As the second millennium culminated, the somber dilemma was: a relatively inadequate multilateral system of consensus or the unilateralism of a super power, prosecutor, and judge of world conflicts. The tragedy of September 11, 2001, has been utilized as a catapult to proclaim, as a doctrine of national security, the preventive war of the powerful against the weak. It did not cost the current U. S. government much effort to dismantle the fragile international structures of conciliation and assume the Texan role of self-designated sheriff of weighty affairs belonging to all humanity. It is a posture that, on occasion, as in the invasion of Iraq, egregiously neglects international law.

Hobsbawm does not emphasize, however, three crucial points of the twentieth century basic to its warlike obsession: the concentration of wars in areas of humanity most afflicted socially, insensibility regarding the pain of the "other," and intense ideological passion.

1. There was in the twentieth century a tragic succession of minor wars, often cataloged as "low intensity," but of enormous human and social cost for the populations involved. The "cold war" was accompanied by innumerable bellicose conflicts that darkened extensive sections of the planet. Korea, Vietnam, Cambodia, Laos, Angola, Mozambique, Israel, Palestine, Jordan, Lebanon, Nicaragua, El Salvador, Guatemala, Colombia, Rwanda, Sierra Leon, Algiers, Liberia, Ethiopia, Eritrea, Iraq, Iran, Afghanistan, India-Pakistan, Bangladesh, among other countries, were scenes of armed confrontations that caused grave harm to their population. The chilling nuclear shield seemed to preserve peace only for the Euro-Atlantic nations incorporated in the two big political-military pacts that at that time shared world domination. The rest of humanity, already suffering the scourge of social and economic misery, remained free for countless wars, incited by exogenous and endogenous causes and fed by a fierce competition in arms sales. After the dissolution of the Soviet Union and the Warsaw Treaty, peace did not prevail. War assumed other profiles: national, ethnic, cultural, and religious exclusions. In Rwanda, Croatia, Bosnia, Kosovo, Armenia, Azerbaijan, Georgia, and Palestine the ethnic and cultural differences revived ancestral grudges. The hatreds did not subside; they only muted their shades and disguises.

2. Upon examining the image of the "enemy," designed to incite hatred and mass slaughter, one can discover, buried under the discourse of vital interests and national security, a profound disdain towards the pain and affliction of those human beings particularized by their different race, color, language, or culture. By undervaluing the visible marks of their being, their subjugation or extermination is facilitated. Only thus can be explained the atrocious cruelty that ordinary human beings perpetrate against those who they recognize not as fellow beings but as enemies because of their different skin pigmentation, ways of praying, language, national memory, or cultural traditions. Serbs, Croats, and Bosnians; Hutus and Tutsis; Armenians and Azerbaijanis; Jews and Palestinians; Ladinos and Mayans; Irish Catholics and Calvinists; Sudanese Christians and Islamists; Turks and Kurds; Russians and Checheskens—the list is endless, submerged themselves in an abyss of hostility that seemed to capture their hearts and minds. The Shoah is perhaps the greatest expression, but not necessarily the only one, of this immense hostility against the "other" in the twentieth century.

3. Ideological passion in that tragic century was a carnival of homicidal convictions. In the name of racial purity and national supremacy, social equality and the abolition of classes, party or proletariat control, national liberation, the global hegemony of the free market, democracy and human rights and, finally, in the name of jealous and irate gods, peoples and nations launched themselves with fervor and passion into the dismal enterprise of violent destruction. The century of immense scientific and technical advances was also the epoch of intense homicidal passions. Only two centuries after the European Enlightenment proclaimed the triumph of serene rationality and Immanuel Kant foretold cosmopolitan peace and the conversion of religiosity into ethical solidarity,[2] passions of blood and soil, irate gods and violent religious devotions, bloodstained the face of humanity.

That bloody twentieth century, marked by the memory of Auschwitz, Hiroshima, the Gulag, two global wars and hundreds of regional conflicts, can be summarized in "The Second Coming," the famous poem of W. B. Yates, with its plethora of religious and apocalyptic resonances:

> Things fall apart; the center cannot hold;
> Mere anarchy is loosed upon the world,
> The blood-dimmed tide is loosed, and everywhere
> The ceremony of innocence is drowned;
> The best lack all convictions, while the worst
> Are full of passionate intensity.[3]

Terror in the Mind of God

Paradoxically, in the twentieth century war was waged countless times with the pretension of ending war. Declarations and actions of war were accompanied, unfailingly, with devout proclamations of universal harmony. From the Russian-Japanese war of 1904 to the recent invasion of Iraq, perpetrators of human massacre have invoked sacrilegiously the ideals of global peace. It seemed to invoke Sisyphus's fate: make war for the sake of peace.

Each scientific and technological military advance was thereby justified, like a new sacrament of world peace, culminating in the horrifying system of nuclear destruction of human civilization, erected paradoxically to protect it. The threat of universal destruction, it was alleged, would be the guarantee of global security. A bipolar frightening strategy that curiously parodies the religious myth according to which the horror of hell leads to the threshold of heaven.[4] The possibility of absolute war is seen as baptismal rite of universal peace.

It seemed initially the century of the secular war, in which ideological passion would proclaim the dawn of profane gods: the supremacy of the nation, the equalitarian society, the apocalyptical class war, national liberation, globalization of the free market, and the reign of universal and secret suffrage. It was the profane devotion to irreverent and heterodox altars of secularization. Religious tribulations seemed to be restricted to the intimate corners of the devout soul and the tranquility of the temples.

Nevertheless, the jealous and implacable gods of olden times were preparing their return in spectacular sacred confrontations. At the end of the century, pious adorers of Yahweh, Jesus Christ, and Allah proclaimed divine wrath and declared holy wars. The volcano of religious passions was revived. Those who thought that with the Peace of Westphalia (1648) we had freed ourselves of religious wars, face with perplexity and horror the resurgence of sacred bellicosity.

Many theoreticians of secularism and modernity are surprised by this renewal of belligerent religious passion, what one French scholar has aptly called the "revenge of God."[5] Those who studied the growth, in the middle of the last century, of Arab nationalism, secular and socialist, are perplexed by the strong challenge that Islamic integrism presents in the battle for the Muslim soul. Jihad recovers its darkest shadows. Something similar happens in Zionism. Many Zionists abandon their socialist, democratic, and pluralistic heritage and adhere to dogmatic postures about the alleged divine promise, inscribed in the Tanakh, of a Greater Israel. On the Indian subcontinent, violence among Hindus and Muslims is revived, threatening the national paradigm of a tolerant and pluralist society sponsored by Gandhi and Nehru. In Sri Lanka, the matrix of the violent civil war of two decades between Sinhaleses and Tamils can be found not only in their ethnic and cultural differences, but also the fact that the first are mainly Buddhist and the second Hindus.

Even peaceful Buddhism can be a source of inspiration for sacred terror, as shown in the attack with chemical substances against the Tokyo subway system perpetrated by the Japanese sect Aum Shinrikyo, in 1995. In splintered Yugoslavia, the religiosity of Orthodox Serbs and Macedonians, Catholic Croats and Muslim Bosnians and Albanians has functioned as criterion for exclusion and antagonism. Idolatry of the sacred letter, archaic millenarianisms, and the national tradition of "Manifest Destiny" converge in militant American fundamentalism. Despite the economic opulence and military might of their nation, the American fundamentalist right conjures with terror satanical axes of cosmic evil. It is the paradox of religious violence: the simultaneity of piety and cruelty, of intimate communion among the faithful and intense hostility against the infidels.[6]

As José Saramago wrote on the occasion of the September 11, 2001, attacks:

> Memory has been lost of human beings killed the worst ways that we have been capable of inventing. Of these, the most criminal, the most absurd, the one that offends most simple reason, is that which, from the beginning of history and civilization, commands to kill in the name of God.[7]

In this postmodern epoch, one of whose pillars seemed to be the Nietzschean proclamation of the "Death of God," irate and devout religious passion springs up anew in many latitudes and cultures. Religion matters—and in such a way that many adherents are willing to kill and die for their faith.[8]

It is a topic that has been studied by some authors. Let us review some of the more outstanding.

1. José Casanova, in his *Public Religions in the Modern World*,[9] has radiographed skillfully this vigorous irruption of religious mentality in the public area. He calls it the "deprivatization" of religion; the rejection of the secular claim to restrict religious piety and creed to the intimacy of souls and temples. In the name of God, religious institutions enter with vigor into the public arena to shape the profiles of morality and legality, disobeying the secular paradigm of modernity. Radical theologies of liberation, reactionary integrisms, or public reformist theologies: despite their profound differences, they join in their common

pretension of political and social protagonism. The author notices the risks of that incursion in the political debate, but he also perceives in it a prophetic critique of the efforts to structure society prioritizing calculations of economic benefit established by a financial market that excludes ethical considerations from its conceptual horizon. Casanova restricts, however, his analysis to countries with relative social stability. Moreover, his study is limited to Christian churches and organizations, leaving out the rejuvenated versions of the crusades against the infidels. The global conflicts that provoke the "warriors of God" remain outside his critical look.

2. Regina Schwartz published in 1997 a sharp and finely written critique of the possessive and excluding dimensions of the monotheism of the three great religions of the Near East, Christianity, Judaism, and Islam. Her book, *The Curse of Cain: The Violent Legacy of Monotheism*,[10] unveils the sinister side of the affirmation "my God is the only true God." The ironic look of Schwartz, charged with ethical density, analyses the risks that a metaphysics of unity and totality within Semite monotheism represents for those who sustain different religious perspectives from the one outlined in the biblical confession of faith (Deuteronomy 6,4: "Hear, O Israel: The Lord our God, the Lord is one"). It is a suggestively heterodox critique of the potentially totalitarian and homicidal dimensions of the Semite monotheism to which the majority of the inhabitants of the planet belong.

3. *The Battle for God*, by Karen Armstrong, is a very suggestive analysis of the current integrisms of the three great monotheistic religions born in the Near East.[11] The belligerence of integrist Christians, Jews and Muslims, according to Armstrong, proceeds from their apocalyptic perception of finding themselves in a decisive moment of history: the final confrontation between the hosts of light and the forces of darkness. It reacts against diverse enemies: the secularists who believe that social laws depend on consensus and not on sacred texts; the coreligionists who promote some type of reformist arrangement that might restrict religious piety to the private sphere; and, finally, the infidels, devotees of other religions and deities. It becomes a dramatic and cosmic battle for God, on the verge, constantly, of passing from verbal offense to holy aggression. It also increases, by invoking the Sharia, the Torah, or the New Testament Epistles, the repression of women and of all men and women who opt for alternate styles of sexual orientation,

as the Egyptian writer Nawal El Saadawi has so finely perceived.[12] There is a discursive continuity between the dogmatic integrisms, the patriarchal cloistering of women, and homophobia.

4. *Terror in the Mind of God: The Global Rise of Religious Violence*, by North American professor Mark Juergensmeyer,[13] studies the mental and ideological mechanisms of the transition to holy war and its conversion into religious terrorism. His exposition illuminates three key areas.

a. The retrieval, in contexts of profound social crisis and community humiliation, of images and symbols of sacred violence found in many religious traditions: divine rage, cosmic confrontation among children of light and darkness, extermination of the transgressors of divine law, exclusion of infidels, idolaters, heretics, and gentiles. Devout piety, nourished by the sacred "texts of terror,"[14] generates implacable cruelty against the enemies of the faith. It is the resurrection of gloomy religious exclusivity. The "warriors of God" militarize religiosity. The enemy is now a satanical agent, who should not only be defeated but could also be exterminated.

b. Action against the enemies of faith is transmuted into a "theater of terror." It becomes a dramatic performance symbolic of a cosmic transcendent war. Divine violence produces theatrical rituals perceived as preludes of the dreadful final conflagration. The mythical apocalyptic images in many sacred texts are revived and applied to concrete historic conflicts. The events of September 11, 2001, are dramatic symbols of such a 'theater of terror": an intensely dramatic attack, in the name of divine wrath, of the economic, military, and political icons/idols of Western infidelity.

c. These religious integrists reactivate the tradition of "redeeming martyrdom." The struggle against secularism, infidelity, and heresy demands disposition towards the supreme sacrifice: one's own life. The blood of the martyrs is the source for the eschatological renovation of the creation. Timothy McVeigh in the U.S., the Hamas militants in Palestine, the ultra-orthodox Zionists in Israel, the Sikh bodyguards who assassinated Indira Gandhi in India, the young men who flew the airplanes into New York's twin towers, and the insurgents who today exact a costly payment for the invasion of Iraq, assume their death as a ritual of sacrifice, a sublime consecration of divine ire against those who contaminate creation. It is the resurgence of human sacrifice, clothed in the prestige of martyrdom, that linked with images of holy war mutates into atrocious homicidal suicide. It is not the traditional sacrifice that, according to Rene Girard's theory of sacred violence,[15] seeks to restore social order and cosmic harmony. It is a sacrifice/martyrdom that seeks to unleash the hoped-for universal eschatological cataclysm, a testimony of blood that pretends to purify the cosmic scene for the ultimate holocaust.

When the nation to which we offer our patriotic loyalty goes to war, the superficial secular facade dissolves and in many altars and pulpits pious entreaties of victory to the "God of Armies" are recited, as Mark Twain satirized with brilliant irony in his poignant *Oration of War*.[16] Praying to different and opposed deities, variations of the dismal hymn of death and eschatological desolation are intoned, the gloomy liturgical chant of the office of darkness:

> *Dies irae, dies illa*
> *solvet saeclum in favilla . . .*
> *Quantus tremor est futurus,*
> *quando judex est venturus,*
> *cuncta stricte discussurus.*[17]

Between Terror and Hope

Yet images of holy terror are peripheral to the great traditional religions. Central to them are the reverence towards the sacred, the affirmation of human life in all its plural manifestations, and the preservation of nature as divine creation and human hearth. Genuine religiosity tends to rebind human beings with their fellow beings, seeking lasting dignity that might overcome the awareness of our ineludible transience.

Thus the strong empathy that resonates so naturally among profoundly spiritual souls as Isaiah, Jesus, Muhammad, Thomas Merton, Martin Luther King Jr., Mahatma Gandhi, Desmond Tutu, the Dalai

Lama, Rigoberta Menchú, and Teresa of Calcutta, despite their enormous doctrinal and cultural differences. They concur in their delicate tenderness and prophetic passion. We face a surprising paradox. These densely spiritual human beings incarnate divine and reconciling love for humanity, with all its defects, and, nevertheless, on occasions they are seized by prophetic uncontainable indignation against oppression and injustice and exclaim:

> Woe to those who make unjust laws,
> to those who issue oppressive decrees,
> to deprive the poor of their rights
> and withhold justice from the oppressed of my people,
> making widows their prey
> and robbing the fatherless of reckoning,
> What will you do on the day
> when disaster comes from afar?
> To whom will you run for help?
> Where will you leave your riches? —Isa. 10: 1-3

One can, doubtless, find in many sacred canonical scriptures, dark images of divine exclusion and holy violence against those who allegedly contaminate the integrity of religious identity. Israelite holy wars, Christian Crusades, Islamic Jihad, oppressive servitudes, despotic hierarchies, and intolerances of all dispositions have claimed legitimacy by allusion to sacred texts. The "Word of God" too often has been used to devastate solidarities, consciences, and hopes.

But, those "texts of terror" are neither the decisive nor the predominant ones in most religious myths and symbols forged by human imagination. Genuine religious thought, reflecting over the destiny of human history, does not emphasize the gloomy symbols of Armageddon and its horsemen of terror but rather empahsizes the hopes for human liberation and universal reconciliation.[18] Certainly, writers of somber apocalyptic mentality, like Tim LaHaye and Jerry B. Jenkins, have mined during the last decade the vein of eternal terror in a series of very popular novels among fundamentalist evangelicals.[19] The literary and theological mediocrity of these texts do not compare with the exquisite manner in which James Joyce describes pious terror inspired by the traditional images of eternal hell in his classic, *A Portrait of the*

Artist as a Young Man (1916). What is sublime tragedy in the great Irish writer is reduced in the American apocalyptists to superficial farce.

Central in most sacred writings is neither the images of terror nor the violence of a jealous and excluding God. It is, rather, the vision of "a new heaven and a new earth" (Isaiah 65 and Apocalypse 21), where human beings can sow wheat and eat bread in peace, harvest grapes and drink wine in shared joy, build houses and sleep with tranquility. That aspiration of universal peace and solidarity responds to the deepest level of creative religious imagination. It is an expression of the perpetual dialogue between the human mind and heart, determined to forge earthly analogies of the genesic myth of paradise and the apocalyptic aspiration of the New Jerusalem.

The thesis of an alleged "clash of civilizations," of an unavoidable hostility between Western Christianity and Eastern Muslim cultures, so in vogue in certain North Atlantic circles[20], is nothing but another variant of anachronic hostility against Islam. It is ironic that American political leadership, with its allusions to total war against those whom it stigmatizes as incarnations of absolute evil, reproduces the Manichean cosmic rhetoric of its enemy. Such confrontation resembles rather a "conflict of fundamentalism," as Tariq Ali has sagaciously suggested.[21]

Those who today make "preventive war" a fundamental dimension of the foreign policy of the world's most powerful nation, utilize in their public declarations a vocabulary that tends to demean the alleged enemies of the nation as adversaries of God. Thus, earthly conflicts acquire cosmic dimensions, dressed up as the mythical perpetual confrontation between children of light and those of darkness. Epochs vary, but the ambition of power, prestige, and profit continues its camouflage as religious devotion.

The complex internal diversity of Islam contradicts the distorted image of the Muslim enemy that some apologists of a new crusade project. Moreover, in its central canonic traditions, Islam shares ethical perspectives not very different from those of the followers of the Gospels or the Talmud. Also misleading, it seems to me, is the thesis outlined recently by some Christian scholars that a notable difference between Christianity and Islam is rooted in the absence of a sacred language in the first, while the sacred canon of the second is unfailingly linked to Arabic. From that distinction they deduce an essential difference between Christianity and Islam, attributing to the latter rigidity and inflexibility with respect to cultural diversity. These are sophisticated subterfuges that preserve the hostile posture toward Islam fatally spanning the history of Western Christianity. Those apologists forget the excessive frequency with which in Christianity and Judaism the idolatry of the sacred letter became abominable and repressive for those who did not share its precepts, something that Baruch Spinoza already judiciously pointed out in the seventeenth century, that splendid heterodox Jew,[22] stigmatized by both church and synagogue, of whom Jorge Luis Borges, with deserved admiration, writes:

> A man engenders God. He is a Jew
> With saddened eyes and lemon-colored skin;
> Time carries him the way a leaf, dropped in
> A river, is borne off by waters to
> Its end . . . .
> From his disease, from nothing, he's begun
> To construct God, using the word.[23]

The idolatry of the sacred letter led, too often, to the execution of women considered witches (Exod. 22:18, "Do not allow a sorceress to live") or of non-virginal newlyweds (Deut. 22:20-21). Men with social power and violent souls read those texts with profound devotion before proceeding to cut down afflicted feminine lives. Today, many dogmatic believers cite canonical texts to justify their repression of homosexuals with a cogitative logic very similar to what their ancestors wielded against the abolition of slavery or the emancipation of women. Idolatry of the sacred letter has been the inspiration of holy wars, crusades, and jihads. Numberless human beings have been sacrificed on the altar of jealous, excluding, and implacable deities.

Global peace requires intercultural and interreligous dialogue and the silencing of bellicose and degrading confrontations. Otherwise, we run the risk of promoting the globalization of sacred violence. It behooves us to forge bridges and channels of dialogue, mutual recognition and reciprocal respect, and, especially, bonds of solidarity and compassion among distinct historic religiosities. Nothing less than the future of humanity is at stake. It is of special importance today to promote a creative dialogue among the three great religions that consider the city of Jerusalem as a sacred metropolis. Is it too utopian to dream that someday Jerusalem, with its tragic and bloody history, will be a symbol of coexistence in peace and harmony between adorers of distinct incarnations of the sacred? Is it viable to imagine that not far from the Wailing Wall could one day be erected a monument to peaceful concord among Christians, Jews, and Muslims, in celebration of the end of holy wars, crusades, and jihads? Is it illusory to think of a future in which, finally, Jerusalem, the sacred city that during millenniums has witnessed so much violence and devastation, honors the etymology of its name, "city of peace?"[24]

Maybe the time has come to forge what the Catholic theologian Johann Baptist Metz called the "*ekumene* of compassion," an inclusive project of solidarity with human affliction that transcends the frontiers of Christianity.[25] By compassion we understand here not merely indulgence or tolerance, but "to suffer with," "to share the passion with," the identification and solidarity with those who suffer the dreadful "mystery of wickedness" (II Thessalonians 2:7). Regarding diverse cultural and religious traditions, the challenge is to overcome mere tolerance and to learn to estimate and appreciate the dignity of difference.[26] The Latin root of the word "tolerance" suggests that its semantic range is limited to endure diversity. What is needed today, however, is to value and enjoy cultural, ethnic, and religious diversity. It is the only way of abrogating modern racism, whose most disastrous expression was the celebrated phrase of Carl Schmitt, Nazi political and ideological philosopher: "Not all who have human faces are human beings."[27]

Is such ecumenism of compassion a dream, a utopia? Indeed, but human beings are constituted by the nobility and boldness of their dreams and aspirations. I have always preferred *Utopia*, by Thomas More, to *The Prince*, by Niccolò Machiavelli, both texts written during the birth of Western modernity. When faced with the lethal pragmatism of the realists forged in Machiavelli, Hobbes, and Clausewitz, on the one hand, and the apocalyptic atrocities of bellicose fundamentalisms on the other, is it not preferable to dream about the passionately erotic instant in which "justice and peace kiss each other," as prayed in the biblical psalm (Psalm 86:10)?

Christians should never forget that the Jesus portrayed in the Gospels never construed the adhesion to dogmas, ecclesiastic hierarchies, or ritual prescriptions the decisive tenets of his message. He was rather heterodox in his predilections. Jesus preferred the solitary and compassionate Samaritan to the pious Levite or the devout priest (Luke 10:29-37). His radical challenge calls us to assume full solidarity and compassion with those who Franz Fanon called "the wretched of the earth."

When religious leaders proclaim holy war against those who they stigmatize as "adversaries of God," we should remember the sensible warning of John Locke: "I ask how shall any one distinguish between the delusions of Satan, and the inspirations of the Holy Ghost?"[28] Regarding different doctrines, valid is the norm affirmed by Umberto Eco in his dialogue/debate with Cardinal Carlo Maria Martini: "in conflicts of faith, Charity and Prudence should prevail."[29] Only thus can men and women of faith place limits on the voracity of those who seek to continue the legacy of death and destruction of the past century. Only thus those who today live between terror and hope can intone the biblical hymn of peace:

> "How beautiful on the mountains
> Are the feet of those who bring good news,
> Who proclaim peace!" —Isa. 52:7

Endnotes

[1] Eric Hobsbawm, "War and Peace in the 20th Century," *London Review of Books,* Vol. 24, No. 4, 21 February 2002, 16-18. See, also, his book *Age of Extremes: The Short Twentieth Century, 1914-1991* (London: Michael Joseph, 1994).

[2] Immanuel Kant, *Perpetual Peace, and Other Essays on Politics, History, and Morals* (Indianapolis: Hackett, 1983).

[3] William Butler Yeats, "The Second Coming" (1919/1920), in *The New Oxford Book of English Verse, 1250-1950,* chosen and edited by Helen Gardner (Oxford: Oxford University Press, 1972), 820.

[4] Luis N. Rivera-Pagán, "*Nuclear Apocalypse and Metánoia: Christian Theology in the Light of Hiroshima and Nagasaki,*" in *Images of the End & Christian Theology,* ed. Roger Williamson (Uppsala, Sweden: Life and Peace Institute, 1990), 41-52.

[5] Gilles Kepel, *La Revanche de Dieu: Chrétiens, juifs et musulmans à la reconquête du monde* (Paris: Seuil, 1991).

[6] David G. Bromley and J. Gordon Melton, *Cults, Religion, and Violence* (Cambridge, UK: Cambridge University Press, 2002).

[7] José Saramago, "O fator Deus," *Folha de São Paulo,* 19 de setembro de 2001, E8.

[8] Oliver McTernan, *Violence in God's Name: Religion in an Age of Conflict* (Maryknoll, NY: Orbis Books, 2003).

[9] José Casanova, *Public Religions in the Modern World* (Chicago and London: The University of Chicago Press, 1994).

[10] Regina M. Schwartz, *The Curse of Cain: The Violent Legacy of Monotheism* (Chicago and London: The University of Chicago Press, 1997).

[11] Karen Armstrong, *The Battle for God* (New York: Knopf, 2000).

[12] Nawal El Saadawi, *Walking Through Fire: A Life of Nawal El Saadawi* (London: Zed Books, 2002), *The Innocence of the Devil* (Berkeley and Los Angeles: University of California Press, 1994), *The Fall of the Imam* (London: Saqi Books, 2002).

[13] Mark Juergensmeyer, *Terror in the Mind of God: The Global Rise of Religious Violence* (Berkeley and Los Angeles: University of California Press, 2000).

[14] Phyllis Trible, *Texts of Terror* (Philadelphia: Fortress Press, 1984).

[15] René Girard, *Violence and the Sacred* (Baltimore and London: The John Hopkins University Press, 1977).

[16] Mark Twain, *The War Prayer* (1923) (New York: Perennial, 2002).

[17] *The day of wrath, that day*
which will reduce the world to ashes . . .
What terror there will be,
when the Lord will come
to judge all rigorously!

[18] Miroslav Volf, *Exclusion and Embrace: A Theological Exploration of Identity, Otherness, and Reconciliation* (Nashville: Abingdon Press, 1996).

[19] The titles of those novels are *Left Behind, Tribulation Force, Nicolae, Soul Harvest, Apollyon, Assassins, The Indwelling, The Mark, Desecration, The Remnant, Armageddon, Glorious Appearing,* published between 1995 and 2004 by Tyndale House, in Wheaton, Illinois.

[20] Samuel Huntington, *The Clash of Civilizations and the Remaking of World Order* (New York: Simon and Schuster, 1997). See the careful critique of Huntington's thesis by Errol A. Henderson and Richard Tucker, "Clear and Present Strangers: The Clash of Civilizations and International Conflict," *International Studies Quarterly*, June 2001, vol. 45, No. 2, 317-338.

[21] Tariq Ali, *The Clash of Fundamentalisms. Crusades, Jihads and Modernity* (London: Verso, 2002).

[22] Baruch Spinoza, *Tractatus theologico-politicus* (Leiden: E. J. Brill, 1989).

[23] Jorge Luis Borges, *Selected Poems*, ed. Alexander Coleman (New York: Viking, 1999), 383.

[24] Amos Elon, *Jerusalem: Battlegrounds of Memory* (New York/Tokyo/London: Kodansha International, 1995).

[25] Johann Baptist Metz, "La compasión. Un programa universal del cristianismo en la época del pluralismo cultural y religioso," *Revista Latinoamericana de Teología*, año xix, núm. 55, enero - abril 2002, 25-32.

[26] Jonathan Sacks, *The Dignity of Difference: How to Avoid the Clash of Civilizations* (London: Continuum, 2002).

[27] Quoted by Claudia Koonz, *The Nazi Conscience* (Cambridge, MA: Harvard University Press, 2003), 1-2.

[28] John Locke, *An Essay Concerning Human Understanding* (1690), bk. iv, chap. 19, par. 13.

[29] Carlo Maria Martini and Humberto Eco, *In cosa crede chi non crede?* (Roma: Liberal Atlantide, 1996), 80.

Celebrating Our Youth

Engaging youth and younger generations is an enormous and yet exciting task. Because youth is the most vulnerable developmental stage in life, there is a great deal of immediacy and seriousness attached to the task of talking about war. Youth, especially those of a lower economic status, are the most targeted audience of recruitment for the military. So it is imperative that the church address these issues in her communal life. Eric Anderson, a youth pastor at heart, has put together this essay seeking to address how to speak with and for youth in times of war. By looking at context and including theological reflection, Eric provides us with a fresh look at the work of youth ministry.

Postmodern Peace

Some Thoughts on War and the Church's Responsibility to Our Youth

Eric Anderson

Any full and complete treatment of the modern Church's relation-ship to its youth in the context and face of war could certainly fill an entire book. It would address the full range of arguments supporting active and vocal advocacy for a more peaceful future; the content and substance of the dialogue that we should be having with our youth; the vast spectrum of practical strategies for engaging young people from varied socioeconomic strata, diverse ethnic backgrounds, and unique regional cultures. Given the constraints of time and space, however, this chapter must settle for more modest ambitions. It will rest upon the assumption that the reader is fairly well convinced, whether by the quality of her own personal and/or religious education or through the persuasiveness of the other contributors of this book, that the most au-thentic Christian stance on war is that, with very few and extraordinary exceptions, war is an indignity to the human spirit, antithetical to the teachings of Jesus Christ, and a blight upon the glory of God's creation. Building upon this assumption, this chapter will present, using a combination of anecdote and essay, some suggestions for the content and approach of a ministry that addresses the complexities, management, atrocities, and injustices of war to, with, and for contemporary youth.

A Voice for Youth

Free at Last?

I had the chance recently to have dinner with three old friends of mine, friends I hadn't seen for several months. This probably doesn't seem terribly remarkable, except that we were celebrating their recent graduation from high school, an achievement that had never been a foregone conclusion for any of them. We had all met while I was working at an after-school academic support center that they began attending in the eighth grade, and I saw each of them nearly every single weekday for the better part of the next two years. The center was operated by an unusually progressive housing authority that had endeavored to level the academic playing field for students living in public housing by providing access to tutoring and technology often available to their more affluent peers. On the evening of our dinner, two out of the three celebrants still lived in public housing, characters in the familiar story of immigrant families whose responsible adults work long hours for low wages.

As is customary at any graduation dinner, the topic of conversation moved promptly to their plans for the future. From the very first days they began attending the Learning Center, I had asked them regularly about these plans, hoping that by refocusing their typically myopic adolescent eyes I might provoke more inspired scholastic performance. In this instance, however, the question had no ulterior motive; since I hadn't been able to communicate with any of them within the last five or six months, I was completely unaware of whatever schemes they had cooked up for themselves during their final months of high school. In that conversation, nebulous plans to take classes at a nearby community college began to emerge; so did a much clearer sketch of the summer work schedule at Men's Wearhouse. All three were in pretty much the position one would expect of nearly any adolescent male left almost entirely to his own devices for most of his high school career. None of them had ever excelled in school, and none of their parents had the experience, training, or available time to guide these teenagers through the college application process. For any of them to have well-defined plans for a university experience already secured would have required clear and brazen defiance of the statistical odds. As it happens, none of these guys would have ever won very much at the slot machines.

At one point, Guiv—tall, athletic, handsome, and mostly soft-spoken—-asked if anyone was considering joining the Army.

"Hellllll no," replied B.G., "I ain't going over there to get killed." As always, B.G was quick with the punch line and ever frank.

James laughed in acknowledgment. "It don't matter if I have to spend my whole life at Men's Wearhouse; at least I'll *have* my life."

Though communicating his point, James' statement was really only a half-truth. The fact was that James had no intention of spending his life in Men's Wearhouse. Despite never earning stellar marks in school, James had the savvy, drive, ingenuity, and intellect to find ways to make life work out for him. Guiv's situation, however, was another matter. For two or three years, Guiv had been talking to me about the possibility of enrolling in the Armed Forces; because of his particular circumstances, it represented an option to which he needed to devote serious consideration. While B.G. and James had long personified academic potential unfulfilled, Guiv's scholastic shortcomings were the product not of undeveloped work habits but undiagnosed cognitive deficits. Unlike his two friends who had at least tasted, if only occasionally, the fruits of authentic academic success, for Guiv the option of prolonging his education beyond what he had endured these last twelve years seemed to him mostly masochistic.

"I don't really want to go to war," he later told me, "but I don't really got no choice."

Guiv's story parallels that of many young Americans who lack either the academic credentials or the economic means to pursue higher education. The best, most viable route to a career or vocation where they won't have to spend their lives staving off poverty with low-paying jobs is through the Armed Forces. Did any of us ever wonder about the disproportionate percentages of men and women from lower socio-economic strata we see represented in the United States military? Some might be tempted to suggest that this simply reflects a greater predilection towards violence among our more impoverished citizens, but we recognize this response as being as preposterous as the alternative hypothesis that people of lesser financial means are more patriotic, honorable, and proud of their country than society's more affluent members. And while there are no doubt significant numbers of individuals who do enlist who are motivated primarily by patriotism or a sense of duty or honor, we must not forget the thousands who are there because they had few other choices.

It is for these young people, those with few viable options to the Armed Forces, that the Church must speak. Guiv's story brings the phenomenon close to home and makes it personal, but the fuller reality is that for many of the youngest members in our Armed Forces, war is not a choice but an unjust outcome of economic circumstance. When the desire simply to cultivate a better future for oneself forces the decision to kill or be killed, it is incumbent upon us as Christians to struggle for a more humane alternative; to argue that a well-trained Army of Peace funded by tens of billions of dollars might, just might, effect better outcomes than an Army of War; to speak out against war because it is completely exploitative of a great many young people who are there only because they are young and just beginning their lives and simply can't afford not to be.

Just to keep us honest, perhaps we should consider, just as the bumper sticker reminds us, "what would Jesus do?" As I recall, Jesus didn't involve himself too extensively in matters of war. Even so, the New Testament provides little reason to believe that a Lieutenant Jesus would have ordered the lepers and the harlots, especially the teenage lepers and harlots, off to battle.

A Moral Compass for Youth

"That's over there, we're over here"

"What do you think about the war in Iraq?"

"I don't know. I guess it's, like, good because it's, like, helping protect us against terrorists and stuff."

"What about the U.S. soldiers in Iraq who are being killed by terrorists? They're U.S. citizens, and the war certainly isn't protecting them. And what about all of the Iraqi citizens, who used to live in relative, albeit oppressive, peace, but who are now also being killed by terrorists as a result of the American invasion on Iraq?"

"Yeah, but that's, like, over there, and we're over here."

My best guess is that if one lived in an affluent suburban neighborhood anytime between March 2003 and July 2004 and had any prolonged exposure to or meaningful conversation with a teenager, one would have access to a dialogue not unlike this one. It is the perspective of the disengaged over-programmed postmodern youth (or DOPY), a perspective shaped by some combination of attention-deficit media, seven-second sound bites, instantaneous access to breaking global news and information, regular participation in largely anonymous Internet communications, overexposure to gratuitous violence, and overbooked parents so overwhelmed by the demands of their downsizing professions or so immersed in driving each of three children to each of three different activities in each of three different locations on each of seven different evenings (we *all* know that Sundays are no longer exempt) that they lack the time or energy to engage their children in provocative conversation. Is there any way we could reasonably expect these young people to have really thought through the circumstances, the consequences, the justice, or the theological ramifications of war in a postmodern era? Hardly. But neither does it absolve us of a responsibility to figure out a way to engage them on the topic.

Do not be deceived, though; this is not merely an academic discussion we're advocating. This discussion has ramifications on at least two different levels. On the one hand, it has implications for the development of authentic and comprehensive personal Christian faith for the younger generations in our Church. What kind of Christianity are we nurturing if we address only Christian faith and sex, Christian faith and partying, Christian faith and peer pressure, Christian faith and alcohol, Christian faith and your parents? A fairly narcissistic Christianity, it seems. Guiding young people into and through thoughtful, informed, and open dialogue about the Christian stance on violence against humanity, on the bases for that stance, and on the most powerful applications of that stance represents an important step in cultivating active faith that is empathetic, compassionate, and philanthropic.

Nurturing within our young people a personal faith that incorporates these effective qualities and Christian ideals has implications not just for the individuals themselves but for society as well. Not only *are* they the future, but this particular cadre will also most likely be the ones *steering* the future. Statistically speaking, these affluent suburban teens are among those most likely to hold positions of influence and decision-making power thirty years from now. Imagine a future in which our nation's leaders, having been DOPY throughout their formative years, have had no direct exposure to war, no direct exposure to the suffering and manifold other consequences of war, and no meaningful exposure to a thoughtful, cogent, empathic, Christocentric stance on war. If you're reading this in 2004, this vision will perhaps resonate all too clearly already.

It is therefore essential that the Church identify ways to engage this cohort of young people in a meaningful dialogue about Christian perspectives on war. It is certainly essential for the health and well being of their souls, and probably for the future health and well-being of our planet and its inhabitants.

Onward!

A Call to Action

Too often in contemporary American society the Church is hushed, when the lost need to hear its voice. Too often the Church is complacent, when the indigent require urgency. Too often the Church remains camouflaged, when society needs to see it at the podium. Too often the Church is a set of disconnected parts, when the world could use a unified whole.

The challenge before us is immense. Even if we do endeavor to counteract the momentum of wars and violence spanning the entirety of recorded human history, we must first roust ourselves from a very comfortable seat. And what man do you know who is quick to jump out of his La-Z Boy™ when fifteen hours of hard labor await? How many devoted mothers out there wouldn't allow their in-laws to take the four children for the day if it meant for mom a relaxing respite at the beach? In early twenty-first century America, most of us are at the beach, sitting in the La-Z Boy™. But if in the matters of war we are to hold any hope of ministering effectively and authentically to and for our youth, our first step must be to get out of that chair.

And we can do it, with God's help. As Martin Luther King Jr. so eloquently articulated in his sermon before the Riverside Church, "Human progress never rolls on the wheels of inevitability, it comes through the tireless efforts of [people] willing to be co-workers with God."[1] We must heed the call from Jesus to walk with him and take better care of the indigent and the oppressed and the subjugated. Now we must be willing to cast away our nets and walk with Christ, even if it means relinquishing our plush, comfortable chair. And we must bring others with us. The shepherds must join together and then guide their flocks along, too. For the youth in America who lack a better option, we must shout. For the youth in America blinded by over-stimulation, we must lead the way.

Strategies for Ministering to Youth

Once we get beyond the motivational rhetoric, though, how do we put our best intentions into practice? First, I would argue, we must band together. We must make wrest ourselves out of the comfort zones of our individual churches or parishes, to not only attend local clergy council meetings as a way of cultivating fellowship but also to begin utilizing them as a forum for developing a concerted, unified, and *sustained* effort to minister in ways that counteract the injustice of war. We can broaden this effort by making creative and shrewd use of the Internet, using grassroots movements like FaithfulAmerica.org as a prototype for our efforts. To the extent that we are able to unify our voices through thoughtful consideration of the teachings of Jesus, the content of Scripture, and the inspiration of prayer, we will then be able to amplify our voices through the megaphone of unification.

With our voices loud, we can begin to shout for the youth who lack any real choice. "Is there justice when our children with the fewest opportunities must go to fight for the ones with the most?" we might ask. However, not content simply to illuminate the problem, we will work to address it as well. The Church might, for instance, consider collaborating with, or at least learning from, organizations like the Austin-based Nonmilitary Options for Youth (NMOY). Though secular in nature, NMOY uses its belief in nonviolence as the basis of their efforts to counterbalance the military options presented to struggling adolescent youth with viable alternatives that might be available to those young people. They work to educate youth on alternative opportunities for skills training, job procurement, and college financial aid, and to promote careers in peacemaking and social change. I know Guiv would (or perhaps more accurately, will) leap at any of these alternatives, and I'm confident several thousand other Christian youth would (or perhaps more hopefully, will), also.

We remain mindful, though, that the Church is more than just a social service agency, and has something unique to offer, something that isn't available at the otherwise wonderful organizations like NMOY. The Church, of course, offers spiritual guidance and direction. It can, and should, offer this ministry to the young people who *do* opt for military service and for the violent, and sadly more conventional, means of international conflict resolution. We must equip them with a faith of broad perspective, a faith that offers spiritual support in times of physical and emotional duress, a faith that is consistently renewed by individual prayer and group fellowship, a faith that is keenly attuned to and grateful for the miraculous gift of Divine Grace.

And what of the DOPYs? In my experience, this group actually represents the greatest challenge for the Church, for it is to them that matters of faith, social injustice, and war seem largely expendable. With soccer practice and music lessons and television and ballet recitals and Scout meetings and music downloads and skateboarding and video games and instant messaging and sometimes even homework, little time remains for youth group, or for Sunday School, or spiritual reflection, or God. Furthermore, once we do have their attention, the challenge can be finding a way to keep it. Often times I think we youth leaders succumb to the temptation to fight fire with fire, to bombard our young people with games and music and videos and flashing lights and space-age sounds. To be sure, media and exciting activities can certainly help; a carefully-selected movie can provide a very effective foundation upon which to build a discussion of the atrocities of war, the emotion toll it takes on its participants, and the value God places on all of their lives, regardless of the side of the conflict they represent. The universal ability of music to stir our souls can be employed to help establish a mood of contemplation and reflection. But in the end, I am convinced that what our young people need, crave, and deserve, is to discuss openly, thoughtfully, and honestly the topic of war. Lectures sedate and activities distract. Perhaps rather than compete with the myriad distractions of the postmodern world, we should instead be offering an alternative: a place where our young people can engage real matters of life, death, faith, and human dignity.

Conclusion

After I resigned from my position with the after-school academic support centers in the public housing developments where I worked with Guiv, B.G. and James, I moved to New Jersey and accepted a challenge to build a new youth fellowship at a church in an affluent suburban community. It had been nearly ten years since I had last participated in youth leadership with this demographic, and so I came to the challenge with considerable uncertainty. Only two or three young people at this church had committed to participating in a youth fellowship, so I decided that my initial strategy would be to make our weekly youth fellowship gathering as fun and zany and exciting as possible, hoping that the opportunity to behave unconventionally in a controlled environment would attract every young person in the county. This went on every week for several months, and the group ballooned to five or six participants, each of whom, it should be said, attended sporadically.

Throughout those months, however, I also happened to be participating in an adult fellowship that was studying the Acts of the Apostles, and in that context spent considerable attention focusing on the living power of the Holy Spirit. Somewhere during that time span it occurred to me that maybe, just maybe, I could entrust more of each week's youth-group session to that living power and just a little less of each week's youth-group session to whip-cream pies and water balloons. Progressively over the next several weeks, more of our time was devoted to Scripture readings, reflection, discussion, and prayer, and considerably less to bells and whistles. And you know what? Not only did this deepen our conversations and our relationships with one another, but it also intensified the commitment of the young people who were attending and even attracted several new participants. As the group grew both in number and in their commitment to faithful lifestyles, I realized that never had I witnessed a clearer testimony to the power of the Holy Spirit and to the capability of this generation of young people to apprehend challenging issues, even those which fall outside the realms of their everyday experience.

And so, emboldened by our faith in the Holy Spirit, let us challenge our young people—challenge them to consider experiences beyond their own; challenge them to consider carefully what course of action an authentic Christian faith might dictate when confronted with war, both now and in the future; challenge them to care about the greater welfare of humanity. Who knows, they might just rise to that challenge.

Endnote

[1] Martin Luther King Jr., "A Time to Break Silence," in *A Testament of Hope: The Essential Writings and Speeches of Martin Luther King Jr.* (San Francisco: Harper SanFrancisco, 1986), 231-245.

Testimonies

Our section of testimonies is a revolutionary place of sacred story telling. Testimonies give voice to where God is at work in the midst of injustice and oppression. We will hear from the social locations of refugee communities, African Americans, military chaplaincy, and the nonviolent activist Mahatma Gandhi. It is in these locations that we find places of unique engagement with creating an ethos of peace. Rev. Stacy Martin, Rev. Everett Mitchell, Rev. Gregory Guice, Rev. Jackson H. Day, and Ajit Prasadam will develop for us a framework of resistance to war and allow us to envision the stories of various communities so that we may embrace them as our own.

No Suffering [One] Is [an] Alien[1]

War, Displacement, and the Ethics of Advocatory Hospitality

Rev. Stacy Martin

Theirs are stories of mythic scope and, although their individual voices span continental distances, many tales of flight share the same origin: war. Regardless of the euphemisms used to describe the impetus for the journeys of an estimated twelve million refugees worldwide[2]—civil conflict, armed uprising, ethnic clash, escalated tribal tension—their realities are that of war and its legacy of displacement. Although necessary for survival, escape from war's atrocities does not denote victory; rather the loss of nation, community, and home that results from flight characterizes a unique form of victimization that opens its sufferers up to a radical vulnerability.[3] Everything is a burden for the refugee.[4] Stripped of the basics that, together, provide a sense of security, self, and place, the refugee is no longer "citizen," no longer "resident," and is dependent upon strangers for relative safety and provision.[5]

To about three hundred refugees, the resettlement office in which I work is one of those strangers. And, for the past year, I have been the privileged witness of the kind of resurrection presence that only refugees can embody as ones who have survived unthinkable horror, escaped almost certain death, and lived in the incomprehensible limbo that defines existence in refugee camps. This experience—as a "cultural broker"[6] for refugees during their initial stage of transition from life in limbo to life in the United States—has elevated my level of consciousness relating to war and has altered my perception of a faith that does justice. I no longer view international news with the superfluity I once did; my encounter with refugees in the U.S. has revealed to me how interconnected life on this planet is. When I read of refugees fleeing the Darfur region into Eastern Chad, or of the Burmese in Thailand, or of any other global humanitarian hot spot, I can no longer indulge in the fallacy that these are distant events happening to people I have no connection with; chances are that I just may know a brother, a mother, a lover, or a friend. Those international news stories now present moral implications that I can no longer ignore.

The reflection that follows considers the ethical challenge brought to our doorstep by those refugees in our midst and offers a possible direction for further consideration. It does not represent an experienced resettlement professional's perspective, nor does it reflect an expert's judgment on matters of international law. I am merely one who stumbled into a refugee community and, through that community, has been confronted by the major social evil of our day and, because of that, has glimpsed a possible paradigm for creating an ethos of peace. This reflection is divided into three parts: the current refugee situation in the context of the United States and its refugee policies, my experience with refugees, and the implication this might have for communities of faith.

The Social Location of Refugees in America

As a New Jersey resident, I go to Ellis Island and the Statue of Liberty quite often. Visits from friends and relatives always entail a compulsory excursion to the icons that typify the American spirit and its accompanying mythology. Each time I take that ten-minute ferry ride from Jersey City to Ellis or Liberty Island, I imagine myself a would-be American on an ocean-worthy vessel in 1924. And, in accordance with what I learned in the fifth grade, I sense the excitement, exhilaration, and eagerness that every individual en route to the Promised Land of America felt. When I arrive at Lady Liberty's feet and read Emma Lazarus' poem, or when I enter the main hall at Ellis Island, my most American of beliefs is affirmed: every person to reach U.S. soil after the Civil War yearned for this land and aspired to be an American. Such an assessment is the preferred historical perspective of many native-born Americans, most of whom, when asked why people continue to move to the U.S., offer, "Because it's the greatest country on earth," or, "Because, if you can dream it, you can do it in America," or the like. Americans generally posit ourselves as the envy of the world and assume our ascendancy among the nations. Political rhetoric echoes these sentiments and employs them as conviction. As Charles W. Taylor described, "The fundamental American story asserts that the United States is the land of opportunity for all; the melting pot open to all those willing to contribute."[7]

But, what happens when newcomers' stories strike a discord with the preferred American narrative? When the newly arrived report that they've *not* chosen this place, that they *don't* believe in its maxims and that they *distrust* its promises? What happens when newcomers' ways clash with the American ideals of self-reliance and self-sufficiency? The very presence of refugees challenges American sensibilities. Steeped in an ethos and mythology that tells us the entire world aspires to live in America and to be American, it is difficult for Americans to understand the social location of refugees in our midst, to understand that no one flees voluntarily.[8] That America would choose the refugee rather than the refugee choose us, is an almost incomprehensible notion, given the story that guides our national identity. The seemingly latent xenophobia of American domestic and foreign policies also makes incomprehensible the concept that America would actually choose to resettle the potentially threatening stranger.

There are an estimated 35,000,000 refugees or displaced persons in the world today[9]; of that 35,000,000, the United States, through the Bureau of Population, Refugees, and Migration, under the Department of State, has chosen to allow about 50,000 refugees to enter the U.S. during the 2004 fiscal year.[10] Most refugees who eventually make it to the United States have been forced to flee across international borders because of persecution and its resultant violence. Only when a refugee has crossed into the relative safety of a neighboring country, often doing so traveling on foot, does she become a refugee as defined by the United Nations High Commission for Refugees (UNHCR) and, subsequently, the United States. Persecuted persons in war-torn states who are unable to flee to a bordering country are not protected under international law and do not qualify for resettlement in the U.S.[11] For those who do qualify and eventually make their way to America, theirs was not a journey for the sake of adventure or employment—theirs was a journey of forced flight; and America, in stark contrast to its national myth, is not their chosen home. America, for many refugees in the context of resettlement, is simply a place that will provide protection until a safe return home can be made.

Part of the United States Refugee Resettlement program entails special privileges for refugees that entrants under other visa statuses do not enjoy. For example, U.S. law mandates that each refugee arrive eligible for a Social Security Number, with an Employment Authorization Card, and with eight month's eligibility for public assistance through TANF, Medicaid and food stamps.[12] These benefits come with responsibilities on the part of the refugee. Within ninety days and with only the $400.00 one-time grant to every refugee by the government, refugees are to be fully self-sufficient; they are to have secured housing, employment, enrolled any minors in school, and learned enough English to be a participating member of the community, all within three months of arrival. Obviously, this is no easy task, especially in states such as New Jersey, where affordable housing is virtually non-existent. Add to that the stress of adapting to a different culture, one that includes institutionalized racism, and the unresolved psychological and physical pain caused by years of living in war zones, and attaining self-sufficiency becomes even more of a challenge.

Although refugees are protected under U.S. law, in my experience, most native-born Americans are unaware of refugees' legal status. This lack of awareness leads to confusion, misunderstanding and, often, discrimination, another hurdle of resettlement. Employers, fearful of hiring "undocumented, illegal aliens," are hesitant to accept applications from any foreign-born person, even when presented with proper documentation certifying legal status. Welfare caseworkers, unfamiliar with the legal distinction between immigrant and refugee and the mandate to serve refugees under federal law, often deny refugees' welfare applications, citing disqualification based upon immigrant status. The Department of Homeland Security (DHS), which is responsible for a portion of the processing of refugees for arrival in the country, is itself confused about what "refugee status" means.

A few months ago I had to contact the supervising DHS representative at an area international airport because of a mishap that had occurred with a recent arrival. When I spoke with the representative, I was told that there are no refugees in the United States, that refugees live in other countries. When I explained that the United States actually has an Office of Refugee Resettlement (ORR), that it is part of DHS' job to process background checks on all refugee entrants, and that I receive government funding to help refugees resettle in the U.S., the representative transferred me to another DHS official, who has yet to return my calls. Imagine how confused lay people are when the government entities responsible for processing refugee entrants do not even know what a refugee is or that there are any who live here.

This general lack of knowledge about who refugees are and their presence in the United States keeps refugees shadowed, remaining on the margins, virtually unseen by the broader public. When and if refugees are spotted at the margins of American life, perceptions about who and how they are are often dictated by centuries-old prejudices, pigeon-holing refugees into a prescribed existence based upon racial biases and bigotry.[13] This, of course, only functions to further marginalize refugee communities. And although the task of refugee resettlement is carried out by a good number of Christian denominational entities, in a public-private enterprise with the federal government, few church-goers or clergy know that such partnerships exist, adding to the dimension of near secrecy that clouds the refugee's entry into American life. Whether misunderstood because refugees have not chosen America (rather America has chosen them), or mistaken for "illegal immigrants" because of a general lack of knowledge about refugee and immigration legislation, or simply invisible because of historic American prejudices, the marginalized status of refugees in America further continues refugees' experience of displacement and rejection. Such is

the social location of refugees in America: they are simultaneously welcomed and rejected.

My Experience with Refugees

Admittedly, before stumbling into the community I now serve,
I had only the vaguest notion of who a refugee is. My understanding
of "refugee" was broad and uninformed. I was blind to the refugees
around me. And, on the rare occasion I had any contact with a refugee,
I had no knowledge or appreciation of his or her struggles past and
present. The assumptions I made about refugees were often misguided
or downright false. It was not until my livelihood depended upon in-
terfacing with refugees that my eyes were opened. I have described
above the situation of refugees in our midst. The following is a general-
ized account of my brief, but meaningful, contact with refugees, who
have made a profound impact on my moral and religious life.

As stated in the introduction to this reflection, refugees come to
America having lost nation, community, home, and social position. In
addition to these losses, many have lost parts of themselves to torture,
starvation, disease, rape, and/or damaged memory. Many arrive the
sole survivor of family and tribe. Indeed, "loss" in every sense of the
word best describes the experience of a refugee. Perhaps it is because
of their overwhelming experience of loss and the constant threat of
losing still more, that refugees master the art of survival. Not all of
these acquired survival skills are virtuous or even lawful. Nevertheless,
the courage and tenacity of these ones, who are often described as the
"most vulnerable," is nothing short of inspiring.

The sheer determination of refugees can only be explained as an
abiding commitment to life over death. Because refugees must forego
all the things that most of us consider necessary for life—things such
as country, a physical home, family, friends, employment—they value
life all the more. This is what the staff in my office often term "the great
refugee paradox": the people who come nearest to death cling impos-
sibly to life. Their very presence challenges me and my perceptions.
The more refugees honor me by sharing their stories, the more I understand that it is only when humans are faced with the formidable choice
between life and death that they discern the essence of life. Refugee
friends and clients speak of camp life as if I were talking about the town

in which I grew up; they had the imagination and survival instincts to view refugee camp life as "home," transforming it from the impersonal to the personal. They started businesses, planted cassava and corn, created sacred spaces for church or temple, made music, held social dances, decorated tents with dried leaves and flowers. They carried on with life in spite of the death that surrounded them. They fell in love, married, had children, celebrated birthdays, held funerals, commemorated holy days; they invested in life when everything around them reminded them of the risk of such an investment. A few of them have pictures or have rendered drawings of their memories of camp life, and as I peer at their pictures and listen to their stories, I witness rebirth, new life. Theirs are not lives like mine, not an inherited existence with a reality worth possessing, but a life created out of sheer resolve and imagination so that their realities are worth bearing.

Not only do the refugees that I have encountered vigorously choose life when common sense might say otherwise, they optimistically persist in their general trust of humanity. For people who have been victimized more times than one can possibly count, it is indeed a miracle that they are not completely bankrupt of trust. Family members may have turned on them, neighbors may have victimized them, governments may have used them as pawns in political diplomacy, churches may have deceived them, but they continue to engage others and extend the hand of friendship. The refugees who have befriended me have chosen to trust despite what past experience dictates. They disregard the risk, opting instead to trust humanity.

In the midst of the worst the world has to offer, my refugee friends choose to find hope and rely upon trust, regardless how tenuous. Over and over again, their stories demonstrate the reality of resurrection by staking a claim for life over death and hope beyond despair. This is not to say that every refugee who comes to our door makes the same choices. Refugees, like any group of people, represent a cross-section of humanity: among them are con-artists and those who have committed unspeakable acts, often in the name of sheer survival. Refugees' experiences cannot be romanticized nor camp life glamorized. The warehousing of people in refugee camps is, in fact, an extension of the immorality of war. However, the humanity and valor I discover in my daily encounters with refugees forces me to question my own values. Refugee stories challenge me to consider how I would be without official identification or citizenship. How would I be in their situations? Would I opt for life over death, hope over despair? Would I offer myself in friendship to anyone? Would I handle the incidentals of war with as much grace? Would I fear the stranger?

Refugees have experienced the most evil of evils and yet are able to display a belief in life, trust, and hope that I, who have had more than plenty to share and know only goodness in comparison to the evil that refugees have witnessed and known, do not. My unbelief is a reflection of my cultural upbringing as a white American. My encounters with refugees have encouraged me to question the most American of assumptions. My refugee friends ground their sense of selves, of being human, in the choice for life, for trust, and for hope. The culture of white Americanism, of which I am a product, grounds sense of self in selected ignorance of the world beyond North America, in the equation of material wealth with self value, in a preference for naïveté in the face of evil, and in avoidance of ambiguity. Refugees have challenged this sense of self and have inspired personal questioning on religious and moral levels. The implications of these questions raised during my encounters with refugees have encouraged me to consider my faith in the context of the refugees in our midst.

A refugees' deepest desire is to return home. Her estrangement from her homeland and her alien status in her new land elicit two of the most powerful themes of the Christian faith: the centrality of land as symbol of God's sovereignty and hospitality to the stranger.[14] Land is a central symbol in the Hebrew Testament; it represents God's sovereignty and represents human unity and God's favor. Accordingly God summons humans to use the gift of land for God's good purposes. Thus those who use God's gift as a tool for limiting community by creating boundaries are unfaithful to the sovereign God. It is those who share the gift of land with and for God's people who are faithful to God and to the law. Shared land, then, means solidarity among God's people and is considered one of the most concrete and profound ways to express one's faith and commitment to God and God's commands.[15] In other words, to be landless is to be powerless, for solidarity with God and others is most appropriately expressed through the shared use of land. My experience with ones who long for the land they call home, who have been denied the safety and solidarity that shared land allows, reminds me that the ancient symbol of land as God's gift for the building of community is still as meaningful as ever before. In an era in which loss of land is a crime committed on a daily basis, God demands that we reclaim the land for its intended purpose, that it no longer be used to divide, that land once again be used for the sake of building solidarity. The refugees in my community are, perhaps, the most marginalized of the marginalized, having been denied all that homeland symbolizes; their very presence in my community mandates faithfulness on the part of God's people.

Faithful action in response to those who have been denied God's good gift of land involves living out the biblical call to display hospitality to the stranger, the alien, the refugee. Hospitality, like land, is a prevalent theme in scripture; it is this act of egalitarian welcome that begins the process of creating solidarity. Hospitality, in the biblical sense, is not composed of isolated acts of entertaining guests in one's home. Through the example of Christ, God beckons us to recognize the outsider, to listen, to hear, to view the stranger as friend. In my encounters with refugees, I have experienced such hospitality. I have been considered friend before I was even known and, even as the stranger, I have been welcomed as equal. Christ is made present in my encounters with refugees who, having experienced the rejection and marginalization of hospitality denied, offer themselves in friendship, embodying the faithful hospitality to which we are all called. Their lived hospitality runs counter intuitive to their experiences and compels me to live beyond my limits, providing a model from which I can begin to embody hospitality as well.

What a gift my experience with refugees has been. Through these encounters, I have been challenged in my faith and in my sense of self. I have experienced true hospitality and the resilience of life over death and hope over despair. This in and of itself is indeed gift enough, but refugees' social location within the United States and my personal and professional experiences with refugees also has implications for the church in its quest for ways to faithfully make ways for peace and justice.

Implications for Communities of Faith

For many Christians, our faith is one of action in love. Christ exemplified this, as did other biblical characters in both the Hebrew and

Greek Testaments. The refugees in our midst beckon us to act faithfully in love on their behalf, for they confront us with the realities of
war, as they are war's products and survivors. If our response to them
as individuals, to their stories of war's horrors and realities, is to be a
faithful witness to a commitment of peace, our response must take into
account the factors that brought the refugee to our door. Our response
cannot begin and end with those few refugees who find safety in our
midst. In a culture that avoids confronting evil, refugees stand as witness to the effects of war and urge us to act on behalf of those whose
immediate safety is still jeopardized by persecution, no matter how far
away they may still be.

The implications that refugees have for communities of faith can
provide the larger church with the narratives and the persons to compel
us as God's people to seek peace. Confrontation with the refugee situation and what this situation displays about the long-ranging effects of
violence must not paralyze us with guilt. The statistics are staggering.
Thirty-five million refugees or displaced persons in the world seems
an overwhelming, unsolvable problem, one that places guilt on all of
us. But there is more than enough guilt to go around, and if churches
merely feel guilty about the plight of contemporary refugees, peace will
never become an overriding reality for humanity. However, if churches
can accept the hospitality that those refugees among us offer, solidarity
with the alien, the stranger, the refugee will begin to occur and, in that
solidarity, we will be able to mourn the refugee situation. The implication here is that the choice to mourn rather than remain paralyzed with
guilt allows voice to be given to the suffering and sorrow of those whose
lives are most impacted by war. A collective act of mourning claims
that such suffering is not God's intention and that as God's hands and
feet in the present kingdom, the church will carry the refugees' sorrow
as its own until enough voices resound the cry for peace.[16]

This is not merely a call to recognition; although recognition of
refugees' presence in our communities, of the injustices they have suffered, is a prerequisite to action, taking on their sorrow is not an effective end result. Mutual suffering breeds solidarity and, as theologians
have been teaching for decades, justice relies upon solidarity, on recognizing the ties that connect all human beings together. Injustice then
becomes something that happens to *us*, not just an unfortunate something that happens to others. In a most tangible, real way, the refugee

reminds us that we are, all of us, interconnected—that the suffering ones in Sudan or Liberia or Tibet are not strangers, they are our next-door neighbors. Our insistence that refugees be given sanctuary in our homeland is an act of solidarity that announces a preference for peace. If churches not only provide friendship, shelter, and other basic needs for the few refugees in our communities but also extend that provision to advocacy on behalf of those refugees whose safe presence in the U.S. is denied, we are acting on God's call for faithful action in love. We are claiming that peace is not only necessary but possible. When we harbor the stranger, we denounce the evil that caused the flight. When we are befriended by the refugee, we no longer perceive war as a problem beyond our scope of concern.[17]

Congregations that intentionally involve themselves with refugees open themselves up for potential transformation. Encounters with refugees generate compassion; this compassion, then, leads to service, and service to advocacy. Refugees bring to the U.S. innumerable gifts, but, perhaps, the most important gift that refugees bring is to give a face and a voice to the suffering that we try so terribly hard to ignore. And in their faces and voices, through their stories, we can no longer remain silent about issues of peace and justice, for we have been confronted and we will never again be the same. Refugees offer us the opportunity to practice an advocactory hospitality; in our act of solidarity with refugees, we advocate on their behalf and we display a statement of peace.

Conclusion

Part of the Christian tradition involves the recitation of the Lord's Prayer during collective worship. In that prayer we ask that we be delivered from evil. Having viewed war through the eyes of my refugee friends, I have learned that I can no longer evade the struggle toward peace or be afraid to confront the evil that inherently defines war. Refugee stories give witness to the ineffectiveness of using violence to suppress violence—the methods of war, of evil, can never resolve conflict. In the reflection above, I outlined the marginality of refugees, in particular those who have been resettled in the U.S.; I described in general terms my experience with refugees and how that experience has shaped my moral and religious life; and I sketched how the refugee situation compels us toward peace and provides a tangible avenue for such work to occur. In his introduction to this book, Chad Abbott described our history as an American people who are, first and foremost, war-like. The refugees among us and the worldwide contemporary refugee situation mandates that our collective thirst for war be renounced. Refugee stories and the powerful testament they provide give us the courage and vision to no longer simply talk of peace but to act on our call to work toward justice and peace in this world. Refugee stories and the refugee presence in the U.S. make us believe in the need for peace and enable us to strive for it in the kingdom here and now. They indeed make true the claim that no suffering one is an alien.

Endnotes

[1] Dorthee Sölle is said to have coined the phrase "No suffering is alien," from which the title comes.

[2] This startling number only represents part of the story: another 23.6 million people are internally displaced. See U.S. Committee for Refugees, *U.S. Committee for Refugees World Refugee Survey 2004* [book on-line] (Washington DC: Immigration and Refugee Services of America, 2004, accessed 26 May 2004); available from http://www.refugees.org/wrs04/pdf/key_statistics.pdf; Internet.

[3] Elie Wiesel argues that by definition a refugee is, primarily, a victim. Of course, refugees are more than mere victims; however their unique vulnerability should not be overshadowed by their courage, savvy or perseverance. Elie Wiesel, "Who Is a Refugee?" in *American Refugee Policy*, ed. Joseph M. Kitagawa (San Francisco: Winston Press, 1984), 17.

[4] *Ibid.*

[5] Dana W. Wilbanks, *Re-Creating America: The Ethics of U.S. Immigration and Refugee Policy in a Christian Perspective* (Nashville: Abingdon Press, 1996), 25.

[6] See Mary Pipher, *The Middle of Everywhere: The World's Refugees Come to our Town* (New York: Harcourt Press, 2002). She uses the term "cultural broker" to define the work of resettlement in the United States. It seems a most appropriate and helpful term when attempting to explain the services our office provides to newly-arrived refugees.

[7] Charles W. Taylor, "Race Ethnicity, and the Struggle for an Inclusive Church and Society," *Pastoral Care and Social Conflict: Essays in Honor of Charles V. Gerkin*, ed. Pamela D. Couture and Rodney J. Hunter (Nashville: Abingdon Press, 1995), 157.

[8] See Dietmar Mieth, "Social and Ethical Reflections on the Distribution of Rights and Duties," *Migrants and Refugees*, ed. Dietmar Mieth and Lisa Sowle Cahill (Maryknoll, NY: Orbis Books, 1993), 73.

[9] Statistics about refugees and displaced persons are often imprecise and controversial. This figure represents a sound estimate made by the U.S. Committee for Refugees. The politics involved in deciphering these statistics often result in a lower figure than most experts in the field believe there to be. As aforementioned, only twelve million of these thirty-five million are considered refugees under the law. The international community has agreed to act collectively to aid and protect refugees;

however, these international protections, because of the concept of jurisdictional sovereignty for nation states, do not apply to internally displaced persons. People uprooted within their own country remain the responsibility of their own government. See U.S. Committee for Refugees, *U.S. Committee for Refugees World Refugee Survey 2004* [book on-line] (Washington DC: Immigration and Refugee Services of America, 2004, accessed 26 May 2004); available from http://www.refugees.org/wrs04/pdf/key_statistics.pdf; Internet.

[10] Since 1991, the refugee admittance figures have been on a steady decline. In FY1990, the number of U.S. refugee arrivals was at 199,317; by FY1999, the number dropped to 72,515. After September 11, 2001, the number plummeted to 26,317. Only when taking into consideration the fact that the United States still accepts more refugees than all other Western countries combined does that minute figure appear significant. See U.S. Committee for Refugees, *Refugee Reports*, vol. 23, number 9, by Immigration and Refugee Services of America [on-line] (Washington DC: Immigration and Refugee Services of America, December 31, 2002, accessed 9 June 2004); available from http://www.refugees.org/world/articles/RR_December_2002_Admission.cfm#admissionsNatl; Internet.

[11] There are exceptions to this general rule. The legacy of the Cold War dramatically affects the U.S. refugee resettlement program: Cubans and citizens of the former Soviet Union are allowed to enter the U.S. as refugees without having fled to a country of initial refuge. In other words, they come directly to the U.S. from Cuba or the former Soviet Union. On paper, Haitians are allowed this same privilege, but statistics show that a comparatively small number of Haitian entrants are allowed in under the resettlement program. Furthermore, not every international "hot spot" is a refugee-producing nation state under governmental definition. For example, citizens of countries such as Guatemala and Zimbabwe, where persecution is systematized and institutionalized, are not allowed refugee status, even when able to flee. Neither are Palestinians considered for the refugee resettlement program. See U.S. Committee for Refugees, *U.S. Committee for Refugees World Refugee Survey 2004* [book on-line] (Washington DC: Immigration and Refugee Services of America, 2004, accessed 26 May 2004); available from http://www.refugees.org/wrs04/pdf/key_statistics.pdf; Internet.

[12] Eligibility differs from state to state, depending upon individual state income guidelines, but if income guidelines are met, refugees are able to access publicly-funded social services under federal mandate.

[13] Charles W. Taylor, "Race Ethnicity, and the Struggle for an Inclusive Church and Society," in *Pastoral Care and Social Conflict: Essays in Honor of Charles V. Gerkin,* ed. Pamela D. Couture and Rodney J. Hunter (Nashville: Abingdon Press, 1995), 157 ff.

[14] The Lutheran Immigration and Refugee Service (LIRS), a national voluntary agency through which my office contracts, addresses the issues of land and hospitality in their mission, vision, and goals. See Bruce Birch, Walter Brueggeman, Terence E. Fretheim, and David L. Petersen, eds., *A Theological Introduction to the Old Testament* (Nashville: Abingdon Press, 1999).

[15] Bruce Birch, Walter Brueggeman, Terence E. Fretheim, and David L. Petersen, eds., *A Theological Introduction to the Old Testament* (Nashville: Abingdon Press, 1999), 190-196.

[16] See Joan Maruskin, "Ministering to the Refugee Christ," *Mission Studies,* no. 1-2, Vol. XVI (2000), 196-206.

[17] Richard D. Crane, "Discipleship and the Church's Struggle for Justice and Peace," *In Essentials Unity: Reflections on the Nature and Purpose of the Church: in Honor of Frederick R. Trost,* ed. M. Douglas Meeks and Robert D. Mutton (Minneapolis: Kirk House Publishers, 2001), 157-162.

If I Speak

The Prophetic Voice as an Alternative Narrative

Rev. Everett Mitchell

"I ain't gonna study war no more, study war no more, study war no more." —Spiritual

"Every gun that is made, every warship launched, every rocket fired, signifies in the final sense a theft from those who hunger and are not fed, those who are cold and are not clothed." —Dwight Eisenhower

"For this is your home, my friend, do not be driven from it; great men have done great things here, and will again, and we can make America what America must become." —James Baldwin, *The Fire Next Time*

When nation raises up sword against nation, a narrative is written. This narrative is often produced by those in power to convince others of the necessity of war. Narratives, therefore, require drama, a set of characters and events that demand a solution to a complex problem.

The narrative of war is only necessary when those writing the script need to place a common "enemy" to defeat at the forefront of the stage. It is the portrayal of the epic struggle of good over evil. Most observers are attracted to these narratives because such stories are true to the extent that we as human beings are often forced to overcome obstacles. One problem. Not all narratives turn out to be true to experience, especially narratives claiming the necessity of war.

What is it about the current war in Iraq that makes it so necessary for the church to examine the narrative being written? I am concerned that the war in Iraq has been based upon false narratives. Such narratives include claims that Iraq has weapons of mass destruction or has ties to Al-Qaeda or will welcome America's presence with open arms. When Colin Powell presented his case before the United Nations Security Council he put forth a narrative, a story. It was a narrative of abuse, pain, nuclear weapons, chemical bombs, and mobile lab units. It was a narrative seeking to justify and promote, not only to Americans but also to the world, that the war with Iraq was inevitable. It was a promotion of intimidation suggesting that people are either for the United States or for the terrorists. Such a narrative creates an ethos of war and fear.

Narratives are powerful because they have the capacity to impart a vision of reality.[1] What can be different about the Iraq war from previous wars is the potential for the voice of the church to propose an alternative narrative, a narrative that imparts a vision of reality other than the one presented by those in power, a vision of peace and nonviolence. It seems, however, as though the church has fully digested the dominant narrative of going to war and has not brought an honest critique to this story. As a result of our silence in the church, lives of young men and women have been lost and are being placed in further jeopardy. When the first bombs fell upon Iraq, I listened for the prophetic voices to arise from the church, calling for a narrative of peace in the midst of war. Much to my dismay, many remained silent, as silent as a gust of wind moving through an open field, preoccupied more with issues of self promotion and wealth than with critiquing the false narrative of war placed before the American people and the world.

The intention of this book is to provide pastors and lay leaders with the necessary tools that they can use to address the construction of false narratives regarding war and violence. The church must provide a vision of a world in which peace does not extend from false narratives perpetuated by fear and terror. If the church is going to remain relevant, then it must address narratives that have been delivered justifying war, search for the reasons behind such motivations, and offer a radical vision of God's kingdom that welcomes and embraces an ethos of love rather than that of hatred and fear.

The primary claim of this chapter is that the mainstream church has largely remained silent regarding the narrative justifications surrounding the Iraq war. As I researched countless sermons on the issue of war, many mainstream preachers chose to act as if the war was not an issue that they must address. Silence only aids in injustice. *The church must reclaim a prophetic alternative narrative voice that both critiques the current narrative and offers a vision of society that is based upon the theological sacrifice that Jesus made on the cross for all of God's children.* I maintain that the primary role of a prophetic voice is to resurrect within the church the imaginative possibilities of an alternative narrative in which there is a world without war. I suggest throughout this essay that in order to reclaim the church's prophetic voice, clergy and lay leaders must reflect upon the challenges to a prophetic voice and seek strategies in which to construct narratives of justice and freedom for all humankind. This essay will 1) examine the barriers of prophetic imagination, 2) explicate the prophetic task, and 3) provide a theological model for creating an alternative narrative against war.

The Prophetic Barriers

A prophetic voice is a voice crying in the wilderness, an alternative voice to those in power. It is a call for acts of justice within the community. In this book, we are called to acts of peace and not war. However, there are many barriers that keep us from entering into such a prophetic ministry. Walter Brueggemann, in *The Prophetic Imagination*, describes the prophetic tradition and its role in challenging the dominant narratives within society. Brueggemann examines the prophets of Israel, the evidence of the Old Testament, and the contemporary situation of the church. For Brueggemann the contemporary American church is so enculturated in the American ethos of consumerism that it has little power to believe or to act.[2] If this is the case, then the initial question that the American church must address is in what ways "has our (the church) consciousness and imagination been so assaulted and co-opted by the royal consciousness that we have been robbed of the courage and power to think an alternative thought?"[3] This is an essential question because it suggests that there are barriers to prophetic ministry that dominate within the church.

First Obstacle: Well-Being and Affluence

One of the major obstacles to the church's prophetic voice is that of well-being and affluence. Ecclesiastes 5:10-11 says, "Whoever loves money never has money enough; whoever loves wealth is never satisfied with his income. This too is meaningless. As goods increase, so do those who consume them. And what benefit are they to the owner except to feast his eyes on them?" I know there are many pastors that would object to wealth being a major obstacle to prophetic vision. But if the church does a serious self examination, there is a connection between affluence and the compromise of prophetic vision.

Under the reign of Solomon, Israel was in a position that it had never been before—that of extreme wealth. Never in Israel's history had there been enough consumer goods to supply the people with a surplus. The problem arises when Israel, once solely dependent upon God, relies more upon its surplus. As a result of this excess the prophetic consciousness of the people is replaced with the desire for the accumulation of more things. This is the primary reason the writer of Ecclesiastes states that the only true benefit for the accumulation of things is so that one can stare at them. Consequently, one's eyes are drawn away from the social issues of suffering and oppression that may have sneaked into the community. Brueggemann recognizes that "all it takes to counter a prophetic consciousness is satiation. It is difficult to keep a revolution of freedom and justice under way when there is serious satiation."[4]

A true challenge to prophetic consciousness within the church is that the United States, and as a consequence the American church, has become a culture obsessed with materialistic gain. To the extent to which mainstream religious culture has legitimated material prosperity as a sign of God's favor, the "spirit" of capitalism has diminished into materialistic self-determinism. I am aware of the breadth of such a contention, but I think in order for Protestant churches to remain prophetic in hopes of impacting culture, the church must come to grips with its role in not only justifying the desire for material wealth but also its perpetuation of this drive within the lives of God's children. The American church has become satiated with the material goods of cars, houses, and golfing, which suggest that it in order for a pastor to preach a sermon using the rich young ruler, (Sell all you have and give to the poor) the challenge of Christ becomes a metaphorical sacrifice rather than getting rid of all of one's material possessions in order to build up the kingdom of God. It is this satiation and affluence that ultimately leads a society to trade covenanting with consuming.

In Israel the communal ethos was based on the principle of covenant. When one enters into a covenant it is a promise to ensure the well-being of brothers and sisters in the community, the poor, the orphan, and the widow. But in the new Israel the desire for material goods outweighed the covenanting principle, which had been established by the post-exilic community. Such is also the case in America, where values have radically shifted and more emphasis is placed on things than on people. Martin Luther King Jr. understood this when he suggested that "America has shifted from a 'people-oriented society' to a 'thing-oriented society.' One in which machines and computers, profit motives, and property rights are considered more important than people."[5]

Where there is no alternative narrative to replace such a transition, the triplets of racism, materialism, and militarism will thrive. It is difficult to sustain an alternative consciousness in a consumer-based society, but if the church is to be prophetic, it must recognize the grip material wealth has upon the lives of its parishioners. As long as the church simply acts as though the problem does not exist, then the issues of war cannot be addressed because the church does not see itself in covenant with people across the world. Wealth needs to be addressed within the church in order to liberate the church's prophetic voice.

Second Obstacle: Oppressive Social Policy

Another obstacle to the prophetic voice in the church has to do with oppressive American social policy. According to Brueggemann, since Israel had abandoned its previous principles, the people set up oppressive social policies in order to maintain their wealth. For the first time in Israel, "the affluence was undoubtedly hierarchical and not democratic in its distribution."[6] What was once a society in which all people benefited from God's provision, now there were those who lived off the efforts of others. In this sense, we are reminded, "there were those who built houses and did not live in them, who planted vineyards, and did not drink their wine."[7] As a result of this desire to accumulate wealth, an exploitative appetite developed an insatiable momentum, so that no matter how many goods or how much power was obtained, it was never enough.[8]

In Israel, the prophetic voice with its demands for justice, compassion, and equality were replaced by a social policy that was bent on ensuring its insatiable desire to maintain control over the lives of people. The United States, much like Israel at points in her history, has become a place in which civil liberties and the ideals of freedom, justice, and compassion are replaced by fear, doubt, and social control. When politicians decide to hold prisoners without due process in Cuba and the Supreme Court upholds such a decision, it speaks to the very corrupt character and nature of United States social policy. The essential principles on which the United States was founded are being completely ignored at the expense of men and women who are looked upon as enemies rather than brothers and sisters in a global struggle for the realization of freedom and justice. It is in this political oppression that the cries and pains of the marginal are not heard or are dismissed as the noises of kooks and traitors.[9]

Third Obstacle: Stagnant Religion

Affluence and oppressive social policies are the ideas that identified Solomon's reign. But these policies would not have been in place unless there was theological sanction for such actions. The third obstacle is the most severe because it proposes the most dramatic challenge to the prophetic alternative voice. The primary reason for the severity of stagnant religion is that God and temple have become a comfortable part of the royal landscape in which the sovereignty and love of God have been subordinated to the purpose of the king. God is no longer free to be wherever and active with whomever God pleases. God is held captive by a regime to the extent to which God is 'on call' to the king and his administration. This has one important function. It gives the king a monopoly so that no marginal voices may approach this God except on the king's terms. In such a society God is so present to the regime and to the dominant consciousness that there is little chance of "over-againstness," and where there is no "over-againstness," there is no chance of newness.[10] Any idea of an alternative consciousness is perceived as a threat against the social structure.

God has become a God who protects the liberties of Americans as the country goes into unjust wars in order to "protect the freedom" of people across the world. God is no longer a gracious, compassionate, and caring God, loving all people within the cosmos. No, God works to ensure the material prosperity of Americans. This radical revisioning of God provides for the continued marginalization and oppression that many people encounter within the United States and in the world. If God is only on the side of the rich, the prosperous, and the powerful, then it diminishes God to a welfare genie. That is not the God who holds back the cascading waters of the Red Sea in order to ensure the survival of a people who had been exploited and oppressed by a regime that thought it was God. This is the challenge for prophetic pastors and teachers in the church. It is to find the voice, the determination to liberate and recapture the God who is active in the world not simply on behalf of the rich and powerful but for *all* those who are sitting on the margins pushing their way forward, determined to get their voices heard.

It is time that the church breaks her silence and speaks to the world about a God who is free to love, free to advocate, free to empower, and free to change the world. It is not up to a political administration to align God with their purposes. People of faith must remind any oppressive regime that God cannot be co-opted and that rushing into wars, which will destroy hundreds and thousands of God's children is not now, nor will it ever be, acceptable. My challenge to the reader is not to necessarily agree with every idea in this book. The challenges listed above by no means exhaust the ethos of war or the entire consciousness of the American public. Rather, my plea is to begin a serious dialogue in which consideration of these barriers to the prophetic and the various implications that arise from them are given serious thought and prayer. The task before us is complex to be sure, but dialogue at least gives the church a starting point, a place to dive into the abyss of problems that plague our world.

The next task of prophetic ministry is to inquire into what are the primary tasks of prophetic voices. How do prophets attempt to discover an alternative narrative in which the community of people can participate? I will now turn my attention to describing the task of a prophetic pastor, preacher, or lay leader.

Task of Prophetic Imagination

The first task of providing an alternative vision to war is to cultivate a counter-conscious congregation. Brueggemann suggests Moses was concerned with the formation of a counter-community with counter-consciousness. He was concerned with dismantling the destructive and often pessimistic consciousness or narratives that underlaid the thoughts of the people. In order to bring about a liberation of their consciousness, Moses concerned himself with completely dismantling the narrative structure the people used for defining their existence.[11] In a congregational setting this may require exposing members of a church to the streams of consciousness that inform their beliefs systems and to how dominant cultural narratives fit together to support this system. Therefore, as did Moses, pastors and lay leaders need to be concerned with creating a body of believers that take seriously the task of unearthing the ways in which they are connected to the negative images within society.

I remember when I first attended a dominantly European-American church. One of the members of the congregation came up to me and admitted that she did not know anything about my African American culture or our history within America. Our conversations regarding race, class, and privilege led her to a new consciousness about herself and the role she played in perpetuating white privilege. This was a new vision for her. The same should be considered when dealing with congregations that may not readily understand what it means to be influenced by the dominant cultural consciousness. If prophetic means anything, it demands that the prophet be committed to the task of developing an alternative consciousness in the lives of the people of God.

Secondly, Moses was concerned with developing a narrative of community, which criticized and energized the people by reflecting upon the special memories that embraced discontinuity and genuine breaks from empirical reality.[12] The primary tool Moses used to dismantle the socially constructed oppressive narrative was that of a critical and constructive discourse. As pastors and lay leaders begin this prophetic task, it is important that they do so with an openness to criticize the things that have been accepted as the norm. Brueggemann suggests "that the dominant culture, now and in every time, is grossly uncritical, and cannot tolerate serious and fundamental criticism, and will go to great lengths to stop it."[13] Therefore, as Moses critiqued the dominant social narratives of Israel, he was revealing that such narratives had both flaws and inconsistencies that had led and continued to lead to Israel's further destruction and oppression. I think this is the hardest task of prophetic ministry because it requires pastors and lay leaders to take a risk of faith and challenge every detail of why we think and act the way we do. For example, when I work within my own African American community, I notice that the majority of mainstream preachers have largely ignored preaching about the negative and false narratives that were being told regarding the war in Iraq.

T. D. Jakes, a prominent pastor from Dallas, Texas, was recently asked his opinion regarding the war in Iraq. He responded, "Preachers should not speak about these things. Those events should be left to the politicians as preachers focus on the souls of people."[14] This sort of response completely ignores the legacy of advocacy that the Black church and African American preachers have fought for throughout history. The African American church has historically been a foundational resource for the American community by providing spiritual hope in which to critique systems of injustice such as segregation and civil and human rights. By linking the struggle of the oppressed with God's emphasis on liberation found within biblical stories of Israel and Jesus, the Black church radically appropriated the message of God into every aspect of the church's mission. One important dimension in which the African American church involved itself was in the area of politics. By politics I mean the involvement in social critique of institutions that denied all people access to the freedoms promised in the Bible and in the United States constitution. This sort of self-critical attitude coming from the African American church regarding racism and segregation must also take into consideration the brutality of war.

It is easy for those in the United States to be extremely critical of Saddam Hussein and the mass graves that have been uncovered. A similar critical discourse seems appropriate, then, regarding the role everyday Americans play in the perpetuation of injustices against millions of men, women, and children within our own country and around the world. If the United States desires to be critical of mass graves then we need to seriously consider the oppression and continual marginalization of the Native American community and the urban poor within our own borders. Perhaps as in the days of the Civil Rights movement, the African American church, through her own historical communal narrative of struggle, can once again find her prophetic voice in a time of unjust war.

Thirdly, Moses knew that the communal narrative of a prophetic voice must reflect upon the one thing that has not been taken over or caricatured by empire: God. The task of prophetic ministry may be the most difficult, but it is the most necessary. It is reflecting upon a God that is not held captive by the imperial forces who simply use the terminology of God to invoke trust in the minds of people. This God is the one who is free and active, not just in America but also in the world, empowering men and women of all cultures with the wisdom to demand justice and freedom. When Moses invoked the memories of God to the people, he was reminding the people that God cannot be contained within the limits of our conception. It is God's freedom that allowed for the people to be liberated from the control of the Egyptian rulers. So, how did the people leave Egypt? They followed God's leadership and guidance. Each step required an act of faith on the part of the Hebrew people, but with each step, God provided. There were difficulties and insecurities within the process, to be sure, but at the Red Sea, God provided the children of Israel with a new opportunity to experience their freedom.

Being prophetic, therefore, is more than simply preaching a good word. Rather, it is about awakening within individuals, whether personally or historically, a narrative memory of empowerment that seeks its definition not from society alone but from a higher source, namely God. The primary role of prophetic preaching is to resurrect within the church all the imaginative possibilities of what the world can become if it embraces an alternative narrative of peace and justice for men and women around the world. For Brueggemann, "the prophet does not ask if the vision of society can be implemented, for questions of implementation are of no consequence until the vision can be imagined. The *imagination* must come before the *implementation*."[15] The challenge to true prophetic ministry lies in the reality that society does not want imagination to occur within the world and, as a result, does everything it can to shrink or dismantle any form of imagination.

When people began critiquing the war on Iraq, for example, the major media outlets silenced their voices so that an objectionable point of view was not projected upon the minds of people. These ideas stressed alternatives such as allowing the weapons inspectors to do their jobs or to work with the United Nations in bringing liberty to the Iraqi people. When the narratives of the Iraq war were being laid out by the Bush administration, it should have been the role of the church to question whether or not this narrative was one that provided justice and equality. The church has the task of raising the imaginable possibilities that can provide an alternative vision that takes into consideration the devastation that will occur to our brothers and sisters throughout the world if war is supported. It is often the most difficult and tiresome task to preach about an ethos where justice, love, and harmony are the dominant stream of consciousness. The imagination of this type of community provides a picture to be painted, words written, and a dialogue assigned. If the church is to recapture its prophetic voice, it must first rescue a prophetic imagination from the limits of social reality.

What is more, being prophetic requires the capacity to construct imaginable possibilities even in the face of "royal"[16] consciousness. The characteristic expression of a prophet in Israel was poetry and lyric. Using these two forms of prose, the prophet was able to construct alternative narratives that offered the possibility of communal alternatives for people. The prophet did not ask if the vision could be implemented because the imagination must come before the implementation. Brueggemann points out that the royal consciousness seeks to make it impossible for people to imagine. Therefore, anything that cannot be implemented is seen as irrational and, in turn, every totalitarian regime is frightened of the artist.[17] It is for this reason that the prophet is not merely a speaker but is also an artist constructing new possibilities of the world regardless of their practicality or possibility of realization. In essence, it is the vocation of the prophet to keep alive the ministry of imagination, to keep on conjuring and proposing alternative futures to the one the king desires as the only viable option.[18]

Moreover, the royal consciousness leads people to numbness, especially numbness about death. Brueggemann writes, "It is the task of prophetic ministry and imagination to bring people to engage their experiences of suffering to death."[19] This may seem somber because prophecy has often been co-opted to become popular statements against society. But prophetic ministry within the church can bring people into an awareness of death, primarily because the narrative of Christ has a symbol of death—the cross—as its core theological orientation.

In the United States, the idea of death has become so easy for us to discuss because we have become numb to its reality. The primary reason for this denial is that if Americans were to embrace the reality of death it would mean that the United States is not in charge, that things will not forever stay the manageable way they are, and that things will not finally all work out in the end.[20] The finality of death is ignored, and we would rather buy into royal consciousness than address the reality: Death is final. American politicians and mainstream media would rather the American people remain ignorant of death. When the photographs of the soldiers who died in Iraq and Afghanistan were released to the public, for example, many were enraged, claiming that such pictures should not be shown to the American public. Why? The American government did not want the American people to come to grips with the reality and finality of death. As long as the American public remained numb to the reality of death, they would support a "war against terror." As long as they could pretend that the soldiers being brought home in caskets were defending their rights to shop at malls, buy cars, and live in their nice homes, then it made their deaths a little more bearable. This, however, is the deception of the dominant consciousness. It puts the majority of men and women asleep so they do not have to deal with the reality of death and violence. In many ways those who accept war as the final answer to social and political conflict have become numb to death. The final assessment of the royal consciousness is that it does not want to know. The prophet, then, must invite not only those who seek a redefined narrative but also the *king* to experience what he most fears to experience, namely, that the end of the royal fantasy is imminent.[21]

Finally, the prophet must use the hope-filled language of amazement. As Moses developed a narrative of imagination, his message was filled with a language of hope. This is a language that engages the community not simply in old realities but also in new discernments and celebrations, just when all hope seems lost. This language is important because it counters a language of both grief and numbness that people experience under royal consciousness. This is the most critical stage of a prophetic imagination because it asserts that words of hope have the capacity to transcend the limits of reality both imposed and accepted by the dominant narrative. What hope does a prophetic moment produce? Hope is an alternative narrative construct replacing numbness with a celebration that guides and instructs the lives of those who choose to participate in this imagined community. At times such hope seems fantastical, but there is a hope that provides the catalyst for worldwide and communal church action. It is a hope that says "to wait is too late." It is a hope that radiates within the lives of the church when our alternative vision of a world of peace and justice seeks to replace a narrative of war. Hope does not diminish the self-critical nature necessary within the prophetic imagined community, but it does provide the capacity to feel our way through the reality of these critiques with a freedom of self that may not have been available otherwise. While the prophet must proclaim this hope, she or he does not become the sole voice of the community. It is necessary that he/she point towards the new song, the new life, the new consciousness that is made available as individuals and communities attempt to enter into this new imagined community with all the anticipated pitfalls and struggles that this entails.

Theological Model

Up to this point we have explored the barriers and tasks of prophetic ministry. Now let us look at the theological model, which is the foundation for this prophetic vision. The model that informs the foundation of the prophetic voice is the cross. The cross provides us with a way to describe Christian responsibility to God and to our brothers and sisters throughout the world. It is the model of the cross that proclaims that we ought not rush into violence and war. It is this model that causes us to pause when contemplating sending young men and women to fight in the streets to defend a liberty that some never felt a threat of losing. It is also this model that allows us to feel safe, not because there are soldiers searching for Osama Bin Laden, but because we trust in a God who loved humanity so much that this God was willing to risk all to save us. Therefore, this final section will address the cross as a theological model for prophetic imagination in three ways: 1) the cross as a symbol of reconciliation, 2) the cross as a symbol of listening, and 3) the cross as a symbol of liberation.

In most churches, the cross has become a mere symbol the church points to in order to justify God's salvation of humanity from the finality of sin and death. However, this view is limited because the cross is not simply God reconciling the world unto God's self. Rather, the cross also signifies God's concern with reconciling human relationships and community. Human relationships and communities throughout history have been severed because of religious beliefs. Even in twenty-first-century pluralistic America, most religious communities are rhetorically, socially, and theologically in conflict. In many churches, a rhetoric is preached, taught, and promoted that is fueled by a Christian puritan ethic denying the capacity of God to be active outside of the church. This rhetoric becomes a philosophy that is then converted into unfair and unjust actions against human beings. Because the church remains silent in the face of U.S. social policy and unjust actions, Muslims are singled out as terrorists. Men, women, and children are placed in prisons and denied the right to due process and justice that others are allowed. These extreme examples signify that humanity suffers from a sickness caused by an incomplete interpretation of the cross.

The cross, in essence, changes not only the Christian's understanding of the relationship between the individual and God but also of relationships with other people. To experience the cross is to understand, as Shirley Guthrie writes, "there is no such thing as reconciliation with God without reconciliation with our fellow human beings."[22] Guthrie continues, "God in Christ reconciling the world to himself, means inevitably and inescapably to take the initiative to do what is necessary to achieve genuine reconciliation in all the human relationships in which we live—reconciliation between children and parents, husbands and wives, Christians and non-Christians, people of all races, classes, and national heritages."[23] If the world is going to become a place where human relationships are valued, then Christians must take up their cross and take the initiative to learn from others about how God's love is operating in the world. God's desire is for all people, regardless of religious difference, to appreciate and love one another.

Second, the cross is a symbol for listening to a diversity of perspectives. As Jesus hung on the cross, two thieves began a conversation with Jesus. Within this interaction, Jesus did not correct or stop the dialogue between the two men. Rather, he listened, not only to their words but also to their hearts. Therefore, listening is multifaceted. Listening involves suspending assumptions about the other. Too many American Christians do not listen to the constructive criticism of others because they already have preconceived assumptions informed by their limited Christology. But Christians must learn to listen if there is to be peace in the world, particularly among religious traditions. Listening encompasses much more than words. Listening is a way of being in the world. The conversation Jesus has with the men on the cross exhibits that learning how to listen to and speak with each other are essential skills for creating relationships that lead to mutual respect, dialogue, understanding, and peace.

The question most Christians raise is, "For what should I be listening?" Listening is a practice in understanding. Thus, we need to listen for how others express God's love and hope. Just as Jesus listened to the hearts of the men on the cross, so Christians should listen to how God's love is operating in the world. In his speech "A Time to Break Silence," Martin Luther King Jr. insisted that the true meaning and value of compassion and nonviolence is when human beings strive to hear one another. It is in hearing one another that we begin to honestly see the weakness of our human condition and discover the resources needed to mature and profit from the wisdom of our brothers and sisters. We must reflect upon the cross in order for genuine listening to occur.

Lastly, the cross signifies liberation. As I enter into my United Methodist church for worship, I always take a moment to look at the empty cross signifying that Jesus is no longer on the cross but free to put into practice the promises he has given. This freedom is a symbol of liberation. Such liberation suggests God has not freed the Christian simply from sin and death but that God has freed us so we can be "for" and "with" other human beings. According to Dietrich Bonhoeffer, "Freedom is not something I have at my command like an attribute of my own . . . Because God in Christ is free for humankind, because God does not keep God's freedom from God's self, we can think of freedom only as being free from to be free for."[24] For Bonhoeffer, this means that as God's creation, humanity is inextricably bound to one another. The freedom Christ provides in defeating death on the cross signifies that a human being "is free from in order to be free for another human being."[25]

The freedom that exists in the cross is the realization that God commands all Christians to pick up their cross and follow Christ into the areas of life that need God's justice and love. Bonhoeffer implies that regardless of the religious, social, economic, or national location of another person, we still have a charge to be "for" that person, which is a symbol of the liberating cross. This includes the voiceless children within Iraq whose homes are bombed daily or any whom we have labeled as "other" or "enemy."

I will never forget the time my father described the brutality and pain that he experienced during the Vietnam War. He recalled that he had been told that these were barbaric people who needed to be destroyed in order to preserve freedom in the world. But as he became familiar with the culture and people, he realized that the narratives being told to him were false. When he told me of a Vietnamese friend that was killed by American soldiers, tears began to run down his face. He said, "Son, there is no true enemy in this world, only stories about them and what you choose to believe."

The empty cross in the church continues to remind us that Jesus is not hanging on the cross but is active in the world. What is this activity going on in the world? It is an alternative reshaping of community that lives out a way of peace as a "theatrics of counter-terror," as suggested by theologian Mark Taylor in his book *The Executed God*.[26] Taylor suggests that Jesus' death on a cross was a political act of rebellion, turning over the tables of power on imperial Rome because the cross became a symbol for Jesus' followers of organizing a community in opposition to oppression and injustice. It is the cross that reminds us that the key to a world of peace and liberation is found in the liberating acts of the community when they speak out in opposition to injustice through nonviolence. The way of Jesus' cross, then, is not only a way of nonviolence; it is that still more excellent way of love.

The power of God's love has the capacity to transform hate into peace and war in to harmony. Let the church hope for the day when nations lay down their weapons of mass destruction and pick up belief in the absolute survival of all humanity. It is up to us to embrace

God's activity in the world and experience the revelation of God in all places in the world. Truly this is not an easy task, but if Christians can begin thinking of themselves as incomplete without their brothers and sisters in Iraq and across the world, then we just may see the liberating impact of engaging the prophetic voice with the creative imagination of a world of peace.

Endnotes

[1] Cheryl Mattingly and Linda C. Garro, *Narrative and the Cultural Construction of Illness and Healing* (Los Angeles: Chicago Press:, 2000), 260.

[2] *Ibid.*

[3] *Ibid.*, 44.

[4] *Ibid.*, 32.

[5] *A Testament of Hope: The Essential Writings and Speeches of Martin Luther King Jr.*, ed. James Melvin Washington. (San Francisco: HarperSanFrancisco, 1986), 420.

[6] Walter Brueggemann, *The Prophetic Imagination* (Fortress Press: 1971), 32.

[7] *Ibid.*, 33.

[8] *Ibid.*, 34.

[9] *Ibid.*, 54.

[10] *Ibid.*, 40.

[11] *Ibid.*, 28.

[12] *Ibid.*, 27.

[13] *Ibid.*, 14.

[14] For this review, visit the *Atlanta Journal Constitution*, June 25, 2004.

[15] *Ibid.*, 46.

[16] By "Royal," Brueggemann also means dominant. Since people were ruled by royal empires that exhibited dominant consciousness over people, he chooses to use the term interchangeably.

[17] *Ibid.*, 45.

[18] *Ibid.*

[19] *Ibid.*, 46.

[20] *Ibid.*, 47.

[21] *Ibid.*, 50.

[22] Shirley Guthrie, *Christian Doctrine* (Westminster Press: Louisville, 1994), 265.

[23] *Ibid.*

[24] Dietrich Bonhoeffer, *Creation and Fall: A Theological Exposition of Genesis 1-3* (Fortress Press: Minneapolis, 1937), 64.

[25] *Ibid.*

[26] Mark Lewis Taylor, *The Executed God: The Way of the Cross in Lockdown America* (Minneapolis: Fortress Press, 2001).

The Experience of War

A Chaplain's Reflections on Revisiting His Battlefield

Rev. Jackson H. Day

> They shall not labor in vain, or bear children for sudden terror . . . they shall not hurt or destroy on all my holy mountain, says the Lord. —Isa. 65:23,25

I. Holy Ground and Sacred Memories

In June 2004 I joined a tour led by Steven A. Leibo, Ph.D., professor of modern international history and politics at the Sage Colleges, Albany, New York; Dr. Edward Tick, specialist on post-traumatic stress disorder, founder of Sanctuary, and author of *Sacred Mountain: Encounters with the Vietnam Beast;* and Tran Dinh Song, our in-country guide, an educator and veteran of the Vietnam War. Of fourteen participants on the trip, seven of us were veterans.

Places of special significance to the veterans were visited on the tour. For me, it was the ruins of an airstrip on the road west of Tan Canh, north of Kontum. This must have been the location of the Dak To base camp of the First Brigade, Fourth Infantry Division, in 1968. Standing on the airstrip and facing the mountains, once called Rocket Ridge, I recalled the photo that I had taken thirty-five years before of

that base camp. I pointed out to the others where Firebase 5 and Firebase 6 had been, at the two ends of the ridge behind the base camp, and described the bustle of helicopters moving from our area up to these and other firebases in the area. Of all the places I had served as a chaplain in that long-ago year, somehow the feeling I had for this place called Dak To was the most intense. It was my first duty assignment in the war. It was the place I left from and returned to when visiting troops on isolated mountaintops. It was the first place I knew physical danger: it was no accident we slept in underground bunkers. And it had the surreal beauty of mountains that challenged logistics and of sudden mists that closed our links to each other, demonstrating that nature too was a player in this struggle for mastery. The other tour members joined me in lighting incense to honor all who had died in the area of this abandoned airstrip once used by American planes and helicopters.

The next day, we visited the site of Camp Enari, the Fourth Infantry Division Base Camp south of Pleiku. Of the huge sprawling base that once was, only one thing remained—a concrete divider in the road that housed a guard post at the camp's entrance in 1968. I posed there along with Lynn Kohl, who had been a U. S. Army nurse at the 71st Evacuation Hospital in Pleiku. The war was over, and this fragment of concrete was proof.

II. Denial

One way we survive wars is by denying their power. In the midst of war, we shut out the danger posed by enemy mortars and rockets. We may deal practically and intellectually with the reality of hidden enemies outside the perimeters of our camps, but we deny the emotions of fear, anxiety, or anger that come with that reality. On the flight to Vietnam, I showed Ed some photos from the war. This picture struck him. He noted that everything in the picture was dead except for me. He then wrote the following poem, entitled "Highland Vespers," capturing his image of the war behind the photo.

The moaning wounded
the crying dead
are growing quiet.
His weary arms droop
from signing the cross
over these lost.
Where mortars whistled
in the long rice grass
now it is only the wind
and his hymn is of return
© Edward Tick, 2004.

To view the picture through his eyes was a revelation into a new truth. I recalled the moment of the picture—it was a "cold LZ" (i.e., a landing zone without active hostilities) or they would not have invited the chaplain out for services. It was a sunny afternoon and the soldiers welcomed a break from the work of preparing a firebase. The denuded trees were part of the package—an explosive charge would be set off that would clear an area in the center where helicopters could land, and, farther from the explosion, clear the trees of leaves, improving line of sight. All of these things meant life, or a better chance for life, for those who were there. I saw no death in the picture. Ed Tick, who wasn't there, saw no living things but the chaplain.

I knew the chaplain's inner reality—this chaplain was struggling with how to bring the word of God and life and hope. This chaplain felt dead inside and was seeking connection with the life around him. Ed saw a living chaplain making connection with major scenes of death around him. Was he seeing a level of truth I hadn't previously seen?

How much work do we go through trying to hide what is visible when we should be making manifest what is hidden! In 1975 it appeared to many in America that the scenes of death they had been seeing on their televisions for years were now complete, as the enemy tanks and their red flags ended the era of South Vietnam. Where supporters of the North saw life, there certainly was a time of death; but for us who saw only death, did we in fact miss the presence of life? The return in 2004 revealed how much life had been there all along.

III. Betrayal

In Ho Chi Minh City, which was Saigon before 1975, there is the "War Remnants Museum." The word "atrocities" used to be in the title before it was toned down, perhaps in the interests of reconciliation, or perhaps for the tourist dollar. Visiting this museum gives a perspective I had not had before. The pictures of wartime suffering and atrocities are sandwiched between pictures of American-Vietnamese cooperation during World War II against the Japanese and pictures of retired American war-time leaders meeting and reminiscing with retired Vietnamese war-time leaders after the war was over. These pictures before and after the atrocity give a fresh perspective on what we call the Vietnam War and they call the American War: The thirty years between our ill-fated support of the French in 1945 and the defeat of the South Vietnamese in 1975 were an unfortunate aberration. They were an unfortunate detour in the relationship of two nations whose story is one of admiration and friendship, betrayal and restoration.

The Vietnam War betrayed the Vietnamese. It also betrayed the Americans. Like many others, I went to Vietnam feeling part of a noble effort to help a friendly nation turn back Communist aggression. The 1971 revelation of the My Lai massacre shattered the image of the war as a noble effort. The testimony of other veterans in the Winter Soldier hearings of Vietnam Veterans Against the War undermined the notion that only a few "bad apples" made the war a bad thing. Later, the documentation that President Lyndon Johnson had lied to Congress in order to obtain the Gulf of Tonkin Resolution convinced many that the war was based on lie after lie. An expression of this betrayal was VVAW's Dewey Canyon III March on Washington in April 1971.

The Vietnam War was a betrayal in a third way. We had been taught that war was a matter for soldiers—leave civilians out of it. But our bombing of the North indiscriminately killed civilians as well as military personnel, and in the South it was clear to all that there was no way to tell which civilian Vietnamese were friendly and which ones participated in the war effort against us.

Even a humorous road sign suggests another way betrayal involved us. Our very instincts to make things better led us to betray our mission. In theory we were invited guests, helping the South Vietnamese defend their country, and we would leave when that was done. But the same instincts that make Americans proud to beautify their neighborhoods betrayed us. We tried to make Vietnam feel like home. This sign is an illustration. To an American driving west on Route 19 in 1969 and seeing this sign, it would have been a comforting indicator of American presence. To a Vietnamese nationalist, it must have been quite irritating, a sign that foreigners were in the country, claiming it in little (but not subtle) ways for themselves. It seemed inevitable

that we would try to "Americanize" Vietnam in order to make it more comfortable for us—there were so many of us after all. But did that also define what victory would have meant? So many wished we would fight a more conventional war, in which we would fight for territory and once we won it, we would not give it up. Would winning territory on behalf of the South Vietnamese have sufficed, or in our hearts did we not really need to win it for ourselves? There are those who say we should have fought on to win the war. What would a victory have looked like? One in which you knew we had won, because Vietnam was Americanized? Perhaps that only could have happened if we had killed every single Vietnamese man, woman, and child. Nonetheless, it did not happen, and the sign in this picture is no longer seen on Route 19 east of Pleiku.

Dehumanization must be included on the list of betrayals. In the mythology of warriors, a worthy opponent enhances me, and my own warrior skills honor him. In reality, we must diminish, demonize, and dehumanize others in order to kill them. I grew up first in China and then in Southeast Asia—farther south in Malaysia and Indonesia. My parents gave their lives to bringing new life to the people around them in spiritual and other ways. For me to be part of combat in Vietnam, surrounded by Vietnamese, I needed to blind myself to the awareness that these people looked very much like those for whom my parents had devoted their lives. Returning to Vietnam in peace, then, meant the freedom to take off the blinders and to reclaim a part of my childhood that I had had to shut away.

Betrayal is a wound that may heal but leaves indelible scars. Betrayal teaches you that reality—even Ultimate Reality—is not what you had thought. It is thus an intensely spiritual experience that profoundly impacts your relationship with God. Betrayal and the struggle to heal from it are sacred memories you carry with you all of your life.

IV. Making Sense of It

> God's foolishness is wiser than human wisdom, and God's weakness is stronger than human strength. —I Cor. 1:25

War confronts you with questions about the nature and disposition of God. It has been said that God cannot be at the same time all knowing, all loving, and all-powerful. Any two out of the three, perhaps, but not all three. If God is all-powerful and all knowing but doesn't stop the violence, God can't be all loving. If God is all-powerful and all loving but doesn't stop the violence, God can't know what is going on. So I accepted that God is all loving and all knowing but has given up the power to intervene, as God gave up God's power on the cross at Calvary. We weren't helped because God couldn't stop what was going on, but God suffered with us, and perhaps that was enough. Thirty-five years later, looking at the regeneration of the country of Vietnam, perhaps God has some power after all, and we simply had too short a horizon.

> Many who are first will be last, and the last will be first.
> —Matthew 19:30

Paradoxically, in some respects the Americanization of Vietnam is now rapidly proceeding, if you consider the vigorous development of institutions of free enterprise. ATMs and the Internet are already there; can the arrival of McDonalds' be too far distant? Vietnamese leadership that is worried about the explosion of knowledge—even forbidden knowledge—that access to the Internet might bring perhaps need not worry so much; the evenings others and I went to Internet cafes to send messages home, we were surrounded by intense middle-school boys and girls concerned mainly with computer games and instant messaging. But there is a broader message—perhaps in 2004 the United States is actually winning the peace as we could not win the war—in the only appropriate way, through openness and exchange of ideas with a sovereign nation that has the self-confidence of a victor. In losing the war, we paved the way for an appropriate victory, while if we had ever won, we might still, thirty-five years later, be paying heavily for what turned out to be a defeat. Now we are at war in Iraq, and we would like both to achieve our objectives and to have a victory. What if achieving our most legitimate objectives requires that we lose, so that the Iraqis can feel that they have won and expelled the invaders? Are we willing to lose in order to win? Or must we insist on winning, even at the price of long-range defeat?

> Since all have sinned and fall short of the glory of God, they are now justified by his grace as a gift, through the redemption that is in Christ Jesus. —Rom. 23-24

The justification that is central to Paul's faith refers to our powerful desire to be right. We want so much to be right. We want to do the right thing. We want our children to know the difference between right and wrong. But being right can be a mixed blessing. Being right makes us feel clean and pure and it permits—it requires—that we kill those who are wrong. Saul of Tarsus was one of the most righteous people around; he was a killer, and God stopped him dead in his tracks. When he re-emerged as Paul, Christian missionary, Paul, with varying degrees of success, counted his own rightness as loss, and replaced it with the rightness only God's grace can bestow.

It is good to believe that I am created in God's image, that there is something of God in me, that I meet God in others and others meet God in me, that I am an essentially good person, that I am knowledgeable and competent and loving, living in a rich network of those who love and respect me and whom I, in turn, love and respect.

But it is also good to believe that the rightness I develop on my own can be dangerous. I am sometimes wrong. And therefore I—and my group—and my country—do not have the right to kill those with whom we disagree.

Being right is seductive. It is possible to be right about pacifism and nonviolence. Out of that rightness, we can kill those who disagree with us, if not with weapons, then with words. If we truly believe that justification is a free gift of God, then our spiritual lives must include a constant letting go of our own rightness.

A generation of Vietnam veterans felt unwelcome in churches that had opposed the war. Will a new generation of Iraq veterans have the same experience?

V. Healing

It was jarring to see Vietnam's red flag with its yellow star flying everywhere. Thirty-five years ago it was the flag of our enemies. It was the flag of those who sought to kill us and of those we sought to kill. Now it is the flag of our hosts. I took pictures of the flag at many sites just because it was jarring to see it.

It can be healing to go back to the site of a trauma. I looked forward to some form of completion but did not know how it would take place. Seeing the sites where we had had bases, now with just about every trace of war gone, gave the message, "Vietnam has healed, why shouldn't you?" It gave the message, "It's really over." It gave the message, "Life has moved on." After the airstrip at Dak To, we crossed a bridge that I was sure had once been bombed and impassable. We came to a new Vietnamese town in an area that had been uninhabited, dangerous territory. Then the Ho Chi Minh trail had gone through this area and it was often contested. Now the trail has become a paved road and in the town it has four lanes, with a street sign identifying it as the Ho Chi Minh Highway. These are more recent pictures than the ones I have carried in my mind for thirty-five years. My Vietnam "clock" stopped in 1969. This trip started the clock back up and permits Vietnam to be not just part of my past but also part of my present.

On the tour we had a discussion of the Vietnamese concept of *Que Houng*, (pronounced "Kway Hoong") which means the whole constellation of experiences of your childhood, including both the place you were born and grew up and the memories of events at that place. What kind of person are you, the Vietnamese ask, if you become separated from your *Que Houng*? Though I was an adult, the Vietnam War was part of my growing up. Now it is part of my *Que Houng*.

Vietnam has become part of our roots because we fought a war there. Steven Leibo has said, "To me, going to Vietnam for an American should be the same thing as going to see the Grand Canyon or the Washington Monument; it is part of what made us who we are. . . . It is like looking in the mirror and seeing who we are. We are forever going to move in history with Vietnamese society—they were transformed by us, we were transformed by them."

They have treated the wound of my people carelessly, saying "Peace, peace," when there is no peace. —Jer. 6:14, 8:11

Child abuse and domestic violence can persist from generation to generation unless someone has the courage to break the cycle of abuse. Wounds of Vietnam are healing, but the American population carries many unhealed wounds that make violence attractive. Voters wounded by ideological conflicts and local issues elect leaders who carry their own wounds that make violence an attractive emotional discharge. It is crucial to find ways to heal these wounds so that they don't seek their salve in explosions of nationalism and lust for military dominance. If we don't, new generations will experience the pain of the old.

Ben Het at Dusk

Ben Het was the location of a U.S. Army Special Forces Camp astride the Ho Chi Minh Trail west of Dak To during the Vietnam War. We visited the site June 4, 2004. Not much farther west is the border with Laos. You could see where the airstrip had been; vegetation had not yet conquered it. Someone had an aerial photo of the old camp, built on a hillside; we walked the hillside imagining what had once been. It had been a long day, and daylight was fading.

It is still, now.

A breeze brings coolness as we stand
where soldiers once built sanctuaries of sandbags.
Clouds shadow the place where steel flew
and imagination tormented.

We look down at the expanse of green hiding old memories,
Covering the tortured earth, all except the airstrip's skeleton.
The red clay of the airstrip's ruins, long bare of its metal surface
glows brighter as the light fades.

Across the road and beyond the stream, mountains rise,
their tops hidden by clouds.
Those who walked among them are now memories,
ghosts who wait to be invoked,
recalled to life by us who once knew them.

They are gone now, all of them,
both to death and to life;
those in bunkers who faced the mountain,
and their enemies moving quietly through the forest.
Gone the fear, gone the misery, gone the pain.

In their place, settlers have built houses by the road.
Peace has come, and peace's possibilities.
As night falls, families share food in lighted rooms.

In nearby towns red posters celebrate victories and heroes.
The young hope they too may one day know such glory.

The Nonviolence of Gandhi

A Framework and Analysis

Ajit Prasadam

An eye for an eye only makes the whole world blind.
—Mahatma Gandhi

Mohandas Karamchand Gandhi was born on Oct 2, 1869, the youngest of five children, in Porbandar, Kathiawad, in present-day Gujarat, to Karamchand Gandhi, the *dewan* (prime minister) of a small princely state, and Putlibai. For three generations the Gandhis were prime ministers in several Kathiawad states (Gujarat).[1] They belonged to the Modh Bania caste, traditionally grocers. He was married to Kasturba when both of them were 13 years old. He chose a career in law and studied in London at the Inner Temple and was certified as a barrister in 1891. In London he had begun to read the Bhagavad-Gita, the Bible, *The Light of Asia*, and books on theosophy.

On his return to India in 1891 he spent two years trying to learn Indian law and was unhappy with the jobs available to him. But an important meeting at this point in his life was his introduction to

Raychand, who was to be a friend and guide on Hinduism and Jainism. The meeting occurred on the day he learnt of his mother's death.

Through his brother a job opened up with a Muslim firm in South Africa. Gandhi grabbed the opportunity. In 1893 he sailed for South Africa for what was to be a one-year assignment; it turned out to be twenty-one years of life transforming work.

He was awakened to the reality of oppression at the Maritzburg station. He was on a train journey from Durban to Charlestown in the first-class carriage, for which he had a ticket. In the middle of the night he was unceremoniously thrown out, as first class was meant for whites only.

In South Africa the seeds of *ahimsa, satyagraha,* and *sarvodaya* were nurtured in the struggle for freedom and dignity for indentured Indian labor in South Africa. He returned to India in 1915 to join the freedom movement. The principle of *satyagraha* was honed as a political instrument in an early campaign in a labor-management dispute in Ahmedabad. From this point on he moved to center stage in the Indian freedom movement and worked relentlessly till India received her freedom in 1947.

The apostle of nonviolence was assassinated on January 30, 1948.[2]

In this essay, I seek to (1) develop a framework to understand Gandhi's thought and (2) analyze Gandhi's thought and nonviolent action from social-sciences and theological perspectives.

Gandhi's Thought: A Framework

Gandhi's thought developed in response to life situations brought into dialogue with religious texts like the Bhagavad-Gita, the Sermon on the Mount, *Light of Asia,* Tolstoy's *The Kingdom of God is within You,* Ruskin's *Unto This Last,* etc. His speeches and writings were always addressed to a specific audience in a specific context. So, one may detect in his writings confusing contradictions. Erik H. Erikson says,

> There is nothing more consistent in the views of Gandhi's
> critics than the accusation of inconsistency: at one time he is

accused of sounding like a socialist, and at another a dreamy conservative; or, again, a pacifist and a frantic militarist; a nationalist, and a "communalist: an anarchist and a devotee of tradition; a western activist, and an Eastern mystic; a total religionist and yet so liberal that he could say he saw God even in the atheist's atheism. Did this polymorphous man have a firm center?"

The answer to this question is "yes." Erikson gave his unique presence a name: religious actualist, i.e., "that which feels effectively true in action (actuality)."[3]

One might, however, see in Gandhi's writings four distinct fundamentals of his philosophy and creed: *satyagraha, ahimsa, sarvodaya,* and *swadeshi.* In this section I will seek to briefly comment on these basic concepts to help us better appreciate his nonviolent method in a world still challenged by violence and war.

Satyagraha

Gandhi was looking for a word to describe the struggle for dignity and freedom in South Africa. In a meeting with Europeans he discovered that "passive resistance" was too narrowly perceived. It gave the impression of a method of the weak, and it could be characterized by hatred and violence. He offered a prize, in *Indian Opinion,* for the best term to describe the struggle. His relative, Maganlal, suggested *sadagraha,* "firmness in a good cause," and won the prize. He liked the word but it did not represent the whole idea. So Gandhi changed it to *satyagraha.*[4] *Satya,* 'truth' in Sanskrit, is a derivative of *sat,* 'that which is.' Thus, *satyagraha* might be translated as holding firmly to Truth, i.e., "that which is" as opposed to "that which appears to be," or untruth. "It means," he said, "that evil is real only insofar as we support it. The essence of holding on to Truth is to withdraw support from what is wrong."

If enough people do this—if . . . even one person does it from a great enough depth – evil has to collapse from lack of support.[5]

Satyagraha could take the form of civil disobedience, or better still, civil resistance[6]. Gandhi's first object lesson on *satyagraha* as civil resistance came from his relationship with his wife. Shortly after Gandhi and Kasturba were married, Gandhi, intrigued with his newfound power to control, since he was socialized into the patriarchal system, sought to monitor his wife's movements. One night, he told her that she was not to step out of the house without his permission. Kasturba did not respond immediately; she just smiled and went to bed.

Gandhi, like many others, lived in a joint family with his parents, siblings, and their wives. In such homes, men and women perform different duties. Women remain in the back of the house, such as the kitchen, and men engage in activities in the front rooms, i.e., the living room, verandah, and so on. The only times that men and women come together are during meal times and at night.

Kasturba noticed that none of the other women in the home needed their husbands' permission, so she went out with them without asking Gandhi's permission. When Gandhi found out, he was angry and reproached her. She responded calmly but with resoluteness, "You decide, should I obey the elders in the home or you? I have been brought up to obey elders." Gandhi was dumbfounded. How could he tell Kasturba not to obey his mother? Later in life, Gandhi would refer to this incident as his first lesson in nonviolent response.[7]

Ahimsa

A Sanskrit word central in Buddhist thought, *ahimsa* is usually translated as nonviolence. Eknath Easwaran points out that *ahimsa* is the complete absence of violence, "this sounds negative, just as 'nonviolence' sounds passive." But like the English word 'flawless' *ahimsa* connotes perfection." [8] *Ahimsa* is perfect love. Gandhi said that we are caught in the conflagration of *himsa*, violence. Therefore, a votary of *ahimsa*

> remains true to his faith if the spring of all his actions is compassion, if he shuns to the best of his ability the destruction of the tiniest creature, tries to save it, and thus incessantly strives to be free from the deadly coil of *himsa*. He will consis-

tently be growing in self restraint and compassion, but he can never become entirely free from outward *himsa*.[9]

Ahimsa might be translated as unconditional love; one is to grow in it daily. It is the means to get at Truth. The way to Truth is not through rationality but through love. Erikson insightfully states, "Truthful action, for Gandhi, was governed by the readiness to get hurt and yet not to hurt—action governed by the principle of *ahimsa*."

Arun Gandhi[10] identifies the five elements of *ahimsa* as Gandhi practiced it at home, in community, and in all relationships: love, respect, understanding, acceptance, and appreciation.[11] One can see the close relationship here with Carl Rogers' facilitating skills: respect, unconditional acceptance, empathic understanding, and genuineness.[12] Erikson sensed a deep affinity between Gandhi's truth and the insights of modern psychology and its potential to transform both partners. This is possible only where persons learn to be nonviolent to themselves and others. Thus, "reality testing" comprises clear thinking and "mutual activation with others." He understood that nonviolent confrontation can bring to light insights on both sides.[13]

Arun Gandhi distinguishes between reactive nonviolence and proactive nonviolence. Reactive nonviolence is exemplified in Gandhi and King. They responded to discrimination in their societies. Gandhi showed proactive nonviolence by cultivating the qualities of *ahimsa* in individuals and in the community.[14]

Gandhi sought to justify his involvement with the Indian Ambulance Corps in the Boer and Zulu wars in South Africa and in World War I in London. Even though *satyagraha* and *ahimsa* had become firm principles by 1906, he continued to participate as a civilian noncombatant. Therefore one could say he was a pragmatic pacifist at first but later became a witnessing pacifist. In April 1929, during the communal violence between Hindus and Muslims, he noted that weapons of warfare derived their life from a belief in violence as a means for securing justice. He viewed the West as "suffocating the world with a spirit of violence . . ." He explained his compromises as views he held at a time when he was younger and said he would "never revert to his previous position."[15] He was criticized for absolutizing nonviolence because it showed insensitivity to particular contexts that might require a limited use of violence. Aurobindo[16] and Sarvarkar[17] viewed Gandhi's ideology of nonviolence as positively immoral. But both did so for different reasons. Aurobindo from his philosophical basis of Integral Yoga held to both violence and nonviolence as necessary based on circumstances. Sarvarkar based his views of violence on the norm of the Hindu martial code of *kshatriya-dharma*, ruler and warrior's duty. But Annie Besant,[18] Rabindranath Tagore,[19] and C.F. Andrews[20] saw the actions of non-co-operation, civil disobedience, and fasting as possible forms of harmful coercion. They also cautioned that a nonviolent movement could result in violent acts and that self-righteousness could result in blind acts. Gandhi, of course, recognized that *satyagrahis* could become violent and therefore taught people the implications of and conduct of *satya-graha*. He totally disagreed, however, with Aurobindo and Sarvarkar's positions.[21]

He adopted three principles for *satyagrahis* to guide their decisions for resistance to, or participation in, war:

1.   Declare open resistance by boycotting the Empire until it changed its stance to war;
2.   Seek imprisonment by civil disobedience;
3.   Participate in the war on the side of the Empire, and in so doing get the strength to resist the violence of war.[22]

At the time of the Boer, Zulu and World War I wars, he did not think he could follow options 1 and 2 and so participated as a non-combatant.

Gandhi's *satyagraha* campaigns followed these steps:

1.   Impartial investigations followed by a sincere attempt at arbitration. *Satyagraha* is only the last resort of an unbearable situation;
2.   A thorough preparation of all *satyagrahis*;
3.   Wide publicity to induce the public either to intervene or to gain support for the proposed action;
4.   A detailed announcement of the proposed action, with a clear ultimatum and an opening for arbitration at any time;
5.   Form an action committee to select forms of non-cooperation—strike, boycott; civil disobedience, and so on; use minimum force to reach a defined goal. The issues need to be important

for the practical life of the community and symbolic for its future.

6   *Satyagrahis* need to:
   a.   Rely on themselves for their suffering and their triumphs;
   b.   Take the initiative for the movement and take responsibility for all actions;
   c.   Persuade and enlighten and be willing to be persuaded and enlightened; seek to learn, teach, and participate to become truer through action.[23]

In sum, Gandhi's nonviolence is based on deep respect and love for self and others. As he said, "It is quite proper to resist and attack a system, but to resist and attack its author is tantamount to resisting and attacking oneself."[24] *Satyagraha* and *ahimsa* evoke transformation through appeal to the good in others and through self-suffering.[25] Gandhi sought to apply the principles of *ahimsa* to diet, family, government, and international relations.

In the following sketch I will try to show how the *satyagraha* movement, guided by *ahimsa*, was transposed from the early experiments in communal living on the Phoenix and Tolstoy Farms in South Africa, to the *satyagraha* and *sevagram ashrams* in India, to the chaotic and turbulent seas of social, political, and economic life under the growing constraints of Empire.

Gandhi first put *satyagraha* into practice on South African soil, the theater of his actions from May 1893 to July 1914. In 1894 he submitted the first petition protesting against the indentured labor system, a form of semi-slavery. Finally, on July 31, 1916, the system was abolished in India after other Indians made concentrated efforts in the Imperial Legislative Council; the British had procrastinated for almost twenty-two years. In India, Gandhi protested the delay in abolishing the evil system despite Imperial promises, and he made known his plans for *satyagraha*. Gandhi said, "I cannot help saying that potential *satyagraha* hastened the end."[26]

In 1917, Gandhi's first experiment with the *satyagraha* movement in India was launched in a legal campaign to bring justice to peasant farmers in Champaran at the foothills of the Himalayas, near Nepal, now in Bihar. The farmers had complained to Gandhi of violent treatment and "shameless" exploitation by British indigo planters. With Gandhi's intervention, the *tinkathia* system (exploitative slavery) was abolished. It was a system that had forced farmers to work without pay for their planter landlords for almost a century.[27]

In December of the same year he used *satyagraha* in Ahmedabad to bring about peace and justice in a cotton mill to settle a dispute over fair wages between Ambalal Sarabai, the owner, and poor employees. Ambalal Sarabai's sister, Anasuyabehn Sarabai, requested Gandhi to intervene on behalf of the employees. She was Gandhi's friend and benefactor, as was Ambalal later. In this campaign he taught the employees how to put *satyagraha* into practice. He went on a fast on behalf of the workers. Erikson thinks that this event was a major turning point in Gandhi's nonviolent campaigns to help India gain her freedom. This action honed his philosophy of militant nonviolence as a political instrument for use on a large scale, "beyond industrial peace in Ahmedabad."[28]

Next, Kheda immediately caught his attention. The annual crop had failed and famine conditions were rapidly approaching. The government's response was that the usual taxes had to be paid. Only one out of six hundred villages was granted revenue relief; one hundred and three villages were assessed for half the crop share. The rest had to pay the usual taxes. The *satyagraha* campaign ended in a compromise. The rich landlords were required to pay the needed revenue. Thus, we see how *satyagraha* awakened the rural peasant farmers and urban mill workers to their rights of just treatment from employer or government. Gandhi's involvement began to take on momentum in the political arena. From these two projects Gandhi moved to the national stage.

The British did not keep their promise of dominion status for India after World War I; instead, martial law of the Defense of India Acts of 1915 was extended for another six months through the Rowlatt Bills. The bills, which became an Act, summarily dispensed with the civil rights of convicted and suspected rebels. Gandhi perceived the systematic repression in such moves, and in March 1919 spearheaded the first nationwide *satyagraha* in a *hartal*, which brought down the shutters on all Indian shops and establishments. The British Empire was the main counterplayer and world opinion was the awed onlooker on the occasion of the anti-sedition law passed by the British. The repression continued; no one realized that *swaraj* (self rule) would take another thirty difficult years.

Between 1920 and1934, Gandhi revolutionized and led the Indian National Congress; however, he quit the Congress in 1934 when he failed to get agreement for *satyagraha* as the means to *swaraj* and for social reforms to precede political reforms. He believed that nonviolence alone could lead to true freedom, and without social reforms Indian rule would be insensitive to the plight of India's poor millions. [29] His withdrawal from Congress probably set back Indian Independence by almost a decade.

Between 1934 and 1940, the abolition of untouchability, the welfare of Untouchables, and reform of Hinduism were his primary goals. In 1940 he rejoined the Congress to lead the country to freedom on his terms. The Congress backed him, but many did so not out of conviction but because it seemed a pragmatic move. They realized the masses listened to him.

Gandhi cared deeply about Hindu-Muslim unity and took every opportunity to become involved with their concerns. He did not want the country divided and the cause of freedom lost through the British policy of divide and rule. He was also concerned about the Untouchables and wanted Hinduism to reform itself by voluntarily renouncing untouchability and its attendant evils. In 1924, on behalf of the Untouchables, he launched a *satyagraha* to protest denial of temple entry to Untouchables at Vaikom, Kerala.[30]

In 1932, when the British Prime Minister Ramsay MacDonald announced separate electorates for the Untouchables, Gandhi went on a fast unto death to get the decision changed. Gandhi did not want the electorate divided and society fractured; he wanted reform of Hinduism from within. He believed in a conversion of the heart. A compromise, the Poona Pact, was worked out with the leader of the Untouchables, Dr. Bhim Rao Ambedkar.[31] The Untouchables would be part of a single electorate but with reservations in certain constituencies.

In 1933 he undertook a twenty-one-day fast against untouchability to get the upper-caste Hindus to change their hearts toward Untouchables. Ambedkar not only wanted untouchability to be illegal, which he failed to achieve till 1948; he also wanted to annihilate the caste system. Much later, Gandhi saw the need for political power for the Untouchables, when they were routed in a municipal election at Kanpur.[32] On the eve of India's independence Gandhi advised Nehru and Patel[33] to invite Dr. Ambedkar to be a Minister of Law in the cabinet, which would make him the chairperson of the constitution drafting committee.[34] Ambedkar was more than qualified for the position but, once again, Gandhi made a powerful symbolic move.

In 1930, in defiance of the British Empire, Gandhi launched a salt *satyagraha* to oppose the salt tax. This tax netted 25 million pounds to the British treasury out of 800 million pounds collected yearly from India.[35] Making salt on the seashore of Dandi after a twenty-four-day march from Ahmedabad was a symbol to encourage people to make and sell salt without paying tax. The tax was a cruel imposition on millions of poor to whom salt was freely available along thousands of miles of seashore. This symbolic act also demonstrated the power of ordinary people against a mighty empire. The salt *satyagraha* probably marked the beginning of the end of the British Empire in India.

In 1940 a civil disobedience campaign was launched to demand self-rule in exchange for supporting Britain's war effort. In 1942 the British proposed an interim government during the war to be followed by independence. So, Gandhi launched the Quit India movement; the demand was for immediate independence.

Two events broke his heart at this time: the possible partition of India and the Hindu-Muslim riots; as a result, he lost his desire to live. He went on special missions to Bihar and Calcutta to calm the people down and help in Hindu-Muslim relations. Muslims wanted partition because they feared the rule of the Hindu majority.

When India and Pakistan became a reality as separate nations, he saw a new role that would transcend this boundary; he desired to extend *satyagraha* beyond national boundaries.

Sarvodaya

The Sanskrit word *sarvodaya* means "the welfare of all," or literally, "The uplift of all." How did this idea originate in Gandhi? In October of 1904, Henry Polak, one of his assistants, saw Gandhi off at Johannesburg station and gave him a copy of John Ruskin's *Unto This Last*, urging him to read it. The book, which Gandhi read on the overnight journey to Durban, echoed Gandhi's concern for social reform. Ruskin's interest lay in social reform, based on his artistic sensitivity and rejection of Manchester's industrial ugliness and degradation. Three ideals in the book caught Gandhi's attention, and he discovered some of his deepest convictions reflected in them:

1. "The good of the individual is contained in [the] good of all";
2. "A lawyer's work has the same value as the barber's"; and
3. "The life of the tiller of soil and the handicrafts man is the life worth living."

Gandhi translated Ruskin's book into Gujarati and gave it the title *Sarvodaya*.[36]

Within a month of reading the book he purchased Phoenix Farm and implemented Ruskin's ideals there. This farm was the first of four rural communes/*ashrams* that he founded (two in south Africa and two in India). He made an offer to the staff of *Indian Opinion* to live and work on the farm. They voluntarily agreed on a salary of three pounds a month. Within a year Phoenix Farm was a vital and healthy community, a model of social transformation. People of all races, castes, and religions lived and worked together.

The second commune was named Tolstoy Farm. Tolstoy, whom he had read eight years earlier, also had a profound impression on him. It was Tolstoy's "independent thinking, profound morality, and truthfulness" that had impressed him. So he sought to implement Ruskin and Tolstoy's ideas with strict business principles on the farms.[37]

He arrived in India with the aim to carry out his *satyagraha* movement in India. He took Gokhale's advice and from January to April 1915 traveled in India to get closer to the people. He soon realized the need for a base. On May 25, 1915, he established a *satygraha ashram* at Kochrab, a village near Abmedabad (now within the city limits) on rented property. The *ashram* was moved from Kochrab, because there was a plague there, to the banks of the Sabarmati near Ahmedabad, a site Gandhi purchased in 1915. Residents had to take six vows to be part of the *ashram*: truth, nonviolence, celibacy, control of the palate, non-stealing, and non-possession. Three "subsidiary vows" included: *swadeshi*, negatively understood as boycott of British goods and positively affirmed as using hand-spun cotton (*khaddar*); fearlessness; and a vow against untouchability. These new rules were refinements from the Phoenix and Tolstoy Farms, with added emphasis on *swadeshi* and the vow against untouchability. In 1933 the Sabarmati *ashram* was given as a gift to the Servants of the Untouchables Society for *harijan* work. *Harijan* means children of God, a name Gandhi gave to the Untouchables. His major campaigns after that were carried out from the *Sevagram Ashram* in Wardha in Central Province (now in Maharashtra). These *ashram* communities were to be model communities free from racism and casteism.

The concept of *sarvodaya* was exemplified in the life of Vinoba Bhave. Known as India's walking saint, Vinoba was Gandhi's most saintly disciple, whom Gandhi called his son. After Gandhi's assassination, Vinoba devoted himself to a series of socially revolutionary movements across India for the next thirty years. He further concretized and demonstrated the concept of *sarvodaya* that Gandhi had epitomized in his reform movements—uplift of *harijans* and social and moral uplift through the two village *ashrams*.

Vinoba responded to the growing unrest in the eastern half of the former princely state of Hyderabad where the Nizam of Hyderabad, with his coterie of landowners, ruled an impoverished peasant population. The communists preached violent revolution, to which Vinoba responded by appealing to the landlords for "gifts of land" (*boodan*) to be distributed to landless peasants. Along with his disciples, including Europeans, Americans, and Japanese, Vinoba walked from village to village. Even the most hardhearted landlords responded to his appeal, though the donated lands were often either too steep or dry for cultivation and took long to transfer to needy peasants.

In 1954 Vinoba launched *gramdan*, the gift of a village. By 1957 he had walked through Bihar and most of Maharashtra and redistributed land in 50,000 villages among the village tillers and workers.

In 1958 he called for *jivandan*, the gift of life, dedication of a life to selfless service to India's poor and needy. Many joined that idealistic movement, but their numbers remained disproportionate to the needs of the people and the growing ills and inequities in urban areas.[38]

Swadeshi

Gandhi first heard of *swadeshi,* interpreted as patriotism or nationalism, while he was still in South Africa. In 1905 the Bengalis promoted the use of *swadeshi* goods as opposed to British goods in the wake of the partition into east and west Bengal in the name of administrative efficiency. When Gandhi started *Satyagraha Ashram* in 1915 in Ahmedabad he made *swadeshi,* the wearing of hand-spun cloth instead of imported cloth, a subsidiary vow for members of the *ashram.* In 1921 Gandhi adopted the loincloth and *khaddar* (hand-spun and hand-woven cotton) as his regular attire. His condition for accepting the office of president of the Congress Party was that all members wear *khadi* and spin each day where possible.[39] In 1921 Rev. C. F. Andrews criticized Gandhi's move to promote *khadi,* to burn foreign cloth, to use *khaddar,* and to spin yarn every day as a religious duty. He felt it was a self-righteous act to burn foreign cloth and that it promoted narrow nationalism. What was Gandhi's reason for *swadeshi* and the *khadi* movement? He saw *khadi* and the spinning wheel as symbols of India's equality and freedom.[40] It was a means to provide employment to semi-starved and semi-employed women who would clothe Indians with their *khaddar.*[41]

Swadeshi began as a movement to boycott foreign cloth and goods and to produce and wear *khadi.* Later it was defined more broadly: a spirit that restricts the use and service of that which is remote in the interest of using what is found in one's own surroundings.[42] *Swadeshi* was translated into economics. Gandhi visualized economically self-sufficient villages.[43] He was concerned about the poor and viewed industrialization as degrading and helpful only to the urban rich. Perhaps the greatest gulf between Gandhi and Nehru was over forms of social action and industrialization. Nehru's views of social action were based on Marxist-Leninist concepts, whereas Gandhi was influenced by early Christianity and ancient Hindu ideals of love and communal sharing.[44]

The sociology of *swadeshi* was the traditional *varna ashrama dharma* that prescribed *dharma* (duties) based on *varna* (traditional social categories of *Brahmin*—poet, priest; *Kshatriya*—ruler, soldier; *Vaisya*—merchant, agriculturalist; and *Shudra*—worker, tiller of the soil), and *ashrama* (stages of life: *brahmacharya*—student; *grahastha*—householder; *vanaprastha*—renouncer of household responsibilities; forest dweller; and *sanyasa*—hermit). Gandhi sought to abolish untouchability and reform Hinduism from within. B. R. Ambedkar, leader of the Untouchables, regarded Gandhi's view on *varna ashrama dharma* as detrimental to the Untouchables because, he said, "There will be outcastes as long as there are castes."[45]

The politics of *swadeshi* meant nationalism based on village *panchayats* (village councils). *Swadeshi* of religion meant one lived by one's own religion and forbade conversion. He said that if one found any defect in one's religion, then one must reform it.[46] Ambedkar opposed him; he converted to Buddhism and urged the Untouchables to convert to other religions as one means of escape from untouchability, the other means being education. C. F. Andrews also criticized Gandhi's anti-conversion stance as it took away the right of individual choice.[47] Gandhi, a pluralist, was against conversion in actual practice but did not discourage those who had converted.

Rev. Fr. Tiwari of Bishop's College, Calcutta, told me about his first encounter with Gandhi. Sent to Gandhi by his family to dissuade him from following the new faith, Gandhi asked him if he had become a Christian, to which Tiwari replied in the affirmative. Gandhi then asked, "Have you taken baptism?" to which Tiwari said, "Yes." Gandhi responded, "Then be a good Christian, and welcome to my *ashram*." Gandhi used Tiwari's services to teach Sanskrit to Mirabehn, a British Admiral's daughter who was a disciple of Gandhi. Gandhi also asked Tiwari to give lectures on the Gospel of Luke to members of the *ashram*.

In sum, Gandhi sought to actualize *satyagraha*, *ahimsa*, and the related concepts of *sarvodaya* and *swadeshi* in his own life, in that of the *ashramites*, and in the larger community. Gandhi's critics eventually must acknowledge that he powerfully showed the significance of nonviolence on a national scale that affected global movements for dignity and freedom. To gain a greater depth into Gandhi and his thought, analysis from social-science and theological perspectives will be invaluable to learn about personal, social, and cultural transformation amid violence and war.

Gandhi: Analysis from Social-Science and Theological Perspectives

In this section I will seek to analyze Gandhi and his nonviolent method from an interdisciplinary perspective. I will draw on an interactionist, neo-Parsonian, model that seeks to show how socialization and transformation are at work in all domains of human action: organism (body), psyche (ego), society (role), and culture (master image).[48] Changes in one domain affect all other domains, like the shifting of a kaleidoscope. The methodology I will use to study Gandhi and his method of nonviolence will draw, on the one hand, from the social sciences and, on the other, from a Christian theological perspective. I will seek to maintain the integrity of all the disciplines. The purpose of using such an interdisciplinary methodology is to (1) illumine our study of Gandhi and his nonviolent action from diverse angles and (2) draw implications for how Divine action might work in, through, and with human action in a violent world.

Gandhi did not systematically explain the reasons for violence. Nevertheless, his understanding of violence as multifaceted and multilayered may be gleaned from his writings. He saw violence operating in all areas of human action. We could begin our study of Gandhi and his nonviolence from any one of the domains. However, it seems logical to begin from the perspective of the psyche (ego) to try to understand the specific inner dynamics at play in his life that transformed him into a nonviolent person.

Gandhi grew up in a particular socioeconomic, political, and cultural context. Hence, to understand the inner workings in Gandhi's life we need the help of developmental psychology and an understanding of his context. I will attempt to show that Freud, Erikson, Jung, and Fowler help in charting the dynamics of the ego. But they do not penetrate the deeper dynamic of the human spirit, the creator of the ego,[49] which is the agency in human psyche that helps to mediate between the inner and outer worlds of persons.

Freudians might argue that in Gandhi an infantile sexuality, repressed after the Oedipal stage in his identification with his father, erupted in adolescent sexual transgressions. This happened despite his marriage at age thirteen, under the influence of his friend Mehtab, his negative identity.[50] Freudians might argue that a sense of shame, loathing, and morality arising out of a superego conditioned by religion may have restrained his sexual impulses. At age thirty-seven he took a vow of celibacy. It can be argued that he sublimated his sexual energy in the service of humanity. Freudians, who see religion as a projection of human beings, would fail to see anything deeper in the religious thematic in his life. But can it be written off?

Erikson, a Neo-Freudian, who wrote a book on Gandhi, affirms much of Freud but goes beyond him. He believes that Freudian Oedipal drama was at the heart of Gandhi's adolescent turbulence.[51] He goes on to say that Gandhi's life reveals infantile and juvenile antecedents of deep conflicts between phallicism and saintliness, and between paternal power and maternal care.[52] Gandhi's major turning point in his late religious resolution of the identity crisis is the coalescing of the vow of *brahmacharya* (celibacy) with *satyagraha*.[53] This religiosity in Gandhi, and in many Indians, is attributed to the diffusion of the mother in the extended family system. It creates nostalgia for fusion,[54] manifested in the primitive mother religion, a unifying stratum of Indian religiosity, and *moksha* (release from the cycle of birth and rebirth).[55]

Erikson helps us see the religious thematic. But one must not fail to see the cultural, social, and political situation in South Africa that precipitated a crisis that made Gandhi look for a resolution of his identity crisis in religion. I think that if we look closely at Gandhi's response to his mother's death, and simultaneously his turn to Raychandbhai,[56] religion, and later for religion's instruction from him, one may be inclined to agree with Erikson that the religious thematic is related to the diffusion of mother.[57] Gandhi's mother died when he was a student in England. The news of his mother's death was given to him on his arrival back in India. He says,

> The news, however, was nonetheless a severe shock to me. But I must not dwell upon it. My grief was even greater than over my father's death. Most of my cherished hopes were shattered. But I remember that I did not give myself up to any wild expressions of grief. I could even check the tears, and took to life just as though nothing had happened.[58]

That same day he met Raychandbhai who impressed him greatly as a saintly person and later helped him explore his faith from within the Hindu and Jain traditions. About Raychandbhai he says,

> The thing that did cast its spell over me I came to know afterwards. This was his wide knowledge of the scriptures, his spotless character, and his burning passion for self-realization . . . the passion to see God face to face.[59]

Thus we see in Gandhi's experiences of loss an awareness of nothingness and a sense of Divine pervasiveness.[60] Is it possible that this longing for one's mother points to a deeper reality in human beings, beyond ego dynamics, that creates this longing for the face of God?

But before we seek to answer this question let us see Gandhi through the lens of Jung. Gandhi revealed so much of his life; he appears to be an open book. Both the abnormal and supernormal vie with such disarming frankness.

> The shadow is a moral problem that challenges the whole ego-personality, for no one can become conscious of the shadow without considerable moral effort. To become conscious of it involves recognizing the dark aspects of the personality as present and real.[61]

Making unconscious aspects of the shadow conscious leads toward individuation. Gandhi, with his openness and constant repentance, moved beyond individuation. He incorporated the feminine principle, anima, into his personality. Erikson observes, "I wonder whether there has ever been another political leader who almost prided himself on being half man and half woman."[62] This, according to Erikson, is sublimated maternalism as part of the positive identity of a whole man and a *homo religiousus*.[63] Jung says that incorporating the anima, an archetype of the self, moves one toward greater individuation and wholeness. But Gandhi's desire is for more: holiness and closeness to God.

Gandhi's life points to the reality and dynamic of the human spirit in search of its ground in God.[64] On November 20, 1925, in the introduction to his biography he wrote,

> I am still so far from him, who as I fully know governs every breath of my life, and whose offspring I am. I know that

it is the evil passions within that keep us so far from him, and yet, I cannot get away from them.[65]

Simultaneously, we read about inward communion[66] and the "inner voice" in his life.

> Time and again in my life, contrary to all wise counsels, I have allowed myself to be guided by the inner voice—often with spectacular success. But success and failure are of no account. [They] are God's concern, not mine.[67]

While Gandhi recognizes the human spirit has been separated from its ultimate ground in God, he also acknowledges the presence and the grace of God in his life.

Over time, his life's mission expanded from a narrow case for dignity and freedom for Indians in South Africa to include fellow Indians in India to encircle the world. He writes on April 14, 1929:

> My mission is not merely brotherhood of Indian humanity. My mission is not merely freedom of India, though today it undoubtedly engrosses practically the whole of my life and the whole of my time. But through realization of freedom of India I hope to realize and carry on the mission of the brotherhood of man . . . By a long course of prayerful discipline I have ceased for over forty years to hate anybody . . . But I can and do hate evil wherever it exists.[68]

The ego decentered to such an extent that Gandhi seems to be participating in the valuing of the Creator's love for creatures rather than coming from "the standpoint of a vulnerable, defensive, anxious creature."[69]

Thus we see that Erikson, Jung, and Fowler recognize a decentering of the ego in (1) the emergence of a *homo religiousus*, (2) the individuative process, and (3) the valuing process. Erikson shows that Gandhi's late religious resolution of his identity crisis throws him off the normal scale. Erikson, Jung, and Fowler help us understand how the ego also gradually decenters in so-called normal human development. It results, in an Eriksonian sense, in a person with a predominance of integrity over despair and with strengths of love, care, and wisdom. In Jungian terms one moves to individuation and wholeness. Fowler shows how a person in the way s/he values the other might move, like Gandhi, to a stance of principled openness, grounded in one's tradition but open to other traditions and to universalizing ways of valuing others. However, each of them recognizes that the role of religion in human development may have a positive impact on one's growth, probably the way we humans are meant to be.

James E. Loder reminds us that the ego develops its defenses in response to situations that give rise in infancy to fears of abandonment and as absorption. The ego is unable to undo its double bind of fears of absorption and abandonment. It is the "Spirit alone [who] can set the human spirit free" for its participation in God's life. From a Reformed Christian theological perspective he wrote,

> . . . the abyss between the human and the Divine is humanly unfathomable, it must be crossed by the act of God; . . . this has already been done in the paradox of God's becoming fully human while remaining fully God in Jesus Christ. What remains for us is the awakening to this reality and to all it implies for the conviction, illumination, and sanctification of the development of persons.[70]

The Chalcedonian formulation of Jesus Christ as fully Divine and fully human is the paradigm for the human spirit to be in relation with the Divine Spirit such that the Divine guides human action.[71] This is a very significant contribution for our discussion on Gandhi. Gandhi's life, with its preponderance for the spiritual and ascetic bordering on Manichaeism. Underlying his asceticism is a tacit form of spirit/body dualism, even though he shows concern for diet, exercise, and home remedies for illnesses. It seems his emphasis on celibacy and overcoming of the sexual drive is an indication of spirit/body dualism. Yet in his emphasis on the spiritual life, he was critiquing the materialism of the West. It is only through the Chalcedonian formulation (Jesus Christ is fully God and fully human), however, which Loder uses to understand human development, that a corrective may be brought to dualistic tendencies in Gandhi or dualism that emphasizes the material over the spiritual. Both the spiritual and material have to be held in relationship, with marginal control of the spiritual over material, patterned after the Divine-human relationship.

God's action in Jesus Christ is the basis for God's grace to flow toward human beings to bridge the great gulf between God and us. Thus, in our action and through the church, we are called to encourage such practices as will provide opportunities for encounters with God and to nurture a life in the Spirit. "The Book of Nature" and the "Book of Scriptures" are windows to God, who awakens us and leads us to purgation, that illumines us with insights into the life of God that lead to unification through contemplation, always putting us back into the world in the power of the Spirit.[72] *Lectio Divina* (divine reading) needs to be integrated into Sunday school curriculum so that habits of contemplation are formed early in life. Adults who do not know *Lectio Divina* need to be encouraged to participate in all such practices that will support a life in the Spirit.

Let us now turn to the domains of culture, society, and organism to try to grasp Gandhi's understanding of violence in each of these areas. Then, once again, we will pick up the theological thread to weave it back into the discussion in the service of transformation.

The Domain of Culture

The *domain of culture* comprises values and ultimate value, held in the head and in the heart. Cultural values legitimize social structures. Every culture, according to Loder, has a "master image" or root metaphor that captures the ethos of that society. The master image functions at the subconscious and unconscious levels. Any change or transformation in cultural values affects societies and individuals. For example, equality affects social structures (roles), as reflected in diversity of relationships between races, ethnicities, genders, status groups, etc., and opportunities for equal employment; persons (ego)—respect and dignity, wholesome human development; and organism (body)— encouraging space for unhindered access to interact with the environment, adapting to and transforming it.

Gandhi's experience at Maritzburg opened his eyes to violence in racism. This in turn helped him to empathize with oppression of the Untouchables and women.[73] Although he was raised in a patriarchal society, he encouraged the liberation of women from oppression, through education and open participation in society.[74] Racism and casteism legitimate socioeconomic and political structures of domination. Gandhi used reason, based on common civil law and the theology that we are all children of one Creator, to counter all forms of racism and casteism.

In seeking to reform Hinduism and rid it of the blot of untouchability the Untouchables or what he called *Harijans* (children of God). Ambedkar disagreed with Gandhi's approach of reform of Hinduism from within; he wanted the annihilation of a system that perpetuated inequality of status and opportunity. Their approaches to tackling the problem of untouchability were different. One wanted reform from within; the other wanted to make the caste system illegal.[75] I think we need both for the system to collapse over time.

His interpretation of religious texts to support nonviolence was creative and in the spirit of a reformer—whether it was the Bhagavad-Gita, the Bible, or the Koran.[76] "According to Gandhi, in the Koran, 'nonviolence is enjoined as duty, violence is permitted as necessity.'"[77]

The Social Domain

The *social domain* comprises the following structures: economics, politics, religion, law, and education. As stated earlier, the values in the cultural realm legitimize the structures of society. In Gandhi's day, racism, casteism, classicism, and communalism influenced the structures that segregated and dehumanized society into oppressor and oppressed. These structures are not unknown today and therefore seeking to transform society is still relevant today.

Gandhi asserted that economic inequality contributes to violence:

A nonviolent system of government is clearly impossibility so long as the wide gulf between the rich and the hungry millions persist. A violent and bloody revolution is a certainty one day unless there is a voluntary abdication of riches and the power that riches give, and a sharing of them for the common good.[78]

He viewed economic equality as the master key to nonviolent Independence. *Sarvodaya* was extended later through Vinoba Bhave through the *bhoodan*, *gramdan*, and *jivandan* movements. Gandhi disagreed with Nehru's[79] form of socialism and industrialization. Whatever one might think of Gandhian economics (*swadeshi*), his concern for the poor and economic equality is relevant in the context of economic globalization so that the poor do not become poorer.

On the political front, Gandhi upheld the institution of democracy; he saw no efficacy in Bolshevism for India. He believed democracy could not be brought about by violence and mere change of forms:

> The spirit of democracy is not a mechanical thing to be adjusted by abolition of forms. It requires change of heart . . . The spirit of democracy requires the inculcation of the spirit of brotherhood . . .[80]

He led the freedom movement in defense of equality, human dignity, and freedom. He wanted a democratic form of government ushered in by nonviolence. In this same spirit he desired unity between Hindus and Muslims, and between caste Hindus and Untouchables. Dividing British India into Pakistan and India led to bloodshed. It was in a way a failure of the spirit of democracy, where faith in the individual liberty of opinion and action is jealously guarded. Just before partition Gandhi told Rajendra Prasad, who became India's first president, that "what we regarded as a nonviolent fight was not really so . . . Had we followed the path of Truth and nonviolence we would not have seen human hearts so devoid of humanity."[81]

The religious structures are a microcosm of the larger society. In Gandhi's time, temples were closed to the Untouchables. The caste system, with its hierarchical ordering of society, is evident in the religious sphere in temples and places of worship. In 1924, Gandhi's *satyagraha* helped gain temple entry for the Untouchables in Vaikom, Kerala. He entered into debates on Hindu scriptures with the temple priests to assert that scriptures do not restrict anyone from entering the temples for worship. Between 1932 and 1934 he made concerted efforts to remove the blot of untouchability from Hinduism.

He viewed law as an instrument in the hands of the dominant that could be used for suppression and repression. He opposed authority by civil resistance whenever the laws were unjust. A case in point was his opposition to the Rowlatt Bill, the anti-sedition law.

While education can be a powerful instrument for transformation, conversely it can also be an instrument of oppression. Gandhi was not a great believer in textbook learning; he preferred the *guru-shishya* model (teacher-student discipleship). He held that, first, attention needs to be given to character building, and then to vocational, physical, and literacy training. Spiritual training was considered important for the knowledge of God and self-realization. He saw the importance of using one's native tongue for education so as not to create an inferiority complex by studying in a foreign language.[82]

While Gandhi sought to educate people on how to sublimate anger released through awakening, his plans to nurture nonviolent *satyagrahis* was not achieved. Nonetheless, whatever he *did* achieve is laudable. I think that Gandhi's method of nonviolence, with its ability to awaken people, needs to be brought into dialogue with Paulo Freire's[83] conscientization method for literacy training and spiritual theology. This needs to be developed for training in literacy and social consciousness, beginning with primary education and continuing through the adult level. In this way, not only will people be educated in the principles of *satyagraha*; they will also develop literacy and the ability to think, articulate their understanding, and take appropriate action in the Spirit to free themselves.

The Domain of Organism

The *domain of organism* concerns the body and how individuals interact with their environment through their bodies, i.e., the biological, neurological, and cognitive mechanisms. If people are constantly made to conform in their interaction with the environment, it might lead to oppressed and authoritarian ways of living. However, if play and creativity are encouraged more than conformity, then people learn to value freedom and develop the belief that they can transform things around them.

Though Gandhi's form of spirituality considered the body as a source of evil and the spirit as the essential self, he showed nonviolence to the body in his experiments in dietetics and home remedies for illnesses. He used his body as an instrument of nonviolence by taking suffering into himself through fasts.

Gandhi was a man who thought outside the box. He was a reformer. His creativity is evident not only in his interpretation of the Bhagavad-Gita but the ability to understand situations, get to the core of issues, work out a plan of action, and carry it out. He encouraged others to do the same.

Central to bringing about the nonviolent change and transformation that Gandhi envisaged is cultural and personal transformation. So long as the caste system, with its inherent hierarchy is intact, democracy as a way of life and economic equality will be a distant dream. His efforts at reform of Hinduism on the issue of Untouchability are laudable but more is needed. Arun Gandhi thinks that criticism of Gandhi for not working toward abolishing the caste system needs to be understood in the light of his times.

> People today wonder why Grandfather [Gandhi] did not take more radical public measures to eradicate the caste system ... History has largely forgotten that even these simple changes generated such anger that they motivated eight attempts on Grandfather's life. If the changes he proposed roused such strong passions among the powerful Brahmins, what might have happened if he had proposed even more revolutionary changes is frightening to imagine.[84]

Nonviolent struggle is not possible unless people embark on a journey of personal transformation; this is amply borne out by Gandhi's own life. He recognized the value of anger or aggression, which needed to be harnessed for nonviolent action. He was a believer in transformation through change of heart. In this sense, he believed in conversion but not in changing one's religion.[85]

In sum, change in one area of human action, be it personal, social, or cultural, affects all other areas.[86] When conflicts and violence are brought into dialogue with the reality of God's rule disclosed in Jesus Christ, a conscious openness to Divine action in and through human action becomes possible.

Theologically, Gandhi believed that Ultimate Reality is characterized by Truth and Love. Although, some have attributed to him an *advaitic* view of reality,[87] others think his views are more nuanced. Easwaran says, "His God, though a living presence, is an impersonal force—Law rather than Lawgiver; Truth, Love, Goodness, the unity of life."[88] C. F. Andrews held the view that Gandhi's belief in God was experienced through personal existence. "To both of us this belief in

God is as certain and immediate as one's personal existence."[89] It seems that Gandhi's understanding of Ultimate Reality might be better explained as belief in God as a presence. He prayed to a reality outside of himself when his son Manilal was severely ill, and the boy recovered.[90] However, he explained God in ethical categories as one committed to the *karma marga* (the way of action).[91] Thus, God is to be encountered in *satyagraha* through *ahimsa*. At the time of *satyagraha* in Champaran he said,

> It is no exaggeration, but the literal truth, to say that in this meeting with the peasants I was face to face with God, *Ahimsa* and Truth . . . I find nothing but my love for the people. And this in turn is nothing but an expression of my unshakeable faith in *Ahimsa*.[92]

At the same time his understanding of Ultimate Reality cannot be reduced to ethics.[93] In sum, Ultimate Reality for Gandhi was both immanent and transcendent, finding expression in an ethical life. Nonviolence was nonnegotiable for Gandhi since it was based on an understanding of Ultimate Reality as Love and Truth, and also on the ground that it was the law of our species, as violence was the law of the brute.

There is a deep convergence between Gandhi's understanding of nonviolence and Christian theology. At the heart of the Christ-event is the violence of the cross, revealing God's sacrificial love. Jesus Christ's life and ministry disturbed the order of a society based on violence. The world crucified him but he rose again. Christ died to expose the world of violence by standing in solidarity with the victims and offering forgiveness to the perpetrators of violence. Christ has also opened the door for a new future, when seen from the perspective of resurrection. Thus God in Jesus Christ has put an end to all the crosses of history.[94] What does this mean for individuals and communities of faith? It means that it is possible for individuals and communities, through grace, to live in the Spirit rather than to be controlled by sin.

We see that Christian theology and Gandhian thought on nonviolence have an ontological basis and share in the possibility of humanity being humanized by the grace of God. The difference lies in the cross, a historical event through which Christians believe God's sacrificial love was manifested to the world to bring forgiveness, reconciliation, and healing.

Gandhi accepted Jesus Christ as a great teacher and prophet who died the death of a martyr. He could not see Jesus Christ as the only incarnation of God, and therefore his death, according to Gandhi, could be interpreted symbolically, but not literally, as salvific. He embraced the moral influence theory.[95] He said, "I do not seek redemption from the consequences of my sin. I seek to be redeemed from sin itself, or rather from the very thought of sin. Until I have attained that end, I shall be content to be restless."[96] Nearly thirty years later, On November 26, 1925, he concluded the introduction to his autobiography by writing that in measuring himself by the standard of Truth he found himself to be a wretch. Gandhi, aware of a deeper fault line, had a desire for the transformation of his being. A functionalist view of salvation, the satisfaction theory of atonement, did not appeal to him;[97] as a Hindu he was conditioned by the concept of salvation as union with the Divine or Ultimate Reality.

I think if Karl Barth's doctrine of reconciliation had been presented to him, it would have resonated deeply with his search for an ontological view of salvation and affirmed the servant-leader[98] model he sought to follow in the roles of prophet, teacher, and elder. Karl Barth combines the three offices of Christ—prophet, priest, and king—with classical doctrines of two natures, Divine and human, and two states, humiliation and exaltation. This gives rise to three themes:

1.   the Lord as Servant (who as priest redeems us from the sin of pride);
2.   the Servant as Lord (in whom humanity is exalted by grace to be in royal partnership with God, freeing us from the sin of sloth); and
3.   the True Witness (the union of God and humanity in Jesus Christ carries its own prophetic power, dispelling our sin of falsehood).[99]

The doctrine of reconciliation and sin are extremely important in the Gandhi-Christian theology dialogue. The deeper dynamic of sin against God (Psalm 51) and not merely a state of alienation, understood psychologically, needs to be addressed. Violence goes deeper than the defenses and aggression of ego dynamics. Gandhi's view that human beings have the ability to rise above the "law of the brute" and to live by nonviolence[100] seems to have been too optimistic. His disappointment in the failure of *ahimsa* on so large a scale led to his depression at the time of Partition, when Hindus and Muslims rioted and killed each other. Police and the military were needed to quell the mob frenzy. Nonviolent movements require the practice of spiritual discipline to transform anger by living in the Spirit. Otherwise violent eruptions will lead to chaos and further cracks in an already fractured society.

I think, therefore, that Gandhian thought needs a framework of Spiritual theology with a focus on union with God and redemption theology.[101] The deep exchange that took place on the cross between Jesus Christ and humanity has a functional aspect in as much as it is a way for communion with the Trinity. The cross opens the door for personal reconciliation, so that we neither direct anger at ourselves for our role in sin and oppression nor displace the anger onto scapegoats.[102] Opportunity for confession, forgiveness, catharsis, and reconciliation as practiced by the Truth and Reconciliation Commission in South Africa is an example of how to help a community move forward to a more just and peaceful world.[103]

The hope of the resurrection is also a significant contribution in the Gandhi-Christian theology dialogue, since it helps us to see that our struggles are not in vain. The victory has already been won, and we need to awaken to the reality of the Rule of God.

Gandhi conducted his life and work out of communes/*ashrams*. These communities were to be models for how pluralistic society should be structured. They were set up to be free from racism, casteism, classicism, communalism, and regionalism. This model provides an opportunity for a dialogue on Christian theological and Gandhian understanding of community. How does a transformed community reflect God's reality? *Satyagraha, ahimsa, sarvodaya,* and *swadeshi* defined Gandhi's communities. Trinitarian theology, revealed in Jesus Christ, and the work of the Holy Spirit in the midst of community manifest in acts of love, define Christian communities. The concepts of *perichoresis* (mutual indwelling that simultaneously affirms individuality and mutuality)[104] to describe the inner working of the Trinity, and *koinonia* (fellowship created amid us by the Holy Spirit)[105] might provide points for dialogue. Convergence might be found in the concepts of co-equality and mutual indwelling. Possible divergence on the center for a community, *satyagraha* or Trinity, might provide for a healthy dialogue and mutual enrichment. The "inner voice" of Gandhi provides rich opportunity for discussion of the role of God's Holy Spirit and for the practice of discernment.

Gandhi's life and work highlighted the importance of keeping Church and State apart and yet intervening to guide state policies. His critical distance as a servant-leader who did not join the government gave him the opportunity to critique the government when it failed to reconcile warring factions and serve the people. The Church needs to uphold nonviolent action as the more excellent way and work toward it with children, youth, and adults. The Church must continue to learn from its dialogue with Gandhi, particularly on how to get involved in the life of a nation in a nonviolent way in order to bring about transformation of cultures, societies, and persons for a more just and peaceful existence.

In sum, Christian theology and Gandhian thought converge on the understanding of God's sacrificial love and nonviolence. They both recognize the gulf between the Divine and the human. They diverge on the point of Ultimate Reality. Gandhi saw Ultimate Reality as Truth and Love. Christian theology points to the Trinity: ontological Trinity, the way God is eternally in God's self, living in eternal relationship of love; economic Trinity, the revelation of God in Jesus Christ and the Holy Spirit; and doxological Trinity, the experience of the Trinity in the life of the Church. The lynchpin that connects the ontological and doxological Trinity is the person and work of Jesus Christ, who is made known to us by the Holy Spirit.[106] When Gandhi speaks of Ultimate Reality as Love there is a possibility for dialogue with a Christian Trinitarian understanding, as Ultimate Reality cannot be eternally love, unless that Reality is in relationship. I have argued, therefore, that Gandhian thought needs a Trinitarian spiritual theology, which focuses on union with God, without losing the aspect of redemption in Jesus Christ to help humanity find forgiveness, reconciliation, and healing, even as we make our upward journey individually and collectively as a Church to encounter the Triune God. Gandhian thought, with its emphasis on praxis, has much to contribute since no one before Gandhi honed and used nonviolent action in the public arena as he did.

Gandhi's legacy continued in the lives and nonviolent movements he inspired: U. Thant, Martin Luther King Jr., Rosa Parks, Cesar Chavez, Dalai Lama, Kenneth Kuanda, Chief Luthuli, Lech Walesa, Aung San Suu Kyi, Benigno Aquino Jr., Desmond Tutu, Nelson Mandela—the list goes on. In India, Vinoba Bhave and many others carried forward the Gandhian movement for transformation. The Church needs to continue to dialogue with Gandhi's thought and find ways to address the growing violence around the world. Perhaps we can find that dialogue in the violence of the cross, a way of moving and living in the world by a nonviolent Jesus, one who, along with Gandhi, rejected war and violence.

Endnotes

1. M. K. Gandhi, *Autobiography* (Ahmedabad: Navajivan Publishing House, 1927), 3; Stanley Fisher, *The Essential Gandhi: An Anthology of His Writings on His Life, Work, and Ideas* (New York: Vintage Books, 1962), 4.
2. The assassin, Nathuram Godse, a member of the Rashtriya Swayamsevak Sangh, claimed that his "provocation was [Gandhi's] constant and consistent pandering to the Muslims . . ." Stanley Wolpert, *Gandhi's Passion: The Life and Legacy of Mahatma Gandhi* (Oxford: Oxford University Press, 2001).
3. Erik H. Erikson, *Gandhi's Truth: On the Origins of Militant Nonviolence* (New York: W.W. Norton and Co. Inc., 1969), 396.
4. M. K. Gandhi, *Autobiography*, 235.
5. Eknath Easwaran in Preface to Louis Fisher, ed., *The Essential Gandhi: An Anthology of His Writings on His Life, Work and Ideas.* (New York: Vintage Books, 1962), xxiv.
6. Gandhi said he did not get the idea of civil disobedience from Thoreau. The resistance to authority was far advanced in South Africa when he read the title of Thoreau's essay. He initially used the phrase but dropped it in favor of civil resistance as it better conveyed the meaning of the struggle. Louis Fisher, *The Essential Gandhi*, 76.
7. Arun Gandhi, *Legacy of Love: My Education in the Path of Nonviolence* (El Sobrante, CA: North Bay Books, 2003), 32-33.
8. Eknath Easwaran, in Louis Fisher, *The Essential Gandhi*, xxx.
9. M. K. Gandhi, *Autobiography*, 257.
10. Arun Gandhi is the grandson of Mahatma Gandhi. He was raised in South Africa, worked in India, and is the founder and director of the Gandhi Institute for Nonviolence, Memphis, Tennessee.
11. Arun Gandhi, *Legacy of Love*, 12.
12. Carl R. Rogers, *Client-Centered Therapy, Its Current Practice, Implications, and Theory.* (Boston: Houghton Mifflin, 1951).
13. Erik H. Erikson, *Gandhi's Truth: On the Origins of Militant Nonviolence* (New York: W. W. Norton and Co. Inc., 1969), 440.
14. Arun Gandhi, *Legacy of Love*, 124.
15. Stanley Wolpert, *Gandhi's Passion*, 136-137.
16. A civil servant who turned against the British government and later became a philosopher and founder of the *ashram* at Pondicherry, at that time a French colony.

[17] Founder of the *Hindutva* movement.

[18] A British Theosophist who popularized Theosophy in India and wanted Home Rule under British dominion.

[19] Poet, playwright, novelist, and Nobel laureate.

[20] Anglo-Catholic priest who was defrocked for his involvement in the freedom struggle in India, who was part of Gandhi's inner circle.

[21] Julius Lipner, "Conclusion: A Debate for Our Times," in Harold Coward, *Indian Critiques of Gandhi* (Albany: State University of New York Press, 2003), 243-247.

[22] M. K. Gandhi, *Autobiography*, 258.

[23] Erik H. Erikson, *Gandhi's Truth*, 414-416.

[24] M. K. Gandhi, *Autobiography*, 203.

[25] Arun Gandhi, *Legacy of Love*, 132.

[26] M. K. Gandhi, *Autobiography*, 297.

[27] M. K. Gandhi, *Autobiography*, 298-313; Stanley Wolpert, *Gandhi's Passion*, 88-89.

[28] E. H. Erikson, *Gandhi's Truth*, 364-392.

[29] Stanley Wolpert, *Gandhi's Passion*, 174-175.

[30] This was the only *satyagraha*, he undertook to remove a disability for the Untouchables. The twenty-one-day fast in 1933 was to change the hearts of caste Hindus toward Untouchables.

[31] Ambedkar, an Untouchable, had a Ph.D. from Columbia University and a D.Sc. from the London School of Economics. He also used *satyagraha* to work toward abolition of untouchability. He had differences with Gandhi over abolition of the caste system.

[32] Stanley Wolpert, *Gandhi's Passion*, 170-171.

[33] Jawaharlal Nehru was the first prime minister of India, and Sardar Vallabhbai Patel was the deputy prime minister.

[34] Harold Coward, *Indian Critiques of Gandhi*.

[35] Erik H. Erikson, *Gandhi's Truth*, 443.

[36] M. K. Gandhi, *Autobiography*, 220-221; Stanley Wolpert, *Gandhi's Passion*, 54-55.

[37] Stanley Wolpert, *Gandhi's Passion*, p. 55.

[38] Stanley Wolpert, *Gandhi's Passion*, 259-260.

[39] Louis Fisher, *The Essential Gandhi*, 192.

[40] *Ibid.*, 260.

[41] M. K. Gandhi, *Autobiography*, 365.

[42] M. M. Thomas, (drawing on C.F. Andrews) *The Acknowledged Christ of the Indian Renaissance* (Madras: The CLS Press, 1970), 202.

[43] *Ibid.*, 202-203.

[44] Stanley Wolpert, *Gandhi's Passion*, 25.

[45] Dhananjay Keer, *Dr Ambedkar: Life and Mission*. (Bombay: Popular Prakashan, 1954), 220.

[46] M. M. Thomas, *Acknowledged Christ*, 202-203.

[47] Harold Coward, *Indian Critiques of Gandhi*, 162.

[48] My arguments here will be influenced by Parsons' understanding of interacting systems in the context of socialization and enculturation and how in the cybernetics of control, cultural change is significant to account for conflicts, resolutions, and changes that go with them. James E. Loder's neo-Parsonian model enhances Parsons at critical points, introduces transformation, and brings a theological critique to Parsons' grand theorizing on socialization and enculturation.

Socialization is commonly understood as the process by which a society or a culture brings new members into itself. It is the means by which it teaches habits and values and how it measures success and failure. Socialization is interactive between persons and their human environment. Its purpose is to keep that environment in equilibrium; it is as Parsons, via Loder, says a "tension-reduction pattern- maintenance process designed to serve the purposes of adaptation and incorporation [of individuals] into the larger and more complex social milieu." Loder juxtaposes this understanding of socialization with transformation. Transformation, according to Loder, is "the patterned process whereby within any given framework of knowledge or experience, a hidden order of meaning emerges with the power to redefine and/or reconstruct the original frame of reference." The process of transformation uncovers those hidden orders of meaning. While socialization seeks to maintain equilibrium and the status quo, transformation disrupts the status quo to reorder reality, disclose the hidden orders, and bring deep change. Both transformation and socialization are at work in all the fields of human action—organism, psyche, society, and culture. The transforming power of the Holy Spirit seeks to recreate every aspect of human action patterned after God's rule disclosed in Jesus Christ. When transformation in the Spirit is the dominant force ". . . the Holy Spirit works within conflict to disclose new insights, releasing the creative energy of the human spirit, and firing us back into the world as bearers of a redeemed creation." James E. Loder, "Education in the Logic of the Spirit," unpublished manuscript. forthcoming.

49 Wolfhart Pannenberg, *Anthropology in Theological Perspective* (Edinburgh: T. & T. Clark Ltd., 1999). Pannenberg argues that exocentricity which is unique to human beings is named by theology as spirit. It is the spirit that is the creator of ego, culture, and society.

50 Sigmund Freud, *Three Contributions to the Theory of Sex* (New York: E. P. Dutton & Co., Inc., 1962), 51.

51 Erik H. Erikson, *Gandhi's Truth*, 113.

52 *Ibid.*, 402.

53 Erikson calls his late identity resolution characteristic of a *homo religiosus*. The phrase refers to a kind of generic religiosity that has become definitive for the totality of a life. By invoking the term *brahmacharya* and giving up of household responsibilities to enter the stage of *vanaprastha,* Gandhi placed his own development within the Indian paradigm of the four stages of a man's life (*brahmacharya*—student; *grahastha*—householder; *vanaprastha*—forest dweller, i.e., one who gives up household responsibilities; *sanyasa*—hermit, one who renounces the world.)

54 Erik H. Erikson, *Gandhi's Truth*, 42.

55 *Ibid.*, 402.

56 Rajchandra, a jeweler, was a devout Jain, slightly older than Gandhi, a connoisseur of pearls and diamonds. Rajchandra was to Gandhi what Staupitz was to Luther. He helped Gandhi articulate his deeply felt yet inarticulate religious and ethical direction.

57 Erik H. Erikson, *Gandhi's Truth*, 157-158.

58 M. K. Gandhi, *Autobiography*, 64.

59 *Ibid.*, 64.

60 Erik. H. Erikson, *Gandhi's Truth*, 346-397.

61 C. G. Jung, *Psyche and Symbol* (Princeton, NJ: Princeton University Press, 1991), 8. Ulanov explains how a man gradually relates to his feminine principle, anima, in four stages. In Stage 1, anima is experienced as arousal and projection onto one woman after another. In Stage 2, the male is at the disposal of the aroused sex and his life is characterized by a "harem mentality." Fidelity, as described by Erikson, is not yet a part of his life. In Stage 3, anima makes demands on a relationship. It may

170   *Breaking Silence*

come in the form of a woman taking the initiative to relate to him. It is consciously directed love. The woman and anima humanize the man. The man emerges out of domination under the Great Mother archetype. In Stage 4, man assumes relatedness to anima. The aim of the relationship of anima to the masculine in man is not to castrate but to make the male relatable. Man now has accessibility to energy hitherto not known to him. (Ann Belford Ulanov, *The Feminine in Jungian Psychology and in Christian Theology* [Evanston, IL: Northwestern University Press, 1971], 219-220.) The process of how a man relates to his anima is seen in Gandhi's life.

[62] Erik H. Erikson, *Gandhi's Truth*, 402.

[63] *Ibid.*, 403.

[64] See James E. Loder for discussion of the theme of human spirit in search of its ground, in *The Logic of the Spirit: Human Development in Theological Perspective*.

[65] M. K. Gandhi, *Autobiography*, xvi.

[66] Eknath Easwaran in Louis Fisher's *The Essential Gandhi*, xxiii.

[67] Louis Fisher, *The Essential Gandhi*, 271.

[68] *Ibid.*, 167.

[69] James W. Fowler, *Stages of Faith: The Psychology of Human Development and the Quest for Meaning* (San Francisco: Harper and Row, 1981), 69-71.

[70] James E. Loder, *Logic of the Spirit*, 12.

[71] Loder used the word relationality to emphasize a new entity that emerges in a certain quality of relationship. Relationality refers to a reality when two bi-polar opposites are brought into such a relationship that it takes on a life of its own.

[72] Diogenes Allen, *Spiritual Theology: The Theology of Yesterday for Spiritual Help Today* (Boston, MA: Cowley Publications, 1997); James E. Loder, *The Transforming Moment* (Colorado Springs, CO: Helmers and Howard, 1989).

[73] Louis Fisher, *Essential Gandhi*,118.

[74] Arun Gandhi, *Legacy of Love*, 34-35.

[75] Untouchability was abolished in 1948, but not the caste system.

[76] Peter van der Veer, *Imperial Encounters: Religion and Modernity in India and Britain*, 27.

[77] M. N. Srinivas, "Gandhi's Religion," in *Collected Essays* (New Delhi: Oxford University Press, 2002), 358.

[78] Louis Fisher, *The Essential Gandhi*, 247.

[79] India's first prime minister.

[80] Louis Fisher, *The Essential Gandhi*, 192.

[81] Stanley Wolpert, *Gandhi's Passion*, 234.

[82] M. K. Gandhi, *Autobiography*, 245-250.

[83] A Brazilian educator who developed a way to conscientization through literacy training. See Paulo Freire, *Pedagogy of the Oppressed*. trans. Myra Bergman Ramos (New York: The Seabury Press, 1968).

[84] Arun Gandhi, *Legacy of Love*, 93-96.

[85] Dr. Stanley Jones, Rev. S. Aldis, and Dr. D. G. Moses reported a personal conversation in which Gandhi said he was open to conversion if becoming Christian did not mean anti-nationalism, in M. M. Thomas, *Acknowledged Christ*, 234-235.

[86] James E. Loder, "Educational Ministry in the Logic of the Spirit" (forthcoming).

[87] Lipner describes monism as ". . . the philosophy of *advaita* or nondualism, which, badly put, states that differentiation is provisional and is to be sublated ultimately into an underlying unchanging, nondifferentiated, ineluctable One that is identifiable with the deeper self of the individual." Julius Lipner, in Harold Coward's, *Indian Critiques of Gandhi*, 253. Also see B. R. Nanda, *Gandhi and Religion* (New Delhi: Oxford University Press, 1990), 9.

[88] Eknath Easwaran, in Louis Fisher's, *The Essential Gandhi*, xxiii.

[89] C. F. Andrews, *Mahatma Gandhi's Ideas* (London: Allen and Unwin, 1929), 34.

[90] Louis Fisher, *The Essential Gandhi*, 79-81.

[91] The Bhagavad-Gita prescribes three possible ways to *moksha*, freedom from the cycle of birth and re-birth. They are *gnana marga*, way of knowledge; *bhakti marga*, way of devotion; and *karma marga*, way of action.

[92] M. K. Gandhi, *Autobiography*, 304.

[93] M. N. Srinivas, *Collected Essays* (New Delhi: Oxford University Press, 2002), 359.

[94] Daniel Migliori, *Faith Seeking Understanding: An Introduction to Christian Theology* (Grand Rapids, Michigan: William B. Eerdmans Publishing Company, 1991), 158-160.

[95] M. K. Gandhi, *Autobiography*, 98.

[96] M. K. Gandhi, *Autobiography*, 90.

[97] *Ibid.*, 89-90.

[98] I was introduced to "servant-leader" as a hyphenated term by Jim Emrich, who holds that there are times when one needs to say, "Follow me," and at other times one just serves. In this servant-leader relationality, servant is always in marginal control over leader.

[99] Karl Barth, *Church Dogmatics* (Edinburgh: T. and T. Clark, 1936-1977).

[100] Julius Lipner, in Harold Coward's *Indian Critiques of Gandhi*, 243-244.

[101] T. F. Torrance, *Mediation of Christ* (Colorado Springs, CO: Helmers and Howard, 1992).

[102] Rene Girard, *The Scapegoat*, trans. Yvonne Freccero (Baltimore: The Johns Hopkins University Press, 1986).

[103] Mpilo Desmond Tutu, *No Future Without Forgiveness* (New York: Doubleday, 2000).

[104] James E. Loder, *The Logic of the Spirit*, 195 and 276.

[105] *Ibid.*, 194.

[106] T. F. Torrance, *The Ground and Grammar of Theology* (Charlottesville, VA: University Press of Virginia, 1980), chapter 6.

A Journey of Love

A Walk for Peace

Rev. Gregory C. Guice

"Blessed are the peacemakers, for they shall be called children of God" —Matt. 5:9

"Dr. King's speech is a dream for Freedom, a dream for a world where people could walk together and work together and a world where we can pray together, a world where Peace is our mission."—from a sermon entitled "A Call for Peace," by Gregory Guice

A (Hu)Man's whole character is determined by the thoughts for which he allows a place in his mind. A strong man or a weak man is what he is because of repeated thoughts of strength or weakness. —Charles Fillmore, the founder of Unity Principles[1]

Whenever there is talk of war, little reflection is given to the conversation regarding love and peace of all human beings in spite of race. In fact, war is often an outward expression of the evil and hatred being projected upon another group, the "other." In the current Iraq war it is difficult to ignore the reality that the Iraqis are a people of color. Given the historical legacy of racism within the United States, it would be naïve not to think that the negative and often racist stereotypes that seek to enslave people of color across the globe is one possible reason Americans and, consequently the church, are able to accept the rationale for going to war. Therefore, I see it as my responsibility as an African American pastor of a majority white congregation to demonstrate through local and global peace activism that the United States has often ignored people of color, from Native Americans to the Hispanic community. As a result of America's inability to accept and deal with its racist ideologies, many American churches often end up perpetrating these constructs onto other people of color across the globe. It just happens that today's hated group ends up being the "terrorist," in Iraq or in the Middle East in general. It is time for the church to reject the structures of war that are based on false socially constructed models of race that promote hatred, fear, isolation, and power. It is time for the church to open its arms and venture into journeys of love and peace with those communities that do not look or worship as we do.

The legacy of racism has left hideous scars in this country. It is sick because it is based upon the color of one's skin. One of my earliest memories of experiencing racism and a community's fight for justice and peace occurred when I was eleven years old and living in Detroit, Michigan. The environment could be characterized as a hostile situation. Policemen patrolled our neighborhoods beating up on young black men and women, constantly reminding us that they, not us, dominated and controlled our neighborhoods. As a result of this constant pressure, my brothers became frustrated at the limits placed upon African Americans and the injustice we were experiencing because of the color of our skin. At the center of my brothers' passion was their desire for acceptance within the United States as human beings and not simply as colored people. My oldest brother even told us of the time our mother was forced to leave her home in rural Georgia because of the threats to her life. As I listened to their stories of injustice and racism, I felt their pain, which later would become my pain as I experienced these same limitations because I am an African American male.

Looking back, I can recall the moment I first heard about Dr. Martin Luther King Jr. Just the mention of his name created a buzz in our neighborhood because an African American had challenged the racist and unjust system within the United States. He was coming to Detroit in order not only to encourage blacks as they endured racial injustice but also to give a call to action to young men and women. When Dr. King came to Detroit in 1964 he brought with him the inspiration and belief that we as a people, as an American people, could overcome this system of racism and injustice through the acts of non-violence and love. He gave what would later become known as his famous "I Have a Dream" speech that day. It was his words on that day that ignited my social and religious fire in order to fight for world peace and justice. I am still captured by the ringing inspiration of his words:

> I have a dream today. I have a dream that one day "every valley shall be exalted, every hill and mountain shall be made low, the rough places will be made plains, and the crooked places will be made straight, and the glory of the Lord shall be revealed, and all flesh shall see it together." This is our hope. This is the faith that I go back to the South with. With this faith we will be able to hew out of the mountain of despair a stone of hope. With this faith we will be able to transform the jangling discords of our nation into a beautiful symphony of brotherhood. With this faith we will be able to work together, to pray together, to struggle together, to stand up for freedom together, knowing that we will be free one day. And this will be the day. This will be the day when all of God's children will be able to sing with new meaning "My country 'tis of thee, sweet land of liberty, of thee I sing. Land where my fathers died, land of the pilgrim's pride, from every mountainside let freedom ring."[2]

After I heard Dr. King's speech I began my journey toward living and fighting for a world of peace. His words became, and continue to be, the dominant mantra and strength for my fight toward bringing the realization of world peace. I believe that God is requiring the church like never before to address the racist ideologies that prohibit communities of people from being able to work together, pray together, and stand up for freedom together. Dr. King often reminded us that the means of justice and equality must be commensurate with the ends a community is seeking to achieve. It is the responsibility of the community of faith, then, to address these projections that are placed upon people of color and to ask, "What role does the church play in perpetuating the stereotypes of racism and classism?" I maintain that in order for the church to envision a world of peace, it must honestly deal with the reality and the impact of racism in times of war. Racism is a power that has the capacity to distort the images of God's children, and if the church is going to maintain its prophetic voice, it must discover new paths of peace and love.

The Journey of Discovery

An old African proverb states, "When walking inside a jungle be careful where you step because one might discover a brand new path." As a pastor, one of the first areas I believe the church should be committed to is that of discovering new ways to establish a world of peace. The initial question the church must address is, "What must we, as the body of Christ, discover?" Racism within the United States continues to influence and dominate many segments of American life. Many Americans believe that racism is no longer an issue and that African Americans should simply "move on" from these discussions. But racism, in fact, has not departed from the American horizon. Rather, it continues from the days of Jim Crow as the systemic foundation allowing for the perpetuation of illegal and abusive policies on people of color. Joe Feagin writes, "systemic racism is thus a system of oppression made up of many thousands of everyday acts of mistreatment of black Americans (and people of color) by white Americans, incidents that range from the subtle and hard to observe to the blatant and easy to notice. These acts of mistreatment can be nonverbal or verbal, nonviolent or violent."[3] Too often the racism within the United States goes unnoticed because it has been woven into every aspect of American life, especially the court system. One study in New Haven, Connecticut, revealed that when considering 118 local arrests, the bail amounts for the black male defendants were 35 percent higher than that of their white counterparts.[4] It remains clear that the legacy of white racism continues to inform and influence the lives of the American public and by association our foreign policies regarding war.

I recall the moment when, as an African American male growing up in the sixties, racism became real for me. I witnessed what the reality of racism had done to the men and women in my urban community. They had lost something within themselves, causing many of them to question whether or not America could become the nation for which King had given his life. I can remember when the Detroit riots erupted and I watched those fearful moments as people of color poured into the streets releasing years of frustration and oppression. I witnessed people of color desiring freedom and justice at any cost. When the fires of the riots came to my front door, I became even further disillusioned by the reality of a United States where men and women were judged by the color of their skin. It was within these moments of anxiety and fear that I began to search for new paths by which to reach the America that King had envisioned and for which he eventually gave his life. I became committed to a life of peace because I wanted a world filled with violence and war to cease. I desired the African American men and women who had lived their lives dispossessed to experience liberation. For the next few years, I searched for King's America. I wanted the realization of an America that upheld the foundation of its basic principles of life, liberty, and the pursuit of happiness. But with each disappointment I began to ask myself the question, "How could a nation with the foundation of liberty, life, and the pursuit of happiness, fight so hard to keep a segment of a people from achieving the basic rights of humanity?"

The question you may be asking is, "What does racism have to do with war? Why should the church be concerned about the affects of racism in times of war?" The answer is found in the story of José Padilla. José Padilla was arrested at Chicago's O'Hare Airport. The FBI concluded that Padilla had been connected to a "terrorist" plot to destroy an American city, and he became known around the world as the "dirty bomber" thanks to Attorney General John Ashcroft.[5] President Bush even labeled him as an enemy combatant. When he asked for his rights of due process, his request was denied. Fortunately, the courts ruled in favor of Padilla, stating that he either should be charged with a crime or released from prison within thirty days. He was released.

At the same time of Padilla's case, a small story reported about William Krar in Noonday, Texas, a man who possessed a chemical weapon with plans to use it in the United States. Although he was arrested, neither Ashcroft nor the American press gave Krar the widespread coverage they had given Padilla. Krar did not fit the stereotypical "Arab" looking, terrorist profile or storyline set forth by the racist structure of the war on terrorism. This example of how intricately race plays a role in a time of war stands before the church as a realization that the war on terrorism is in reality a war against people of color. It is the legacy of racism that allows hundreds of men, women, and children to be locked away without due process in a United States founded upon the freedoms of right to a trial and a lawyer. The resolution of Padilla's case was a fortunate one, but the heritage of racism can be clearly seen when his legal rights were dismissed because of his so-called "ties to terrorist organizations." The American terrorists Terry Nichols and Timothy McVeigh were given more due process than was this colored man in Chicago.

If the church is going to create a world of peace, it must reflect upon the struggles and the heartaches minorities, such as José Padilla, have endured and continue to endure around the globe. Discovering a new path involves realizing that the church has often silently participated in the marginalization of people of color and as a result, provided a sense of comfort for them. The new path I am advocating involves listening for the stories of the oppressed and being honest about the dreams that have been lost because of the racist and classist structures often justified by our theological presumptions. Too often the church has remained silent about racism, classism, sexism, and homophobia. It is no surprise, then, that the church has remained silent regarding the war in Iraq, the lies surrounding weapons of mass destruction and ties to Al Qaeda. What is one to expect when it remained silent in the face of slavery, Jim Crow Laws, Brown vs. Board of Education, and violation of civil rights? However, if the church chooses not to listen for the voices of the oppressed, then she commits a greater sin against God's children. As a result of not listening for their voices, the church becomes a full participant in the continual marginalization not only of people of color but also of all those who are caught in the web of war. We must travel a different road, one of peace and love.

Journey of Peace

In the book of Matthew, Jesus teaches, "Blessed are the peacemakers, for they shall be called children of God" (Matt. 5:9). The key phrase in this statement is the term "peacemakers." In the Unity Church, the discussion regarding peace begins within the individual state of consciousness. For example, peace is achieved when the disharmony within an individual's consciousness is fully addressed. When one finds his or her mind to be in disharmony, this points toward a deeper issue that must be addressed in order for the entire physical body to find peace. When reflecting upon the legacy of racism within the United States, the disharmony regarding people of color in a time of war points toward such a disrupted state of consciousness. The problem within the church is that it often participates in disharmony rather than seeking to locate the disharmony and work to eradicate it from the body. When Jesus gives the bold declaration for peacemakers, he realizes that the Jews are under Roman occupation and have a limited voice. Therefore, Jesus recognizes that making peace in a time of conflict will not be an easy task. Nevertheless, it is a task that is necessary in order for the Kingdom of God to be manifested on the earth. The racism within the United States will continue to manifest itself in wars as long as church members ignore the "Help Wanted: Peacemakers" sign that is dangling before their faces. It is up to the body of Christ to suggest that preemptive wars are not going to build the kingdom of God for all of God's children. In fact, *not* working for peace is just as detrimental as choosing to keep silent in the face of oppression.

Perhaps the brutal reality is that the church is going to encounter some obstacles on its way to creating a state of peace within the world. But the comfort Jesus offers us is that in building a foundation of peace, God's love will be allowed to penetrate those walls of solitude that have minimized people according to their color. In Unity, the peacemaker is the most sacred of vocations. It is the peacemakers that are able to bridge the gulf that separates people and form new patterns of relationships that seek to bring God's love forward in new and powerful ways. The war on terrorism should not exist. The war should be against systems of oppression, such as racism, sexism, classism, and homophobia, all of which influence the reasons nations have for going to war. The church must enlist peacemakers who are willing to speak up and project an alternative vision to the one that is being placed before their eyes. The church must be concerned with reconnecting with a faith that places people before procedure and covenant before comfort.

Since I have become an advocate for peace and not war, I now understand that the dream Dr. King spoke of was not one of the mind. It was a passion that radiated from his heart, his "Christ center." As a youth I did not grasp that Dr. King's vision and dream of peace was an energy that was fueled by the Christ presence within him, a "soul force." Dr. King's message and life have given us a way to understand a higher spiritual approach to achieving peace. He wanted us to realize that our quest for peace is first born within us. If our mental frame of reference is bounded by hatred or fear and if our reason for civil rights activism is born out of reaction to violence, then we as a people will only return that which was given to us. Dr. King expressed this thought when he said:

> I've decided that I'm going to do battle for my philoso-
> phy . . . I'm tired of violence. . . . We have a power that can't
> be found in cocktails, but . . . it is a power as old as the in-
> sights of Jesus of Nazareth and as modern as the techniques
> of Mahatma Gandhi.[6]

I, too, am tired of the violence, the hatred, and the pain caused by systems of racial oppression whether they are masked with a white pillowcase or disguised as "the fight against terrorism." Therefore, when I think of the power of God and of Christ, I am aware that the power to become a peacemaker is not found in nuclear weapons or in locking up prisoners without due process. The true power of peace is extracted each time the body of Christ seeks the power of God's ability to create a world of peace that is not dependent upon material comforts but upon the covenantal promise that we are participating in a world made for all of God's children.

Journey of Love

The journey of love is the most radical challenge for the church. It is a call for the church to promote a sense of selfless love and tireless dedication to the "other." When one considers the reality of racism, what in essence does it keep individuals from being able to do? It seeks to keep members of various races and classes from truly loving and embracing one another. Jesus said, "This is my commandment, that ye shall love one another, as I have loved you." In Unity, the love that Christ is advocating for begins with a self-love that radiates to others. The reason this chapter has centered on racism and war is because I believe that in order for the racism to stop abroad it must stop within the borders of the United States, the last remaining empire in recent memory. The issue of racism, hatred, fear, and oppression cannot be solved abroad if the church and the rest of America seek to dismiss its influence. Dr. King recognized that only in love could the true power of evil be overturned in this world.

Love is a power so great that it can only be realized when it is truly given from the heart. In Unity there is a belief that suggests that thoughts held within our mind will produce after their kind. In other words if the thought of violence is the central and dominate thought of our consciousness, then one will most likely generate an act of violence. However, if the thoughts are of love, then acts of love will follow from our thoughts. Dr. King understood this reality and continued to express to us the importance of this truth by preaching the goals of non-violence and the quest for peace as the tools for civil action. His rhetoric and philosophy were targeted to emphasize a certain mental approach, designed to unite within us a spiritual movement into a journey of love, a civil action for bringing into this world his dream of freedom and world peace. He said:

> Now let me say that the next thing we must be concerned about if we are to have peace on earth and good will toward men is the nonviolent affirmation of the sacredness of all human life. Every man is somebody because he is a child of God.[7]

The journey of love is a need to walk together as a collective body for world peace. The church as an advocate and instrument of peace must express that the result of this journey of love is designed to move society, churches, and the entirety of humanity in a direction where this peace, this conscious state of understanding, can become a reality. Socially and morally Dr. King and Jesus were asking us to raise our level of understanding so we could see the oneness in this walk for love. Dr. King demonstrated for us in his quest for racial harmony and peace that in order to bring about true change, one must become the change for which one hopes. If the church hopes that this nation will become a nation in which human life and equality is respected, then it must commit itself to conquering injustice wherever it stands, even if the critique leads us to the steps of the White House.

Finally, the church must believe that there can be peace on earth, not as some simple saying or echoed prayer but as a reality that can be achieved. If racism is to be eradicated and war overcome, then the body of Christ must believe in the capacity of the world to be transformed before our very eyes. The church must also be willing to become the change that it seeks. The phrase that the Sunday morning hour is the most segregated moment in the United States must no longer be the descriptive narrative of the church. If the body of Christ wants a world that accepts and respects differences in the global arena, then congregations must be constructed along lines of diversity. In the end, the church must make this journey of love, a walk for peace, by keeping God first in our lives. Thomas E. Witherspoon speaks to peace and love when he writes:

> Love God, all the people on this planet and love yourself. That's it. Oh, so simple. The Destiny of this earth is at stake. Peace in the world is at stake. Peace of mind is at stake—yours and everybody else's.[8]

The simple truths of a journey of love and peace are that the church cannot become a peacemaker without the emphasis upon God's love for all of humanity. The Bush administration has done a wonderful job of placing fear and doubt as the dominant ideas dictating our behavior. But if the church is to make a world of peace, then it must rescue the love of God from being co-opted by the privileged and powerful. Do not the scriptures say, "Perfect love casts out fear"?

May the vision of Dr. King ring in our ears. May Christ's call to a life of love fill our hearts. May the church become a bastion of peace as it works to eradicate racism and the brutality of war from our world. Allow this peace not only to be a desire based upon the eradication of differences. Rather, let it be the hope of all Unity congregations, and all religious congregations around the globe, that the racism and oppression existing throughout the world will be removed when each child of God seeks to love his or her brother or sister not because they are the same but because all of humanity, regardless of skin color, are children of the living and true God. The journey for love and peace is now before all the world, and the call for peacemakers remains open, as the great hymn we often sing proclaims:

> Let there be peace on earth,
> And let it begin with me.
> Let there be peace on earth,
> The peace that was meant to be.

With God as CREATOR
United all are we . . .
Let there be peace on earth,
And let it begin with me.

Endnotes

1 Thomas E. Witherspoon, *The Peace that Passes of MisUnderstanding* (Missouri: Unity Books, 1988), 2 (italics mine).

2 *A Testament of Hope: The Essential Writings and Speeches of Martin Luther King Jr.* ed. James Melvin Washington (San Francisco: Harper Collins Press, 1986), 219.

3 Joe R. Feagin, *Racist America: Roots, Current Realities, and Future Reparations* (New York: Routledge Press, 2001), 139.

4 *Ibid.*, 149.

5 Paul Krugman, "Noonday in the Shade," in *The New York Times,* Tuesday, June 22nd, 2004.

6 Coretta Scott King, *The Words of Martin Luther King Jr. Selections by Coretta Scott King* (New York: New Market Press, 1984), 71.

7 *Ibid.*, 83.

8 Witherspoon, *op. cit.* 144.

Special Selection

Living in an ethos that lives and breathes war, there is no doubt that we are inundated with visual imagery of violence. From bombs dropping and cars exploding to politicians putting forth their ideology, war is a visual reality. In this chapter, Darren Burris explicates for us how images play a role in our politics and in our theology of war. Such images in a time of war create "distant others" with which we experience very little mutual solidarity. Images of war, therefore, are damaging and perpetuate the creation of "the other." However, deeply imbedded within the Christian tradition is a counter-image, an image of a God who came and suffered for and with those who suffer. Humanity is an image of this God and the Church, therefore, has deep theological resources for creating a counter-image of justice and peace from a faith perspective. In a time of war, while "we" all suffer from the images "we" experience through media, perhaps it is refreshing to know that the Church experiences a liberating image in the person of Jesus Christ.

Distant Others:
A Theology of Images

Darren Burris

"Know the image"—Rilke

Cropping (Introduction)

Susan Sontag, in her recent work entitled *Regarding the Pain of Others*, refocuses "our" attention on "our" experience(s) of the photograph[1] (including cinema and television) and examines the meaning of, as well as "our" ethical relationship to, images in a time of war.[2] She illustrates that the meaning(s) of images primarily revolves around the captions that "we" give or are given to images and that the ethics that follow from the dynamics of images emerge out of their peculiar ability to relate "us" to a multiplicity of suffering "others" in a time of war.[3] These two areas, the meaning of images and an understanding of an ethics of the image, are the crucial entry points that I believe U.S. congregations must explore as they come to terms with the ambient images of war. I will briefly take them in turn in the following essay, with the hope that a broad framework concerning a theology of images will promote conversation and thoughtful action in our present time of war.

Although it is beyond the scope and purpose of this short essay, I should also briefly mention another crucial portion of Sontag's book—politics, money, and power. Sontag rightly acknowledges that images do not appear in magazines, newspapers, or on a screen by accident. Images are staged,[4] carefully chosen, manipulated, selectively published, and transmitted via the multitude of organizations and businesses that control the media in the U.S.[5] The images of war that surround "us" have been picked for "us" to see and represent a myriad of interests—both known and unknown. However, images are double-edged phenomena. It is equally true that unapproved and unedited images make their way into the media, and these can serve as powerful windows into and correctives of the suffering they depict.[6] In summary, images in the media can and usually do serve the interests of oppressive, exclusive forms of power, but they can also be resources for critique and empowerment. It is toward this empowerment within our image-rich context that I hope to speak.

Meaning-Making[7] When "We" Are Worlds Apart

The central quandary of the meaning of an image (and ethics) emerges out of the *structure of distance* or absence that images instantiate and reproduce. It is this structure of distance that enables events and peoples to be encountered regardless of the distance (geographical, cultural, linguistic, social, etc.) that separates them while at the same time enabling them to remain absent.[8] As a result, the mediated space[9] in which we live and move and have our being is radically expanded to include a myriad of others and strangely contracted to include these others that also seem, at times, worlds apart.[10] Whether it is prisons in Iraq, the children of Philadelphia, the plight of indigenous populations in India, these once absent actors are now known actors with whom we share a world. In a very real sense, the conception of the "global" (or even, "Iraq" or "Afghanistan") is possible because the globe (and its inhabitants) is mediated to us through a multitude of paths.[11]

Although countless unknown others are now at our fingertips or glance, it does not close the gap of meaning between viewer and viewed; rather, the mediation creates a possibility for the realization of a multitude of different meanings for what is mediated. The structure of distance necessitates the emergence of a "caption" that provides the context and meaning of what is viewed. "We" need captions for the images we see in Iraq, Afghanistan, Colombia, Israel, Palestine, Sudan, etc. (not to mention the countless images from wars of the recent past or re-presentations of the wars too temporally distant to have surviving images), and "we" must also generate meaning as "we" face these photographs and moving images.[12] What is going on there? Who are these people? How is the U.S. handling events there? What is the purpose of this war? Who are "we" fighting against and why are "we" fighting it this way? Meaning is a crucial location of struggle as "we" remember that captions express interests and that the meanings associated and produced through the images can be questioned.

Captions and Counter-Captions

Because there are a multitude of meanings, images of pain and suffering cannot be assumed to build a consensus for one particular cause or to be a means to creating a unilateral meaning. Sontag writes, "[p]hotographs of an atrocity may give rise to opposing responses. A call for peace. A cry for revenge. Or simply the bemused awareness, continually restocked by photographic information, that terrible things happen."[13] The distantly present content of images needs to be explained and their meaning unraveled according to the multitude of individuals and communities that receive them. This peculiar site of reflection is essential to the praxis of communities of faith in a time of war. How will the community of faith understand the overwhelming presence of the pain of so many others? What meaning will a church attach to this suffering?

First and foremost, communities of faith must actively begin to engage the given meanings, question meanings, and create new meanings (whether they be local suffering in the community as a result of war or in this case the suffering of distant people in a time of war). Communities of faith start this journey by reflecting on the images that originate in the "medias" that are laid bare in the sacred texts of the community, the messages from the pulpit, and the sounds of worship.[14] In the Christian tradition these "medias" are rooted in the centrality of the gospel or "good news." The gospel should be taken in its literal sense as "good *news*" or we might say, "good media(s)" or "good images." Christian communities of faith must actively situate themselves betwixt and between the images that surround us and speak prophetically out of the *news* of God mediated to the Christian community through the self-revelation of God in Christ.[15] There are Christian medias that can begin to grapple with and discern the captions that are given to us as well as provide counter-captions to the ones that fill our eyes and ears.

There are two basic registers in which these counter-captions (sometimes co-captions) could be articulated. The first is exemplified in Timothy Gorringe's *Karl Barth: Against Hegemony*, which locates a resistance to fascist propaganda and ideology within the theology of Barth. Barth writes, "It was on the truth that God is that the 'Third Reich' of Adolf Hilter made shipwreck ... Beside God there are only His Creatures or false gods, and beside faith in Him there are religions only as religions of superstition, error and finally irreligion."[16] Gorringe portrays Barth's theology as an articulation of the Word (Christian media) that upholds the particularity of its message in such a way that all captions or meanings that oppose this Word are rendered subservient to the centrality of that Word (in the case of Barth, it was the ideology of Nazi Germany and liberal Protestant theology). In this register, counter-captions are generated by reflection and obedience to the Word of God, which necessarily sets all other discourses and images as false gods and superstition. The differing cries of revenge, peace-making, resentment, and denunciation that emerge from images must first find as their critic this mediation—the message of God in Christ.[17]

The second register for Christian theology is to de-center ecclesiastical or traditional discourse and develop a "theatrics of counter-terror" (or we might say here a "media of counter-captions") that incorporates the meanings that emerge from movements for social justice.[18] Mark Taylor illustrates in his *The Executed God: The Way of the Cross in Lockdown America* that an essential part of Christian reflection is recognizing where justice is being done in the world (the poor are fed, the widow aided, the disadvantaged enabled, etc.) and to find resources for meaning-making there. This register recognizes that the activity of God is not limited to the ecclesial sphere, and that we must discern God's presence outside the church walls.[19] Christian reflection is therefore a humble and dialogical enterprise[20] that listens to others in the face of these tragic images in order to discern the meanings of the images of war that are continually and vividly portrayed to "us."

I will return to these two registers below, but it is important to understand here that I am constituting communities of faith between two modes of being grounded in a singular vision of God who is active in particular communities of faith *and* in the world. The first involves looking inward, which drives the Christian community of faith to wrestle with the images found "within" the Christian tradition itself. The second requires communities to look outward and find meaning in the midst of other communities (primarily, movements for social change and social justice) grappling with the suffering of distant others. The two of these are mutually informing activities and lose their meaning if both of them are not present, active realities. Introspection should drive the church community, equipped with the meanings they have come to, toward those outside of their community, and the movement outward should likewise challenge and reshape the introspection that occurs as the community looks inward. This ongoing dynamic allows the church not only to retain the power of its particular message in relationship to the images of war, but also to find itself criticized and empowered by the work of justice being done by others in the world.

After Acknowledgement

As hinted at above, images set the spectator or viewer in an ambiguously distant relationship to what is being viewed. The distance of what is being mediated in the image (specifically in the case of the war being waged in Afghanistan and Iraq) not only makes the meaning of images difficult to distill, but also challenges a church's ability to respond to the suffering that is being represented. To adequately respond to any of the images of war with particular actions seems to require magic or a means that go above and beyond those at "our" disposal. This overwhelming reality is perhaps the most difficult aspect about the images of war that surround "us" day-in and day-out.

Sontag poses the question in the following way: "What does it mean to protest suffering, as distinct from acknowledging it?"[21] Most individuals could agree that suffering is involved in images of war (i.e.

we can acknowledge suffering), but could they agree on what type of response is appropriate for them, their nation, and their communities of faith? What can "we" do when faced with these images of violence and suffering? Can we protest this suffering, and if so, what will it look like? Even after "we," as individuals or communities of faith, distill a meaning to attach to these images, what then do communities *do* with what "they" have seen and heard?

Beyond the Neighborhood

The distance that separates "us" from all of these others calls for different avenues of action that supersede the conventional understanding of "neighbor."[22] "The neighbor" is implicitly understood to refer to sufferers who are at hand, near, and able to be directly affected by the viewer. The gap between suffering and action in our present context of the image has been so intensified that the word "neighbor" loses this traditional meaning.[23] In addition, the word "neighbor" bears too much conceptual and ethical pressure when it is applied to the multitude of so many distant others.[24] The dynamics of images places Christian ethical discourse in a new context, which requires "us" to imagine an ethics that regards the pain of distant others.

Fortunately, I do believe that within the Christian tradition there is a conception of ethics that can go beyond the neighborhood and engage the peculiar situation of a world grounded in the increasing power of images. The Christian tradition has also conjured ethical activity around the human subject as a being created in the image of God (*imago Dei*).[25] This conception of the human subject as image can be reimagined[26] and I believe reappropriated to not only close the gap between suffering and action, but also to provide an embodied theological ethics that can more fully engage our virtual context. I will take these two components as a humble attempt toward reconstructing theological ethics in the light of the image.

Toward an Ethics of the *Imago Dei*

The terminology *imago Dei* is tantalizing for a theological re-construction attuned to the dynamics of the image because we immediately have the word "image" as constitutive of human being. The phrase "image of God" grants two readings on the relationship of the "image" to God: "God's image" or something that represents God, "an image *of* God." The second connotation is the one I wish to use because it grants a significant portion of the agency and power to the realm of the medium of representation.[27] The image is representing God—it is not held tight or possessed as in the other understanding of this phrase.[28] The human subject is created as an image of God and therefore is an actor in realizing this image in the world.[29]

The image(s) of God as represented through human life must, like all images, bear the distance (the ontological difference between God and humanity) that the image instantiates. The participants in the praxis of the community of faith *are* the representation of a God that cannot be seen or heard without the life of the church or other mediums (e.g., movements for social justice). The church is the image through which the world encounters God and it is through the life of the church that God is made known. The burden of meaning and bearing witness to the reality of God is in the hands of the community of faith. The question becomes how are "we" to represent God in a time of such *known* human suffering. Should "we" remain silent? Should "we" acknowledge the suffering but dwell only in the realm of rhetoric and conversation?

As already stated in our search for resources for meaning-making, images require captions. As these new captions (meanings) are generated within the community of faith, they must *at the same time* become embodied in action. As "images of God" the church not only creatively responds to the suffering depicted in the images by offering counter-captions, but it also offers an image through their collective life and activities. Just as these counter-captions occurred in two mutually constituting registers, so also does the response of the church as it embodies these meanings. As a result, the meanings that are derived from the "medias" of the church and the movements for social justice also become the informing components of the image of God the church is to enact in the world.[30]

The praxis of the church emanates from the centrality of the Word as representation of who God is and who "we" are to be. Within the Christian community there is nowhere else to turn, no other image, except for the image of God as revealed in the life and work of Christ.

This is the central resource for meaning-making and for embodying what it means for "us," now in a time of war, to be images of God.[31] James Cone describes the incarnation and the image of God that is found in the person of Christ:

> The scandal is that the gospel means liberation, that this liberation comes to the poor, and that it gives them the strength and the courage to break the conditions of servitude. This is what the Incarnation means. God in Christ comes to the weak and the helpless, and becomes one with them, taking their condition of oppression as his own and thus transforming their slave-existence into a liberated existence.[32]

In the incarnation "we" find that Jesus Christ, as the foundational image of who God is to "us," comes as one who seeks and acts toward the liberation of individuals caught in oppression and "becomes one with them." This is an image that acts on behalf of those who are suffering and with the caption, "[t]his is my body given for you." This is the burden and opportunity of the image "we" have chosen to bear as "images of God."

Cone guides "us" to recognize that individuals and churches embody the image of God in so far as they "come to the weak and the helpless, and becomes one with them, taking their condition of oppression" as its "own and thus transforming their slave-existence into a liberated existence." This image is one of solidarity with those who suffer and one that works from that position of suffering toward a liberated existence. The distant suffering of humanity did not remain distant to God, but God actively took into God's self the position of suffering at the hands of humanity in order to offer a liberated existence. This is the good news that is to be embodied by the Christian community in this time of human suffering generated by war.

Counter-Images

Where is this image of the church in the world? Where are the concrete actions that demonstrate solidarity with those who suffer? Where is the church that bears the "image of God" to be found around us? There is no serious, relevant or engaged "image of God" being articulated or performed by the majority of churches. As the title of this collection of essays may imply, the church has been too silent and inactive in recent years and has failed to provide any voice for the suffering in Iraq and Afghanistan or offer any effective actions to end the suffering that is occurring on both sides of the conflict. One of the central problems is the distance (geographical, political, social, etc.) that individuals and congregations feel from the situation as well as the enormous amount of suffering that is depicted daily to us (teenage violence, the AIDS epidemic, famine, earthquake, etc.). There is a sense of powerlessness that the images create as we continually hear and see everything that is happening to so many others.

The steps the church could and should take are legion, but it must begin to engage the media and circulate counter-images that demonstrate that there are forces of peace working their way in the world. The church can accomplish this by creating counter-images that bring to the forefront the multitude of actions being taken by the church and organizations for justice.[33] These images of the church and work for justice are what can span the distances that separate other interested groups (including congregations) and can generate the needed awareness to more effectively create an ethos of peace.[34] The following set of bullet points lists practical ways in which churches can begin to engage the various forms of media available and, hopefully, begin to empower the church and larger society to embody images of peace-making in a time of war:

- **Internal Church Documents:** Sunday bulletins and periodic church announcements are important places to begin engaging the suffering that surrounds the community through education and promotion of ongoing or upcoming actions toward peace.
- **Newspaper Press Releases:** Local newspapers are usually very willing to receive information about what local churches think about the current war as well as what they are doing to bring about change. Press releases should detail common human concerns as well as offer venues for discussion and action.
- **Opinion Editorials or Letters to the Editor:** This is an efficacious location for local congregations to express a sustained and effective voice that engages the images being passed down through the media. It also enables churches to provide their own caption and image to the current suffering.

- **Television Press Conferences:** Communities of faith need to establish connections with local media services in order to publicly announce what they believe about the current conflict and how others can participate in what is going on in the local, state, federal, and national arenas. These press conferences can function to awake awareness, provide local ways of addressing this issue, and outline specific actions to be taken.
- **Radio:** Communities of faith can commit to relatively inexpensive radio announcements highlighting their concerns over the present conflict and announcing ongoing actions to effect change (voting drives, letter writing, marches, etc.).
- **Internet:** Communities of faith should also work to provide online resources for their congregants regarding the war and the work that the church and other organizations are doing to transform the current conflict.
- **Organized Media Event:** These are usually planned activities that the community of faith or coalitions stage to dramatize the conflict. These events are the culmination of an ongoing relationship with the media in all of the areas listed above.
- **Alternative Media:** The church must find partners that are generating information and counter-media that voice and portray concerns that appear to be left out in the national media. In addition, congregations should find films, newspapers, books, etc. that address these issues and circulate them as alternative images to the more dominant ones that haunt us (e.g., *Fahrenheit 9/11*).

The images that inundate "us" everyday often bear with them the suffering of countless international forces engaged in conflict. These images shape our world and inform how we experience our everyday lives. The church must find its voice and bring its resources to bear on these images with the hope of entering an embodied disruptive image into and between these images. This disruptive image is an image that goes beyond the necessary questions: "Who caused what the picture shows? Who is responsible? Is it excusable? Was it inevitable?" It is an image centered on dramatic action that closes the gap between viewer and those suffering. It is an image that bears the imprint of God, who is working for justice not at a distance but out of the suffering toward peace. This work begins by living into "our" new context and creating counter-images that will engender and empower us toward an ethos of peace.

Endnotes

[1] Susan Sontag, *Regarding the Pain of Others* (New York: Farrar, Straus and Giroux, 2003). She previously engaged this topic with her award-winning *On Photography* (New York: Farrar, Straus and Giroux, 1977).

[2] For one general history of the emergence, effect, and role of photographs in American history, see Robert Taft's *Photography and the American Scene: A Social History, 1839-1889* (New York: Dover Publications, Inc., 1938). See also the recent monograph by Paul Starr, *The Creation of the Media: Political Origins of Modern Communication* (New York: Basic Books, 2004).

[3] For my use of the term "others," I am alluding to the thought of Emmanual Levinas and the emergence of ethics that he articulates from the claim of the Other. See his two major works, *Totality and Infinity: An Essay on Exteriority* (Pittsburg, Pennsylvania: Duquesne University Press, 1969) and *Otherwise than Being or Beyond Essence* (Pittsburgh, Pennsylvania: Duquesne University Press, 1998).

[4] For example, Sontag mentions the staging of the famous picture of the capture of Mt. Suribachi by Allied troops on Iwo Jima, in *Regarding*, 56.

[5] The influence of politics, culture, and money on the media in the U.S. has been demonstrated by several different authors see Theodor Adorno's *The Culture Industry: Selected essays on Mass Culture* (New York: Routledge, 2001), Noam Chomsky's *Media Control: The Spectacular Acheivements of Propaganda* (New York: Seven Stories Press, 1997), Arundhati Roy's *Power Politics: The Reincarnation of Rumpelstiltskin* (Kerala, India: D C Books, 2001), Peter Steven's *The No-Nonsense Guide to Global Media* (London: Verso Publications, 2004), Andre Schiffrin's *The Business of Books: How the International Conglomerates Took Over the Publishing and Changed the Way We Read* (London: Verso Publications, 2001), Paul Ginsborg's *Silvio Berlusconi:Television, Power and Patrimony* (London: Verso Publications, 2004), and Jean Baudrillard's *Simulacra and Simulation* (Ann Arbor, Michigan: The University of Michigan Press Ltd., 1994).

[6] As the photographs from Abu Ghraib prison may, to some, attest.

[7] See Clifford Geertz's conception in *On the Interpretation of Culture* (Oxford: Oxford University Press, 1967).

[8] Leo Charney and Vanessa R. Schwarts, eds., *Cinema and the Invention of Modern Life* (Berkeley, California: University of California Press, 1995). This book is a wonderful window into how our social life has been changed by "cinema."

[9] I am not suggesting that we did not live a mediated existence prior to the "image," but rather that we should concentrate on this type of mediation due to its proliferation in the twentieth and twenty-first centuries.

[10] Walter Benjamin, "The Work of Art in the Age of Mechanical Reproduction," in *Illuminations: Essays and Reflections,* (New York: Harcourt, Brace, and World Inc., 1968).

[11] This argument is indebted to Bernard Anderson's *Imagined Communities: Reflections on the Origin and Spread of Nationalism* (London: Verso Publications, 1991). See also John Beynon and David Dunkerely, eds., *Globalization: The Reader* (New York: Routledge, 2000), 165-230.

[12] *Regarding*, 10.

[13] *Regarding*, 13.

14 Jacques Derrida, "Faith and Knowledge: The Two Sources of 'Religion' at the Limits of Reason Alone," in *Acts of Religion* (New York: Routledge, 2001). I owe this rendering of gospel to Derrida's analysis of religion in terms of mediation, presence, absence, and the contested boundaries of images within "Abrahamic" religious discourse.

15 This articulation of revelation is deeply indebted to H. Richard Niebuhr's *The Meaning of Revelation* (New York: MacMillan Publishing Company, 1941).

16 Quoted by Timothy Gorringe in *Karl Barth: Against Hegemony* (Cambridge: Cambridge University Press, 1999).

17 See John H. Yoder's *Karl Barth and the Problem of War* (New York: Abingdom Press, 1970).

18 Mark Taylor, *The Executed God: The Way of Cross in Lockdown America* (St. Paul, Minnesota: Fortress Press), 127-163. See also his *Remembering Esparanza: Toward a Cultural Political Theology for North-American Praxis* (New York: Orbis Books, 1991).

19 Barth also hints at this in CD I/I with his often quoted remark concerning the revelation of God through a "dead dog."

20 I use "dialogical" as it relates both to identity as well as narration. I owe the meaning and conceptual underpinning of this term to Mikhail Bakhtin's *The Dialogical Imagination: Four Essays* (Austin, Texas: University of Texas Press, 1989).

21 *Regarding*, 40.

22 Luc Boltanski, *Distant Suffering: Morality, Media and Politics* (Cambridge: Cambridge University Press, 2001). Chapter one is especially interesting as he analyzes the concept of the neighbor in the " Christian West."

23 Boltanski, *Distant Suffering*, 8.

24 See Jacques Derrida's analysis of the neighbor and responsibility in *The Gift of Death* (Chicago: The University of Chicago Press, 1998).

25 The Christian theologian has a multitude of voices to listen to on this issue, from Justin Martyr to Origen, Augustine to Aquinas, and Barth to King. I am most indebted to Augustine's conception in *The City of God* (New York: Random House Inc., 1950), Books XII to XIV, and to Martin Luther King's "'The Trumpet of Conscience" and "A Letter from a Birmingham Jail" in *A Testament of Hope: The Essential Writings and Speeches of Martin Luther King Jr.* (San Francisco: HarperCollins Publishers, 1986), 634-653, 289-302.

26 For a formulation of theological reconstruction and the theological imagination see Gordon Kaufman's *The Theological Imagination* (Philadelphia: The Westminster Press, 1981), especially 263-279.

27 For a theological treatise on images see St. John of Damascus's *On the Divine Images*, (Crestwood, New York: St. Vladimir's Seminary Press, 2000).

28 The theological anthropology that lies behind, within, and in front of my understanding of human being is deeply indebted to the work of Paul Fiddes. See his *The Promised End: Eschatology in Theology and Literature* (Oxford: Blackwell Publishers Ltd., 2000), 1-109, and his *Participating in God: A Pastoral Doctrine of the Trinity* (London: Dartman, Longman, and Todd Ltd., 2000), 3-112.

[29] It should also be evident that if one understands the phrase as meaning "God's image" (which it should also be taken to mean), then the suffering of distant others is seen as the suffering of God's image. Human life is a work of God that bears God's image and should not be effaced, killed, or tortured; rather, the work of God as understood in the person of Christ is the overturning of humanities destruction of the image of God as witnessed in the fullness of the resurrection. See Leonardo Boff's *Passion of Christ, Passion of the World*, trans. R. Barr (Maryknoll, New York: Orbis Books, 1987), 111-112.

[30] In this model there is no space between the meanings the church produces and the activities of the church (image+caption).

[31] Mark Taylor encapsulates this in the word "christopraxis." He writes, "Within Christian religious contexts, theology takes rise from and occurs within what I call christopraxis. It emerges from the acting and thinking that coalesce around lives of commitment to Christ . . . As praxis, christopraxis entails components of action, decision and reflection . . . As christic the praxis within which theology occurs is centered around and substantively concerned with the Christ as symbol," *Remembering Esparanza*, 18-19.

[32] James Cone, *God of the Oppressed* (Maryknoll, New York: Orbis Publishers, 1997), 71.

[33] Actions that can be taken by the church include educational campaigns, study groups, discussion groups, community awareness days, fundraising, letter-writing campaigns (local, state, and federal representatives), coalition building, sponsoring public debates, nonviolent direct action, establishing links with national campaigns and movements, and so on. I am only briefly focusing on ways for local churches to begin a ministry of media advocacy. See Charles Dobson's *The Troublemaker's Teaparty: A Manual for Effective Citizen Action* (Gabriola Island, Canada: New Society Publishers, 2003), 129-154, and Jim Shultz's *The Democracy Owners' Manual: A Practical Guide to Changing the World* (New Brunswick, New Jersey: Rutgers University Press, 2002), 132-156.

[34] Ethos has an intriguing usage in the work of Karl Barth as it pertains to what is traditionally called "ethics." In CD II/2 Barth argues that ethics is the science of decision-making, testing, and critiquing, but that ethos is the actual living into actions and taking responsibility for real decisions.

The Sermon

The sermon that follows was written by a pastor engaged in bringing matters of war into the pulpit. A sermon is an engaging task. It is a task that embraces interpretation of the scriptures, interpretation of the events of the world, and interpretation of a congregation. In this dance of interpretation, pastors and laypeople are led by the Holy Spirit to action and social justice. Rev. Dr. Dave Davis provides us with a framework for understanding the pastoral role of preaching in times of war and conflict.

The Pastoral Dance of Preaching

Rev. Dr. Dave Davis

As a pastor who preaches on a weekly basis, I have often tried to convince students at seminary that it is much easier to preach each Lord's Day than once every six or eight weeks. The Sabbath rhythms of weekly preaching allow a pastor to engage the concerns of life in the world and in the congregation on a regular basis. It is much easier to take the voices of pastoral and public concerns into the study with you when you are engaged in that interpretive dance on a regular basis. Each week in the study, preachers seek an encounter with biblical text, congregation, and world. By God's grace and through much prayer, such encounters bear the fruit of an experience of the Word of God within the context of the faithful gathered for corporate worship.

Perhaps I should subtitle my introduction here as "confessions of a lectionary preacher." While completely foreign to some traditions of preaching and theologies of proclamation, I have been a lectionary preacher for most of the nearly twenty years of my ministry. I have found that the lectionary provides one tool that helps to ground my preaching within the wider context of the congregation's life. The *Common Lectionary* runs on a three-year cycle and assigns four biblical texts for each Lord's Day—a gospel reading, an epistle lesson, a psalm, and an Old Testament text. In utilizing the lectionary, the preacher engages the voice of a broader theological and ecumenical tradition. In that way, preachers can find themselves in conversation with the larger church or other churches in the community. Amid public issues or crises, the pastor knows of others who may be struggling with the same biblical text.

In terms of one's own exegetical context, I have found that the lectionary supports the vital engagement of pastoral or public concerns. As events in the public arena demand attention, the pastor allows such concerns to confront an unsuspecting biblical text. As one pastor is led by the Spirit to select a particular text relevant to the front page of the news, another pastor may well take the front page into the study where the bible is already opened to an assigned text for the day. I, for one, continue to be surprised by the dynamics of such an interpretive dance. For when the horizons of text and context meet, a sermon can exhibit a life and a timeliness that even catches the preacher off guard. All preachers know that a sermon often goes in ways not imagined, even when the text selected seemed quite clear. The use of the lectionary in public issue or prophetic preaching may allow a text to have the first word in an interpretive conversation not yet imagined.

Of course, it is true that on any given Sunday reality in the world could cause a preacher to suddenly shift from an assigned text or a text determined earlier in the week by preacher's choice. Like many preachers I was led to a different text on September 16, 2001. I remember moving away from my previously selected passage after the school shootings at Columbine. However, the sermons to follow are examples where the lectionary served as a fruitful conversation partner in the life of my congregation.

In March of 2003, during the weeks that led up to the Iraq war, the public arena was full of the language of good and evil. The gospel lections for those Sundays came from Mark. As President Bush expounded upon his notion of the axis of evil, a text in Mark introduced us to the Gerasene Demoniac and the community's desire to locate evil. On another Sunday, the story of the Syrophoenician woman and her pleas for the health of her daughter seemed to suggest that the face of humanity could be seen even on those we would choose to demonize or cast as the enemy.

There is little doubt in my mind that in the winter and spring of 2003 the task of preaching and leading public prayer became more difficult than ever before in my ministry. Time and time again, a disciplined encounter with lectionary proved to be more relevant than I could have imagined. It would seem to me that the exegetical process and the practice of lectionary preaching led me to a deeper level of theological reflection in a time of war.

March 23, 2003

Mark 7:24-30

"Dogs at the Table"

Late Wednesday night, like many of you, I sat in front of the television with a knot in my stomach. For weeks we have been listening to news anchors and journalists and politicians and protestors and U.N. diplomats and military leaders and cabinet officials and retired generals completely fill the airwaves with words. On Wednesday night the words could no longer be casually described as the talk or rumors of war. At one point after the President's speech, the television coverage offered a live picture of sunrise over the city of Baghdad. For a very brief moment, there were no words at all but the audio feed came up with the video. I guess the intent was to see and hear any bombs or sirens or anti-aircraft fire. But there was only silence and sunrise. And then the sound of a barking dog could be heard. The anchorperson didn't know what to say. So he said something about the dogs being stirred by the military action. As I saw it, the dog told something of the ordinary, the everyday, of a morning routine in a far-off city, with people getting ready for work and children eating breakfast. The dog told something about life in common.

It may sound strange, but the dog barking reminded me of the common lot of our humanity. The sound of the dog from Baghdad cut through the distance of it all, that tendency to view battle in a safe, sanitized, and matter-of-fact way, the video-game nature of what we watch, the reporters on video phones, the Internet coverage of war available at your office desk, that very odd and troubling tendency of the media to give war a catchy title, a theme song, and a shot clock down there in the corner. Some of you remember that sound of weaponry. The sound must strike deep within you now as you hear it on the news station of your car radio as you drive to the store. But from my life lens, even that sound is distant for me and my experience. It was the sound of the dog that reminded me of our human condition that crosses all boundaries. That as nations once again engage in this state of war it is the common lot of our humanity that will bear the scars. Some time later Wednesday night, I went through my routine that would eventually include turning lights off, checking doors, looking in on sleeping kids. I took out our black Lab and stood in the backyard looking up at the sky. It was something of a prayer time right then under the stars, something of lament. And somewhere, off in the distance, maybe just a few blocks away, I heard a dog barking.

On this Third Sunday of Lent we continue traveling along the Way of Mark's Gospel. Each Sunday when we stop, you and I witness some part of humanity's encounter with Jesus. If you have been following along at home, walking along this path using our daily devotional, which offers a continuous reading through Mark, you will recall that up to this point in the gospel, the ministry of Jesus has included preaching the coming kingdom of God, teaching, and healing. There was the parable of the sower and seed. Jesus healed that begging leper. Jesus gave life to the daughter of Jairus. He restored the man with the withered hand. He cleansed that Gerasene Demoniac. He healed the paralytic who had been lowered through the ceiling by some friends. Jesus called the twelve, and he taught about fasting, the Sabbath, eating clean and unclean foods, a lamp placed under a bushel, and the death of John the Baptist. Here in these early chapters in Mark, Jesus calmed the storm, walked on water, fed the 5,000.

And then right at the conclusion of chapter six, we are told that wherever Jesus went people recognized him. They recognized him at once and rushed around to bring the sick to be healed. In the whole region they would bring the sick to him on mats. People would bring the sick into the marketplace to be healed. They would rush to a place just when they heard he was there. They begged to touch even the fringe of his cloak. And as told by Mark, "And all who touched it were healed" (6:56). That chaos described by Mark—don't you think it is the gospel writer telling of the Messiah's encounter with that human condition? The Lord is being pressed on all sides by the breadth and the depth of our humanity.

So when a foreign woman bursts into the house to ask Jesus to heal her daughter, when the Son of God and the Savior of the World is interrupted there in a house where he went to get away from it all, when Jesus yet again could not escape notice and the reality of our humanity yet again invades his solitude, this is not without precedent. To the leper who begged to be made clean, knowing Jesus could heal him if he chose, Jesus said, "I do choose, be made clean!" To the crowd gathered in the house of Jairus, those people who were weeping and wailing at the death of the girl, Jesus said, "Why do you make a commotion and weep? The child is not dead but sleeping." He said to her, "Little girl, get up!" To those disciples who thought they saw a ghost on the water in the middle of the night as Jesus walked on the water, he said, "Take heart, it is I; do not be afraid." But to this Gentile woman who boldly bowed and begged for her daughter's health up there in that house in Tyre, Jesus said, "Let the children be fed first, for it is not fair to take the children's food and throw it to the dogs."

Excuse me? "Let the children be fed first, for it is not fair to take the children's food and throw it to the dogs." And with the deep-seated resolve of a mother whose child is threatened, the woman doesn't miss a beat. "But sir," some translations indicate she called him "lord," "but Lord, even the dogs under the table eat the children's crumbs." "Oh yes" Jesus said with a nod of his head. Or as the gospel writer records it, Jesus said to her, "For saying that, you may go—the demon has left your daughter." She went home and found the child curled up on her bed and healthy.

The clarity of this encounter with Jesus doesn't exactly leap off the page. The dogs, the children, and the crumbs. It's like an algebraic equation. You and I have to approach the board in the front of the classroom to work it out. The equation reveals the gospel of Jesus Christ extending beyond the people of Israel to include the Gentiles. "Let the children of Israel be fed first. It is not right to take their food, which is the teaching, preaching, and healing touch of Jesus, to take such food and throw it to the dogs. The dogs are the people of the non-Jewish community—the Gentile world." "But, yes, Lord, even those of us on the outside, even those of us beyond the bounds, even a Syrophoenician woman in Tyre pleading on behalf of her daughter, even we are nourished by what drops from the table. Even the crumbs are enough to offer to the dogs." The crumbs of the teaching, preaching, and healing touch of Jesus are enough to sustain the rest of the world as well.

So Mark's telling of the story of the Syrophoenician woman reflects the ever-broadening and inclusive gospel word that extends from the people of Israel to the Gentile world. This discussion of table etiquette that results in a healed child foreshadows the narrative told in the Book of Acts and revealed in the Epistles as the New Testament Church fulfills the Great Commission of Jesus, "Go therefore and make disciples of all nations." And you and I have completed our homework. We can take off the plastic gloves with which we so safely handled the text and analyzed the equation, for we have kept the text at a safe, sanitary distance and we have learned in such a matter-of-fact way. We can walk away reminded once again that in the grace-filled world of the gospel "there is no longer Jew or Greek, there is no longer slave or free, there is no longer male and female; for all of you are one in Christ Jesus" (Gal. 3:28).

The problem, of course, is that there is no such thing as a sanitary interpretation of a biblical text. Here in this story, there's no way to avoid the humanity of it all, hers and ours and his, the humanity of Jesus. The Lord was abrupt, a bit harsh. He called them dogs. Did he change his mind? Did he lose the argument? Does he suddenly perceive the wider scope of his ministry that will embrace the Gentiles? Jesus went into that house to get away from everyone. If he wanted to pray, he would have gone to a mountain. He was looking to avoid people. Perhaps he was tired. Maybe he needed rest, which is to say that he was human, fully human.

Jesus wanted to avoid the pressing flesh of humanity. When that frightened mother fell at her feet before Jesus she bore in her soul the mark of humankind, she brought the dog with her, that common lot of our condition, and she came face to face with the very humanity of

Jesus. We can diagram the equation, the theological implications of it all, and maybe we can even figure it all out, but it is the humanity that drips from this page of Mark's gospel: hers, ours, and his.

We're never really comfortable with the humanity of Jesus. But it is that humanity, that fully human Jesus that offers comfort and understanding and strength. When you find yourself surprised by that anxiety, and on Wednesday night when you kissed your children while they slept and offered a deeper sigh than usual, when you called someone just to talk because no one should really watch a war alone, when you can't find the words to voice the prayers that you offer for your grandchildren . . . it is the compassion of Jesus that gives strength. When you try to understand the complexity of this world that has again spiraled into war, when your heart breaks for families who receive news of the death of a child in battle, when you try to imagine a spouse with children watching this news coverage not to learn the news but to see if she can see her husband, it is the tears of Jesus that will give comfort.

When you watch the division of people out there on the street, when you read of the level of distrust and betrayal in the relationships of world leaders, and when you start to add up the other situations in the world that seem tenuous at best, it is the humanity of Jesus that can speak to your fear. When your stomach turns as some seem to celebrate war a bit too much, when you hear religious leaders demonize entire groups of people, when you try to comprehend a world where nations actually try to develop biological and chemical weapons, when you just want to sit and weep over the utter sinfulness of it all, it is the exhaustion of Jesus that speaks.

It is the humanity of Jesus that tells me that God understands our despair, our fear, our grief. We're never really comfortable with that humanity of Jesus. But when the safe distance is ripped away and you have to confront the messiness of this human condition that crosses all boundaries and nations, when life turns away from any clear-cut, sanitary interpretation, when the press of our humanity comes from all sides, it is then that I find myself turning to his humanity.

We trust in Jesus Christ—fully human, fully God.

March 16, 2003

Mark 5:1-20

Lent II

"Evil Contained"

The discomfort comes as soon as Jesus steps out of the boat in the fifth chapter of the Gospel of Mark. I'm not sure "discomfort" is the term to describe the unnamed man's reaction to the arrival of the Son of God, there on the edge of the burial ground. The uneasiness I mention refers to that gnawing feeling that ought to strike the reader as soon as Jesus steps out of the boat and is met by "a man out of the tombs with an unclean spirit." Mark's attentive audience knows by now that this "Good News of Jesus Christ, the Son of God" involves miracles and healings and casting out demons and calling the twelve and teaching in parables. But this encounter on the other side of the sea, this one-on-one conversation involving Jesus and a helpless soul bound by much more than chains, this meeting that offers the reader an entree into the biblical world of unclean spirits, demons and evil, this healing moment in Mark's gospel seems to evoke a unique reader response. Mark's description of the encounter so quickly fills with detail. Just when the ears are tuned to this gospel writer's brevity, an affinity for fewer words, the reader has to linger here for a while with Jesus and the tormented soul, linger there among the tombs, that place where readers and audiences of all time are supposed to experience discomfort.

The church ought to be uncomfortable as soon as Jesus steps out of the boat. Frankly, when it comes to the Gospel's telling of the story of the man plagued by an unclean spirit multiplied by a factor of several thousand (as in Legion), this gut-level angst I mention doesn't seem to go away too quickly. Maybe it is the detail, like the shackles and chains and a strength to break them that goes beyond human power, or the picture of the man crying out and hurting himself with stones, or the bizarre activity of those pigs that Mark granted the dignity of a number (2,000 of them launched themselves into the sea).

You and I come to expect those short and sweet biblical encounters with demons. As in Mark, chapter one: "and Jesus cured many who were sick with various diseases, and cast out many demons," as in Mark chapter three: "Whenever the unclean spirits saw Jesus, they fell down before him and shouted, 'You are the Son of God'." Is it the extent of this conversation, "My name is Legion, for we are many?" Is it the expanded fleshiness of the narrative that causes the stomach to knot? Putting a name and a face to an issue always causes the church to squirm, even if the face is that nameless man tradition calls the Gerasene demoniac. Uneasiness just seems to hang in the air when the church stands up to read Mark, chapter five, and the story of Jesus and the Gerasene demoniac.

A certain degree of the distaste evoked from this story must come when you and I reflect upon history's portrayal of mental illness and the semantics of evil. That connection between mental illness and the manifestation of evil is rooted deep in our past. Yet our ability to care or show compassion for such hurting souls doesn't seem a whole lot different today than shackles, chains, and tombs. A Hollywood production every few years shouldn't clear the culture's conscience. And so the story of that cemetery tenant tormented from all sides produces something of a chronic ache in the belly of the people of God. But in this world created by the New Testament text, it is a story that tells of Jesus going toe to toe with evil.

Jesus stepped out of the boat into a world that reeked of suffering and death. The land of the tombs would have been considered impure, a place where evil lurked. The exclamation point to such ritual uncleanliness comes in the form of those pigs running around. The literary eye should note the irony builds through Mark's telling of this exorcism, as the unclean spirit petitions Jesus in the name of God rather than in the name of Satan, as the thousands of unclean spirits beg to possess the swine; themselves known to be such an unclean lot, as the animals perish in the sea so recently calmed by the voice of Jesus himself. The literary side of your ear ought not to miss the irony. One New Testament scholar who chooses to remain safely there within the confines of literary criticism even describes some of the details as "especially funny."

Now maybe it is because we have had a long winter, or maybe it is because of Lent, and my family and our church staff have suggested that I have been a bit cranky; but I don't see anything funny here. Maybe its because no preacher can stand before a congregation without seeing more than one individual and more than a few families embroiled in a daily battle with mental illness; or maybe its because the clarity of the Lord's action in healing in the text always produces challenges when trying to offer pastoral care in those instances where such healing is never to be found; or maybe its because the semantics of evil is now a daily part of political rhetoric and discussions of foreign policy; or maybe its because the language of war falls off our tongues so easily while so many who take the name of Christ seek justification in a twisted plot of apocalyptic fulfillment where current events merge with God's ultimate victory over evil. I don't find much "especially funny" in the Son of God's encounter with the forces of evil present in the suffering man from the tombs.

This knot in my spirit, this knot hangs around for a while after I find myself in Mark's audience at the beginning of chapter five. And I have decided that the knot tightens when I ponder Mark's portrayal of the people. After the herd had plunged out of sight, the pig farmers ran to tell in the city and in the country. I take that to mean they told everyone. Mark records that "the people came to see what it was that had happened." The people came to see Jesus. The people saw the man "sitting there, clothed and in his right mind, the very man who had had the legion." It was then that the people were afraid. It was then that the people started talking about it. You know how people are; they probably talked about it endlessly. The people talked about how Jesus took on the presence of evil. And it was then that the people "began to beg Jesus to leave their neighborhood."

If Mark was to have described the anger of the swine keepers, then maybe we could convince ourselves that the community was upset with Jesus because of the economic disruption of an entire herd gone into sea. But Mark tells us about the people, those who arrived from the country and from the city: it was these people and they were afraid. The people were afraid. Jesus takes on the presence of evil, evil multiplied to some factor of ten. Jesus takes on evil multiplied to the "nth" degree, and the people were afraid. It is so much easier when you know what to hate, where to look, where to point. It is so much easier when the evil is contained somewhere, in something, in someone. There is a certain clarity in life when there is an enemy. The people were afraid because Jesus took away their scapegoat, the locus of evil in their town, the village enemy. Jesus took away the focus of their fear. Jesus took away the centrality of evil. And the people were so afraid that they begged the Son of God to leave their neighborhood. The people were so afraid that they turned their backs on the Savior in their midst. The people chose darkness rather than light. The people who walked in darkness turned away from that great light. The people begged "God with Us" to head the other way.

Jesus stepped out of the boat into a world of suffering and torment and terror and destruction and disease and death. A world where no exclamation point is needed, for the uncleanliness of it all speaks for itself. A world where evil lurks. A world where one child is found and many are still missing, where a front page focusing on the Middle East lures us into forgetting the violence and abuse and death that plagues our streets, our neighborhoods, our homes, where disease in a far-away continent is described as epidemic because of the thousands who die, more than a legion. A world where fear translates into plastic and duct tape and terror has forever changed a way of life, where nations seem determined to prove history can repeat itself and humanity will never learn, where bragging rights and power come with weapons of mass destruction, where dictators prove that genocide has yet to be expunged from the dictionary, where reporters talk about calculating loss of life like they're predicting the weather. Jesus stepped out of the boat right into your world and mine.

You and I live in a world where evil is far from contained, as if we thought we could just point here or there. There is a certain appeal to a locus of evil. But that's the problem with foreign policy and the rhetoric of evil. Regardless of your opinion about military action in Iraq, or the tyranny of Saddam Hussein, or the arguments about national security, or the desire for consensus among nations, war and foreign policy cannot eliminate evil. "My name is Legion, for we are many." That's the answer evil gave to Jesus. And when that healed man sat there fully clothed and in his right mind, the people started wondering where to look. They needed to know where to find that identified evil in their midst. The people were afraid but the discomfort came as soon as Jesus stepped out of the boat.

That's the Good News, really. Jesus, the Son of God, stepped into your world, thrust out of Mary's womb bearing our very flesh, a flesh that aches when surrounded by the darkness of this world. As we linger there just outside the tombs with the healed man clothed and in his right mind, another burial ground comes into view for the people of God. That tomb is empty. For this Jesus, the Savior who steps into your world again and again, this Son of the Most High God has conquered death and plunged the depths of hell itself. He has forever broken the chains and the shackles of those powers and principalities. And for those of us who live in a world where evil lurks, in a land of deep darkness, on them, on us, a light has shined.

And so God's people will dare to hope, and the people will not fear, though the earth should change, though the mountains shake in the heart of the sea, for God is our refuge and strength. We will dare to pray endlessly for peace, for one day the people shall beat their swords into plowshares, and nation shall not lift up sword against nation. One day God's people will learn war no more. God's people will work for justice and mercy and compassion knowing that the kingdom in heaven shall surely be coming on earth, a kingdom where they will hunger no more and thirst no more, and the Lamb at the center of the throne will be their shepherd, this "God with Us" will guide them to springs of living water, and God will wipe away every tear from their eyes.

Until that day, here along the Way where Jesus steps out of the boat, you are called to go home to your friends and tell them how much the Lord has done for us, what mercy God has shown you.

Once you were no people, but now you are God's people. And the people began to beg Jesus to never, never, never leave.

Statement of Faith

What has historically followed the sermon in a worship service is a "statement of faith" responding to the preached word. In this essay, Dr. Kathleen McVey provides us with a sketch of how Christians throughout history have responded to the issue of war and violence. Christian response to war is neither simple nor uniform. Dr. McVey offers us a glance into the positions of pacifism, just war, and holy war, each of which has been taken up by Christians in the Western historical tradition. She also provides us with an engaging analysis of the current situation in Iraq, questioning its justification through the criteria of a just war. As Christians living in the twenty-first century, we have a rich environment in which we must interpret our own history of warfare, which leaves us with the question, "What then shall we do?"

What Then Shall We Do?

Pacifism, "Just War," and "Holy War" in Western Christianity

Dr. Kathleen E. McVey

Western Christian attitudes to war and peacemaking have varied considerably over the course of history. Broadly speaking, they fall into three major categories: 1) the pacifist position, which rejects warfare as well as all other forms of coercion and violence, 2) the "just war" position that limits the use of violence by rules applicable in principle to both sides in armed conflict and generally assumes that the power to wage war will be wielded by an authority distinct from the highest religious leadership, and 3) a "holy war" position in which violence is deemed to be the will of God and in which the religious authority plays an instigating and directing role.[1] In both theory and practice, there have been subtle variations and combinations of these three general types. Since the purpose of this book is to provide a brief basic orientation to enable Christian clergy and congregations to engage these issues in the world today, an extensive treatment of these subtleties is both impossible and inappropriate. Instead this essay will be an attempt

1) to describe these broad types and the manner in which each emerged during the first thirteen-hundred years of Western Christian history, 2) to sketch further developments and interactions among the three types, and 3) to suggest some points of contact with contemporary discussions of war and peace.

The Emergence of Three Major Attitudes to War and Peacemaking

The Earliest Christians
Between the Sermon on the Mount and Apocalypticism[2]

As portrayed in the New Testament, Jesus' stance toward violence is a complex dialectic between pacifist and "holy war" understandings set within a strongly eschatological framework. In the Sermon on the Mount he articulates a compelling ethic of overcoming evil by meekly accepting it and refusing to judge others by "turning the other cheek."[3] This is to be contrasted (or complemented) with his occasional portrayal in a prophetic role characterized by zealous actions,[4] harsh words (against the "hypocritical" Pharisees), and parables and sayings on the judgment to come when sinners will be thrown into eternal fire.[5] These two distinct strands may be reconciled by arguing that an apocalyptic time frame is key: Christians are to follow the way of peace, humility, and forgiveness until the Endtime in which God will judge. In this case the meek endurance of persecution by the evil powers of the world is only for a time; the followers of Jesus are to bide their time in the knowledge that divine judgment will come to vindicate them and to wreak vengeance on their persecutors.[6] Symbolized in the Book of Revelation by the conquering Lamb, Jesus himself will return to lead the saints to victory, to execute the defeat and punishment of evildoers, and to rule in the heavenly Jerusalem.[7]

The early history of Christian attitudes toward war and peacemaking (as well as the broader assessment of the legitimacy of violence and coercion) is marked by tension between those who believe that the Sermon on the Mount requires Christians to embrace a new, absolute ethic of non-violence, i.e., pacifism, and those who understand that ethic to be modified, in one degree or another, in the light of a coming judgment that will radically distinguish good and evil persons and requite them appropriately. The implications of these differences come clearly into view only when Christians take hold of political power, beginning in the fourth century under the Roman Emperor Constantine. In the intervening period of the second and third centuries, impelled by persecution, they ponder the working of divine providence, the legitimacy of governmental authority, and the place of vengeance in the context of violence and suffering.

Many early writings stress an ethic of nonviolent, non-judgmental endurance of suffering based on the Sermon on the Mount.[8] This attitude of meekness sometimes extends to a quietist acceptance of authority, both societal and governmental. So they may affirm that Christians willingly pay taxes,[9] that, although they worship only God, they respect the emperor, pray on his behalf, assist him in the promotion of peace and virtue, and even view the Roman rule as providential.[10] New Testament citations mustered in support of these claims include Paul's advice to pay taxes and obey the rulers since they have been appointed by God[11] and Jesus' words, "Render to Caesar what is Caesar's; render to God what is God's."[12] These assertions of good, obedient citizenship appear in the context of apologetic literature aimed to convince educated pagans that Christians are "philosophical people" guided by reason and conscience rather than by superstition or subversive attitudes. The goals of ending persecution and of conversion of the wealthy and powerful are transparent. Yet they also have a confrontational aspect: Christian apologists are not, in their own minds, adapting Greco-Roman philosophies to explain their beliefs and to make them more palatable; they are showing the educated how the best of their Greco-Roman literature, philosophy, and institutions are imperfectly derived from intimations of the true God, the God known to Christians more directly and truly in Jesus Christ.

In the Christian confrontation with persecution, a more apocalyptic strand of thought appears especially (but not exclusively) in texts related either to martyrdom or to Montanism or both, such as the Book of Revelation, the *Passion of Perpetua and Felicity* and the later writings of Tertullian. Without counseling violent resistance to the Roman government, these writings breathe a spirit of utter confidence in the power of God blended with defiance toward those who persecute the innocent. Often through visions and ecstatic prayer the Spirit brings their prophets (both male and female) the power to speak in the name of God on behalf of the weak and helpless and to triumph spiritually over diabolical forces in the present time as well as in the future. Here defiance often spills into hostility toward both government and the persecuting populace: one day, perhaps soon, the tables will be turned, and the persecutors will become the victims of divine wrath. In this spirit Tertullian asserts that "the souls of the martyrs rest quietly under the altar and nourish their patience with the assurance of revenge."[13] After the bloody persecution of Diocletian at the beginning of the fourth century, Lactantius will console his readers with detailed descriptions of the grotesque and painful deaths of the imperial persecutors.[14] The heroic nonviolent witness of the martyrs had an emotional and spiritual cost: the spectacle of the torture and execution of their innocent co-religionists evoked from some Christians not a generous spirit of forgiveness but instead feelings of hatred and a desire for vengeance.

This turbulent inner state troubled Christians who viewed the Sermon on the Mount through Stoic and Middle Platonic philosophical lenses rather than through the lens of apocalyptic prophecy. To "bear witness" (the root meaning of the word "martyr") to Jesus Christ, they thought, meant to be thoroughly transformed by a spirit of peace and love. Thus Clement of Alexandria understood the injunction to "turn the other cheek" as a rejection not only of revenge but also of angry thoughts and words and presumably of fantasies of revenge. To become a true peacemaker, lover of one's enemies and knowing witness to the truth of the gospel, the Christian must fight an inner warfare with the passions, notably including anger.[15] Those who would be martyrs must train not only to avoid desertion of the faith in apostasy, denying Christ by offering sacrifice to idols or to the emperor's image or escaping by bribery, flight or deception,[16] but they must also avoid denying Christ by succumbing to hatred. Similarly Origen insists that Christians are committed to peaceful words as well as peaceful deeds: "revilers shall not inherit the kingdom of God."[17]

Distinctions among the early voices must not be too strongly drawn. The philosophically inclined apologists consistently affirmed the value of blood witness both in word and in deed; they include the famous martyr, Justin, and the famous confessor, Origen.[18] Despite their threats and angry words the most apocalyptically inspired Christians did not take up arms against their persecutors. Finally, all used the language of "spiritual warfare" to describe their combat against evil; the battles to be fought in the present time were inner struggles with the passions and with unseen demons; in them, visible swords had no use.

But what about those Christians who took up arms on behalf of the Roman Empire? Although the New Testament mentions military men who encountered Jesus or embraced his teachings, there are words neither of approval nor of disapproval for their vocation.[19] A few third-century Christian soldiers are known by name through accounts of their deaths as martyrs. Some of them suffer death for refusing to participate in idolatrous worship with no apparent relation to their service as soldiers,[20] but others are killed for refusal to serve in the army, a task they reject explicitly as incompatible with their Christian commitment.[21] The views of the latter, the first known "conscientious objectors," are reinforced by several early Christian writers who claimed for their community the prophecy of "swords beaten into plowshares" as part of a perfectionist ethic. For example, Justin asserts that the Christian community, having foresworn not only war against enemies but even lying or deceiving their interrogators in the face of persecution to the death, has fulfilled the prophecy of "swords beaten into plowshares."[22] Origen adds, "No longer do we take the sword against any nation, nor do we learn war any more, since we have become sons of peace through Jesus."[23]

In addition to these claims drawn from apologetic contexts, early disciplinary manuals instruct communities that soldiers who are baptized must abandon this means of earning a living. Hippolytus' *Apostolic Tradition* (ca. 215 A.D.) declares: "Catechumens or believers who wish to enlist as soldiers are to be sent away, for they have shown contempt for God."[24] Opinions differ on whether the essential issue is a rejection of killing or a rejection of idolatry. In favor of the former view, the same source also insists:

> a soldier in a position of authority is not to be allowed to impose a death sentence; if he is ordered to do so, let him not carry out the order; he is not to be allowed to take an oath. If he does not accept, he is to be sent away. A man with the power of the sword or a civil magistrate who wears the purple must give it up or be sent away.[25]

Thus other kinds of officially sanctioned killing and violence, such as capital punishment, are also to be shunned; gladiators, charioteers, and wrestlers are also unacceptable in Hippolytus' view. Some sources also condemn the common practices of exposure of infants (the abandonment of unwanted children to die) and abortion along with a variety of sexual sins and professions.[26] On the other hand, any profession with a connection to idolatry was also prohibited—not only service in the military and civil government but also in the theatre and in the teaching of children.[27] To put the pre-Constantinian prohibitions of military service in perspective, then, we must keep in mind the comprehensive perfectionist ethic of both the apologetic writings and early Christian codes of behavior. In some cases, Christian identity is defined through separation from a society perceived to be idolatrous to the core.

Christianity in the Fourth and Fifth Centuries

Coming to Terms with the Roman Empire and the Emergence of "Just War"

Constantine's rise to power and his related conversion to Christianity in the early fourth century brought many changes to the church. Among them were the cessation of persecution, substantial financial support that included an extensive building program, and imperial promotion of theological harmony for the sake of providing a unified public prayer pleasing to God on behalf of the Empire. In the face of these changes, Christian writers—notably Eusebius of Caesarea, a bishop and historian personally associated with Emperor Constantine—responded with enthusiastic approval and relief. Later in the fourth century other bishops, such as Basil of Caesarea, John Chrysostom, and Ambrose of Milan, challenged the authority of the emperor on behalf of their orthodox Christian people, but not for the sake of others. By the end of the fourth century, under Emperor Theodosius public worship by Christian heretics as well as traditional polytheists ("pagans") was outlawed. Jews, too, were restricted at least from proselytizing. This legislation was neither systematically enforced nor even efficiently promulgated, nor was it "thought control," for it did not restrict individual beliefs or private devotion. Often while the women of prominent wealthy families converted, their husbands and sons continued to rule and postponed the public embrace of Christianity until their deathbeds. Yet in the mob violence of the 390s, orthodox (catholic) Christians could expect increasingly that government officials—often with ecclesial encouragement—would "look the other way" when Christians were guilty but enforce against the others (heretics, pagans, and Jews) the laws prohibiting rioting and property damage.

The theoretical questions arose afresh: Are Christians permitted to use violence? If so, under what conditions? In a broader attempt to address questions of accommodation to the society that now welcomed them, both Eusebius and Ambrose propounded the view that Christians are divided into the "perfect" and the "ordinary."[28] Like the rich young man in his encounter with Jesus, all Christians are invited to choose between the "perfect" life of radical discipleship and the "ordinary" life of obeying the commandments.[29] The newly popular monastic life was increasingly seen as the embodiment of the "perfect" life.[30] For the "ordinary" Christians a new ethic was needed. Neither the perfectionism nor the apocalypticism of the New Testament was deemed sufficient. Theologians turned, on the one hand, to Greco-Roman tradition, especially to Cicero and to Stoicism, for discussions of virtue, and, on the other hand, to the Old Testament for models of political and military leadership. Neither was entirely new: Clement had looked to Stoicism in enunciating ethical principles for the guidance of wealthy second-century Christians; and all had turned to the Old Testament in search of types and allegories that were fulfilled in the New Testament or in the Church. Now the behavior of Moses, David, and Joshua was to be seen as an ethical model directly applicable to "ordinary" Christians such as governors and emperors. As before, spiritual warfare continued to be the duty of all Christians—whether they were monks in pursuit of the "perfect" Christian life or "ordinary" married people. All must strive for a dignified and anger-free execution of duties. For some those duties might include physical combat (for those in leadership or in the ranks of the Roman army) or the execution of criminals (for governors and emperors, those who had "the power of the sword").

The "just war" doctrine began in the late fourth century with a few brief discussions scattered in the writings of Ambrose and Augustine. Both adopted from Cicero the following requirements: 1) that war be declared by the proper authority, 2) that it be undertaken only to rectify an injustice, 3) that conduct during the war and toward the vanquished be governed by justice and self-discipline rather than passion, and 4) that the guiding principle and goal throughout should be the achievement of a lasting peace. But they made some highly significant modifications as well. First to Cicero's notion of justice, "to render to each what is due," Augustine added that the primary instance of justice must be to render to the true God His due—recognition and worship. This notion would eventually be used to justify punitive violence against heretics and pagans, and in his attitude toward the Donatists Augustine himself began to move in that direction. Second, Cicero's requirement of self-discipline became in Augustine the requisite that physical harm be inflicted only in a spirit of love—that is, love in the sense of wanting what God wants for the enemy combatant, criminal, or heretic, to be understood in the light of the soul's eternal destiny as well as in the full awareness of the tragic, fallen state of the world. Thus, in matters of the state, the love of enemies had been reinterpreted. The mandate to "turn the other cheek" applied now only to private persons, who, in contrast to military and government officials, were forbidden to avenge injustices on behalf of themselves or anyone else. Ambrose concurred in relegating the *Sermon on the Mount* to private disputes and injustices but added that "love of neighbor" required that wrongs inflicted upon the innocent and helpless should be rectified by the proper government authority.

Augustine's critical appraisal of the Roman rise to imperial power (especially in his *City of God*) did not prevent his embracing a very Roman endorsement of measured violence (including judicial torture and capital punishment as well as warfare properly declared and carried out) for the sake of public order and protection of the populace from external enemies, especially "barbarians." Divine Providence assured that all sufferings endured in the course of war would be applied as salutary correction and punishment for sin.

Medieval European Christians and the Emergence of "Just War" and "Holy War" in Tandem

Augustine's formulations were brief, unsystematic, and directed toward the crises of his own time—among them pagan reproaches that the Christian God had failed to protect Rome from the barbarian invaders in 410 A.D. Ultimately his views would assume normative significance for exponents of "just war" tradition. Likewise, Pope Gelasius' articulation (in 494 A.D. to Emperor Anastasius) of the "two powers" "by which this world is principally ruled, the consecrated authority of bishops and the royal power" would eventually be seen as normative.[31] But from the fifth to the tenth centuries these ideas had little effect on the emerging Christian culture. Instead the Germanic tribes, who dominated Europe and gradually came to embrace Christianity, brought the ethic of their gift-giving, warrior culture into dialogue with prior Christian tradition.[32]

The result was a wary and shifting relationship between Christian bishops and barbarian warrior-kings. In an earlier stage some clergy took on secular duties out of necessity in the absence of effective Roman/Byzantine imperial protection. Such were Pope Leo (d. 461), who negotiated with barbarian leaders (Attila the Hun and, later, Gaiseric the Vandal) on behalf of the Roman populace, and especially Gregory the Great (d. 604), who organized the defense of Italy against the Lombards, provided funding to pay the army, ransomed captives, provided relief to the civilian populace, and negotiated peace.[33] Gregory, Bishop of Tours, his contemporary and a fellow Roman aristocrat, described the Merovingians (newly Christianized Franks among whom he lived) with contempt for their violent mores.[34] But eventually, drawn into the gift-giving culture and the realities of Germanic dominance, and themselves drawn from "barbarian" stock, Christian clergy and monks would take a more enthusiastic view of their warrior kings. To the Frankish monk Einhard, Charlemagne was an agent of God as Emperor Constantine had been in the eyes of Eusebius and as King David had been long before. Like his predecessors, Charlemagne counted on military victory as an implied benefit of conversion to Christianity, and he saw no problem in waging an incessant war of conquest against the neighboring tribes and in administering mass baptism to the vanquished.[35] Although his scholarly monastic biographer described admiringly this unabashed wielding of power, neither he himself nor any other Christian clergy or monks played a direct role in the violence.

Thus the "two powers" notion had been effectively transplanted from the late Roman Empire to early medieval Europe. Kings and bishops supported one another in authority though they continued to struggle over whose authority was higher. While clergy and monks abstained from bearing arms, they endorsed the right of the king and his warriors to do so. Yet a shadow of the early Christian reluctance to accept violence remained in the penance commonly imposed upon warriors who killed even in the legitimate execution of their professional duties. Although Einhard portrayed his rough-hewn and illiterate but earnest king as having a fondness for Augustine's teachings, particularly the *City of God*, his attachment may have consisted in assurance that he rightly waged war "to wreak vengeance and exact righteous satisfaction" —a phrase that closely mirrors Augustine's definition of a justifiable *casus belli* and that would become a touchstone for the medieval "just war" tradition.[36] But in reality the dominant ethos in this period, including those factors moderating and limiting violence, emerged from Germanic codes of chivalry. From them would eventually come the principles of non-combatant immunity and proportionality, both of great significance in fully developed "just war" guidelines.[37]

As royal power weakened in the late tenth century, a significant revision of the Gelasian understanding (of the "two swords") emerged in the form of two movements: the "peace of God" and the "truce of God." In an attempt to protect clergy and their property from marauding gangs, bishops claimed the right to enforce (with armed force as well as with the ecclesiastical power of excommunication) an oath to be taken by peasants and warriors to "keep the peace." Eventually this provision was extended to protect unarmed people of all social classes. A second movement, the "truce of God," prohibited the use of arms on certain days—first on Sundays, then on church feast days, eventually encompassing most of the year. By the first measure the bishops protected the unarmed and their property; by the second they restricted the frequency of fighting by the knights. Ironically, because the bishops claimed the authority to impose these measures by armed force, these attempts to restrict violence and to promote peace contributed to the development of a new military ideal defined by the clergy and to full-blown Christian "holy wars," the Crusades.[38]

In the Crusades of the eleventh to thirteenth centuries, all the restrictions on warfare that had applied in the previous centuries were broken: a pope encouraged Christians to fight not as a concession for the sake of order in a disordered world but as "God's will" and a Christian duty; monks and even children took up arms; instead of doing penance for the inevitable sin of killing, warriors were promised a heavenly reward; a first-hand account gloated in the infliction of unlimited injuries on the non-combatant population of Jerusalem; fellow Christians were attacked in their capital city, Constantinople; the killing of

Muslims was sanctioned as "malicide" rather than homicide (killing of evil rather than killing of human beings).[39] In their time these expeditions were understood to be a divinely ordained duty, an "armed pilgrimage to the holy places of the holy land" undertaken under a solemn oath.[40] Because the places at issue were, in effect, chosen by God, special status was accorded to violence undertaken for the sake of their rescue from the infidels; as long as the task was undertaken for the sake of piety rather than for glory or financial gain, it was not sinful but holy.[41]

The "just war" doctrine developed in tandem with these varieties of "holy war"—thus keeping ideology and practice in dialogue, however feebly, with the Sermon on the Mount. Isidore of Seville (d. 636) had begun the systematization and passing on as authoritative of Augustine's views on warfare, but far more important contributions were made in the twelfth and thirteenth centuries. In his *Decretum* (ca. 1140) the Italian monk Gratian compiled the opinions of earlier canon lawyers and presented them as a dialectically constructed textbook of ecclesiastical law, which was quickly adopted by the law faculties of the emerging universities of Europe.[42] In "Causa 23" he addressed the question of warfare and its legitimacy in the light of the Sermon on the Mount and the Pauline injunctions against anger and vengeance in Romans 12.19-20. Thus explicitly posing the dilemma of the pre-Constantinian church, he answered it as Augustine had, invoking both his authority and his arguments.

Medieval theologians as well as canonists continued the discussion, with Gratian's work as their foundation. They raised many questions touching individual responsibility for the actions taken in warfare, such as, whether military service is ever acceptable, what measures were needed to show true penance in the case of a soldier who had committed serious sins, under what conditions a vassal or a subject people might refuse to fight in a war declared by a king, what spoils of war were permitted to those who fought, and whether some weapons (such as the crossbow) were inherently unacceptable.[43] By the mid-thirteenth century, as the full corpus of Aristotle's writings began to show its impact, the conversation about "just war" moved from the "casuistic and penitential" domain of canon law toward more systematic philosophical formulations. Thomas Aquinas, a key figure in this development, set the discussion into the context of political authority.

For him, warfare was "a natural function of political authority" and was thus not only due to sin but "rooted in the nature of communities."[44] The "just war" was an acceptable "means of promoting the common good of a society" and might "be necessary to preserve liberty and territory and to increase dignity."[45] Formulae, such as those now commonly associated with the "just war" doctrine, began to appear. Thomas identified three criteria: 1) proper authority, 2) just cause, and 3) just intention.[46]

In sum, medieval Christian attitudes to warfare varied immensely. They responded to new social realities and drew upon a wide range of writings and customs, biblical, Greco-Roman, and Germanic. While, as we have seen, questions radically critical of warfare were raised within the "just war" discussion, the answers were often more harmonious with the practices of the time and place in question. Thus the twelfth and thirteenth century canonists addressed questions pertinent to the crusades—both those against the Saracens (Muslims) and those against the heretics. Against the former, some justified "any means short of killing them . . . to accomplish their conversion," while others considered that, with the exception of the Holy Land, Muslims might have the right to govern their own lands without Christian interference so long as they refrained from attacking Christians; heretics, on the other hand, were generally assumed to have no rights.[47] As Russell observes, "It remains an open question whether just war theories have limited more wars than they have encouraged."[48]

Post-Medieval Developments and Interactions: A Few Trends[49]

Accepted by Protestant reformers such as Luther and Calvin, the "just war" tradition continued to flourish and develop as distinctive national cultures emerged in late medieval and early modern Europe. Sixteenth-century Spanish Catholic theologians, especially Vitoria (d. 1546), adapted it to meet the needs of an age of conquest. Both Vitoria and the Dutch Calvinist, Hugo Grotius (d. 1645), expanded its natural-law basis so that the rules of "just warfare" might be seen to apply to all nations, not merely those that were Christian. A statesman, jurist, and ecumenical theologian, Grotius synthesized earlier Christian and classical traditions in his *On the Law of War and Peace* (1625) and laid the foundation for international law governing warfare. The transition to a secular basis was so successful that during the eighteenth, nineteenth, and early twentieth centuries the principle discussion of proper conduct in war and peacemaking moved from the theological realm to the realm of international law and military codes of conduct.[50]

In the wake of World War II, the place of "just war" in Christian ethical discourse was strongly reasserted. As it is commonly presented today, the long and complex historical development is encapsulated as a set of criteria arranged under two categories: *ius ad bellum* (criteria that justify embarking upon war) and *ius in bello* (criteria governing behavior in the context of war). All of these criteria must be met for a war to be considered justified. The *ius ad bellum* include 1) significant injustice (defense of a people, often extended to allies and to innocent victims; some say offensive war may be justified if the anticipated injustice is clear); 2) persistence in injustice, such that war is the only solution or the "last resort" (underscoring the necessity of negotiation prior to embarking on war); 3) declaration by the proper authority; 4) realistic expectation of success; 5) proportionality of ends (i.e., the damage reasonably anticipated in war must not exceed the original injustice); and 6) right intention. Two further criteria fall under the *ius in bello*: 7) protection of the civilian population and other innocent persons such as soldiers who have surrendered, and 8) proportionality of means (specific weapons and tactics must be continuously evaluated in the course of war to decide whether the harm inflicted exceeds the good to be achieved).[51]

Although it has played a dominant role not only in modern Christian history but also in the development of secularized Western culture and international law, the "just war" tradition has not gone unchallenged. Machiavelli criticized it in the name of *virtù*—the ancient Greco-Roman ideal of masculine valor.[52] More numerous, and more explicitly Christian, have been the critiques launched from a pacifist perspective. Radical Reformers, such as Michael Sattler, his fellow signatories to the *Schleitheim Confession* (1525), and Menno Simons (d. 1561), refused oaths and military service in the name of the Sermon on the Mount. Like the early martyrs whom they emulated, many of them paid with their lives for their Christian convictions, but now the persecuting state was Christian. Erasmus and others trained in the humanist tradition promoted the idea of peacemaking by drawing on Stoic notions of natural law and the common bonds of humankind in addition to the legacy of the New Testament. The stories of the "peace churches"—the Mennonites, Church of the Brethren, and Quakers

(Society of Friends)—as well as the development of modern humanist theories and movements for peace would constitute worthy supplements to the present essay, but time and space do not permit.[53]

The Contemporary Discussion: Some Points of Contact

The twentieth century brought two devastating worldwide wars, both of which began in Europe and spread via imperial ties and ambitions. Numerous more limited conflicts (equally devastating to the lives of those involved) have continued on virtually every continent and in every decade. The arms races that have preceded and followed wars have fueled the idea of the inevitability of war. They have also enriched the purveyors of munitions, thus fueling technological advances to invent ever more sophisticated methods of killing. Not only nuclear bombs but also anti-personnel devices (such as cluster bombs and napalm) and weapons designed to destroy the environment (e.g., Agent Orange) have compounded the horror of war. The same technological advances (especially toward the end of the century in the United States) have enabled the conduct of war from a distance—sanitizing the killing for televised consumption. At the same time, warring states have been motivated by ideologies such as fascism, communism, anti-communism, Islamism, and anti-terrorism—an encouragement to unlimited violence and reprisal. Revolutions and civil wars have raised more insistently the questions of proper authority and systemic violence perpetrated by unjust regimes. Tactics and technologies have made it nearly impossible to distinguish civilians from combatants and to protect the former.

Christian responses to new realities have drawn on a whole range of earlier traditions. Popes and other Roman Catholic authorities have provided a clear and persistent articulation of the "just war" tradition and have emphasized its normative character. Particularly under the leadership of Reinhold Niebuhr in the face of fascism, Protestant theologians have enunciated a comprehensive "just war" doctrine from a distinctively Protestant theological perspective. Both have insisted not only on justifying the entry into war but also on adherence to the restrictions on conduct in warfare.

The "peace churches"—Mennonites, the Society of Friends, and others—have continued to espouse pacifism. In addition to rejecting military service and resisting militarism, they have developed extensive networks to promote peacemaking and international understanding. African American and African Christians have articulated a distinctive witness to the peaceful pursuit of justice: The American Civil Rights movement (under the leadership of Martin Luther King Jr. and others) and the nonviolent movement against apartheid in South Africa (under the leadership of Nelson Mandela and others) have proven the effectiveness of nonviolent activism as a realistic alternative to warfare as a means for achieving social justice.

Pacifist traditions have increasingly influenced "just war" tradition churches. The question has been raised whether "just war" criteria can ever be satisfied under twentieth-century conditions.[54] Especially in reaction to the Vietnam War and the nuclear arms race, many have asked whether it is possible to protect civilian populations, whether a policy of nuclear deterrence and the ongoing arms race constitute both an immoral squandering of resources and an inherently dangerous provocation to war. On the other hand, the measured use of violence in the name of justice continues to be espoused in our time.[55] Some liberation theologians have advocated taking up arms against the systemic violence of economically unjust and repressive regimes. In another mode, American Christian presidents such as Ronald Reagan and George W. Bush have characterized other nations in apocalyptic language: Soviet Russia as the "Evil Empire" or North Korea, Iraq, and Iran as "The Axis of Evil." Now at the beginning of a new millennium, Christians, frightened by terrorism and Islamist threats of violence, seem to be confused about the proper response.

What can an awareness of the history of Christian perspectives on violence contribute to our current dilemma? It is clear that Christians have embraced a wide range of responses to war and violence. Within that mix, however, certain voices emerge. We hear the insistent refrain of the Sermon on the Mount ever challenging Christians to an obedience they rarely achieve. How many of us who hear that call have responded by taking concrete action against the violence in Iraq, in Rwanda, and now in the Sudan?

The "just war" perspective, which emerged as the dominant voice in most of Christian history, invites us to undertake responsibility for safety and justice in the world, tempered by a need for restraint and guidance by clearly articulated principles and rules. In the past half-century, as noted, many Christians in "just war" traditions have questioned whether its precepts can be applied to justify warfare as it is currently waged. Much of that discussion addressed the problems of nuclear deterrence, which is still an issue today. But how does this apply to the war in Iraq? What questions do "just war" standards bring to an assessment of this conflict?

To me it is clear that the *ius ad bellum* questions that should have received thorough attention before the war were neglected in the atmosphere of anxiety created by the terrorist acts of September 11, 2001, and fostered and exploited by those intent on war against Iraq. The decision to go to war demands reassessment under the traditional headings: 1) Significant injustice: The *casus belli* has changed from "weapons of mass destruction" coupled with alleged support of al-Qaeda to "bringing democracy" to the Iraqi people. As is now evident, there were no "weapons of mass destruction" in Saddam's arsenal; there was no substantial connection between his Ba'ath government and al-Qaeda; and the Iraqi people did not invite us to change their government on their behalf. 2) Persistence in injustice: It was alleged that Saddam's defiance of U.N. weapons inspectors meant this condition had been met. Significant voices at the U.N. as well as in the U.S. government have challenged that view, saying that negotiations were prematurely abandoned. 3) Declaration by the proper authority: The U.S. Congress at the behest of President Bush did declare war on Iraq. Still, we must ask whether this is really "the proper authority" since the alleged threats to our safety ("weapons of mass destruction" and al-Qaeda ties) remain unproven at best, fallacious at worst. The remaining justification, imposing an allegedly better form of government on a sovereign state, has never been recognized by international law (a secular descendent of "just war" doctrine) or by "just war" criteria as a legitimate reason for armed invasion. 4) Realistic expectation of success: Despite the Bush Administration's repeated assertions, their expectation of success was not grounded in reality. The chaos and destruction in Iraq might have been foreseen but were not. It is difficult to see an ethical solution to the tragic and dangerous conditions that the U.S. invasion has created. 5) Proportionality of ends: Again the question of original purpose arises. Is the destruction, which war inevitably brings, offset by the benefits likely to accrue to the people who collectively suffer loss? It appears that now a majority of U.S. citizens as well as of Iraqis would dispute that this condition was met. 6) Right intention: Warriors often allege, as "just war" demands, that their intent is to bring peace. In this case, democracy is added to peace, but the question of unstated monetary motives has been credibly raised. Lucrative contracts for support of our troops as well as for reconstruction of Iraq's infrastructure have been "outsourced" without transparency or adequate oversight.

The results of an assessment of the *ius in bello* criteria are no better. 7) Protection of the civilian population: The American public has not been given figures on the number of Iraqi civilian casualties, but clearly there have been many thousands. Failure to address this question, coupled with the ongoing failure to protect civilians from daily bombings, kidnapping and rape, shows indifference to this criterion. 8) Proportionality of means: The ability to wage war by "surgical strikes" has been claimed especially by Donald Rumsfeld on behalf of the Bush Administration. If it were true, this criterion would appear to be met. But in the absence of a count of civilian casualties and in the face of disagreement about the nature of many targets hit by "smart bombs," the verdict on this "new" kind of warfare is unclear. Further, the use of anti-personnel weapons (e.g., cluster bombs), the arrest without charges of many civilians, and the use of torture (however casuistically defined) at Abu Ghraib prison and elsewhere all indicate this criterion has not been met. In sum, Christians who consider themselves adherents to the "just war" tradition must ask themselves how it applies to the current situation. If this war does not measure up to the traditional criteria—which, in my view, is clearly the case—then we must ask what we are doing to exercise our responsibilities as Christians and as citizens of a democracy.

Those Christians who may be comfortable with a "holy war" perspective may see as their task the sustenance of a vision of divine justice promised to and demanded of God's people in "this world" as well as "the next." Bringing holy battles from an apocalyptic scenario into the conflicts of our everyday world is not without precedent among Christians, as we have seen. Historical study undermines the illusion, perhaps still widespread among Christians, that theirs is a history of peace while others, such as Muslims, have "lived by the sword." We may all be sobered to "see ourselves as others see us." Among Christians who have seen themselves as exercising God's will through violence, the dangers of dehumanization and demonization of "the other" are especially acute. Perhaps, like the medieval Christians who embarked on Crusades against the infidels, often under millennial excitement, American Christians are also especially subject to the lure of apocalyptic enthusiasm as we enter the third millennium of Christian history.[56] If so, all Christians need to address these trends and subject them to ethical evaluation.

As Christians we have inherited sophisticated and many-faceted traditions pertaining to warfare. As United States citizens we have the privilege of living in a democracy. Informed citizenship is a heavy burden in a world in which government may seek to manipulate opinion by simplistic generalizations and slogans and in which the media provide only limited critical perspectives. We must all become students of our own traditions, responsible critics of government policies, and activists in promoting the policies to which our consciences lead us.

Endnotes

[1] The typology is based on Roland Bainton's classic treatment, *Christian Attitudes Toward War and Peace* (Nashville, Tennessee: Abingdon Press, 1979); critical appraisal in David Little, "'Holy War' Appeals and Western Christianity: A Reconsideration of Bainton's Approach," in John Kelsay and James Turner Johnson, eds., *Just War and Jihad: Historical and Theoretical Perspectives on War and Peace in Western and Islamic Traditions* (New York: Greenwood Press, 1991), 121-139.

[2] The issues in the New Testament and early church have been discussed by many; cf. Bainton, Attitudes, 53-84; for a synopsis of more recent discussion, see D. G. Hunter, "A Decade of Research on Early Christians and Military Service," *Religious Studies Review* 18 (1992) 87-94; for a brief overview and more bibliography, see Willard M. Swartley, "War," in Everett Ferguson et al., eds., *Encyclopedia of Early Christianity*, 2nd ed., (New York: Garland Publishing, 1997), 1171-1174. The views expressed in the present essay are based on my own reading of the sources.

[3] Matt. 5-7 and parallels.

[4] Cleansing of the Temple and cursing of the fig tree (Matt. 21.12-17, 18-22, and parallels).

[5] For example, Matt. 18.7-9 and parallels.

[6] Rom. 12.9-21; also the agency of the angels, e.g., Rev. 14-17.

[7] Esp. Rev. 17.13-15.

[8] E.g., Polycarp, *To the Phillippians* 2; Ignatius, *To the Ephesians* 10, *To the Trallians* 8; *Epistle of Barnabas* 19; Justin, 1 *Apology* 15-16; Clement of Alexandria, *Stromata* 4.6 *et passim*. Since there are many English translations of early Christian literature, I cite these writings by author, title, book, and chapter, referring to a specific translation only when I have drawn a quotation from it.

[9] Justin, 1 *Apology* 17.

[10] Justin, 1 *Apology* 12; Tertullian, *Apology* 30-34; Origen, *Against Celsus* 8.63-75, 2.30.

[11] Rom. 13.1-7.

[12] Matt. 22.21 and parallels, cited, for example, by Justin in 1 *Apology* 17; Tertullian gives it a more rebellious tinge in *On Flight in Persecution* 12.

[13] Rev. 6.9, allusion in Tertullian, *Scorpiace* 12.9 (my translation); cf. also Tertullian, *Apology* esp. 47.12, 50.12, 16; *Passion of Perpetua and Felicitas* 18; Polycarp baits the crowd while expressing respect for the governor's authority, *Martyrdom of Polycarp* 9.

[14] Lactantius, *On the Deaths of the Persecutors.*

[15] Clement of Alexandria, *The Instructor* 1.8, 3.12; *Stromata* 4.6-14.

[16] These are concerns of Tertullian in *On Flight in Persecution* and *Scorpiace.*

[17] *Against Celsus* 8.38-41, trans. Henry Chadwick, Origen, *Contra Celsum*, 3rd ed. (Cambridge: Cambridge University Press, 1979), 478, 481, quoting 1 Cor. 6.10.

[18] That is, once arrested, he continued to confess the faith under torture but was released rather than being executed.

[19] The centurion whose slave (or son) is healed by Jesus in Matt. 8.5-13, cf. Luke 7.1-10 and John 4.46-54; and Cornelius, also a centurion, in Acts 10; cf. also John the Baptist's advice to soldiers in Luke 3.14.

[20] E.g., Marinus, Julius the Veteran, Dasius; cf. Herbert Musurillo, *The Acts of the Christian Martyrs* (Oxford: Oxford University Press, 1972), 240-243, 260-265, 272-279.

[21] Maximilian and Marcellus; cf. Musurillo, *Acts*, 244-259.

[22] Isa. 2.2-4, Mic. 4.1-4. Justin, 1 *Apology* 39; similarly Irenaeus, *Against Heresies* IV.4; Tertullian, *Against the Jews* III.9-10. In addition to their apologetic purpose toward educated and powerful Romans, several of these are in the context of anti-Judaic and anti-Marcionite polemics.

[23] Origen, *Against Celsus* V.33 (Chadwick 290).

[24] *Apostolic Tradition* 16, trans. Matthew J. O'Connell, *Springtime of the Liturgy: Liturgical Texts of the First Four Centuries*, Lucien Deiss, ed. (Collegeville: Liturgical Press, 1967), 138.

[25] *Ibid.*

[26] *Didache* 2; Justin, *Apology* 27.

[27] *Apostolic Tradition* 16.

[28] Eusebius, *The Proof of the Gospel* 1.5; Ambrose, *On the Duties of the Clergy* 1.40, 3.2.

[29] Matt. 19.16-30 and parallels; cited by Ambrose, *On the Duties of the Clergy* 1.40.

[30] Cf. Athanasius, *Life of Antony* 2.

[31] Tomaž Mastnak, *Crusading Peace: Christendom, the Muslim World, and Western Political Order* (Berkeley: University of California Press, 2002), 2.

[32] Peter Partner, *God of Battles: Holy Wars of Christianity and Islam* (New York, 1997), 62-66.

[33] Robert A. Markus, *Gregory the Great and his World* (Cambridge: Cambridge University Press, 1997), 97-111.

[34] Partner, *God of Battles*, 63.

[35] Einhard, *Life of Charlemagne* 5-15, esp. 7.

[36] Einhard, *Life*, 24, 7, trans. Samuel Turner, *The Life of Charlemagne*, with a foreword by Sidney Painter (Ann Arbor: University of Michigan Press, 1960), 31. On "avenging injuries" *ulcisci injurias* in Augustine, see Frederick H. Russell, *The Just War in the Middle Ages* (Cambridge: Cambridge University Press, 1975), 18-26 *et passim.*

[37] James Turner Johnson, "Historical Roots and Sources of the Just War Tradition in Western Culture," in Kelsay and Johnson, *Just War and Jihad*, 3-30, esp. 11-12.

[38] Mastnak, *Crusading Peace*, 1-54, esp. 2-6, 26-27.

[39] Hans Eberhard Mayer, *The Crusades*, trans. John Gillingham (London: Oxford University Press, 1972); Mastnak, *Crusading Peace*, 55-128; Partner, *God of Battles*, 59-132.

[40] Partner, *God of Battles*, 85.

[41] *Ibid.*, 110-111.

[42] Russell, *Just War*, 55-85.

[43] *Ibid.*, 86-257, esp. 150-158, 214-234.

[44] *Ibid.*, 267.

[45] *Ibid.*, 293, 264, cf. 213-291 *passim.*

[46] *Ibid.*, 267-291, for this enumeration and further discussion of the meaning of each of the criteria.

[47] *Ibid.*, 195-212, esp. 197.

[48] *Ibid.*, 308.

[49] For systematic treatment of this period, see Bainton, *Christian Attitudes*, 118-268; Johnson, "Historical Roots," 16-30; Partner, *God of Battles*, 185-310; John Howard Yoder, *When War is Unjust: Being Honest in Just-War Thinking*, 2nd ed. (New York: Wipf & Stock Publishers, 1996), 19-70.

[50] Johnson, "Historical Roots," 19-26.

[51] This list combines elements from Johnson, "Historical Roots," 16, and from John Francis Burke, "the Interreligious Dimension: A Global Ethic of Peace" in María Pilar Aquino and Dietmar Mieth, eds., *The Return of the Just War* (London: SCM Press, 2001), 52-61, esp. 53. There are many others, but particularly valuable is the precise and comprehensive compilation from a critical perspective in Yoder, *When War is Unjust*, 147-161.

[52] Bainton, *Christian Attitudes*, 124-126.

[53] As a starting point, see Bainton, *Christian Attitudes*, 127-135, 152-172.

[54] For an overview of this trend, a critique of the very notion of "just war," and a response, see Yoder, *When War is Unjust*.

[55] The essays in Aquino and Mieth, *Return of Just War*, constitute a helpful survey of the possibilities.

[56] On millennial expectations in the context of the Crusades, cf. Mastnak, *Crusading Peace*, 35, 45-47, 76; Partner, *God of Battles*, 112, 156-157.

Prayer

In these chapters, Rev. Frederick Boyle and Rev. Neal Christie demonstrate the need for the peace movement to assess how spirituality and prayer plays a role in working for social justice. The concept of "preemptive peace" arrives out of our deep need to connect and love all of humanity. These chapters aim to teach and mold us into people who live out love, compassion, and resistance to war.

Preemptive Peace

A Spiritual Awakening that Precludes the Nightmare of War

Rev. Frederick Boyle

The journey I began in January 2003 by attending a peace rally in Washington, D.C., to oppose the invasion of Iraq has taken many unexpected turns and produced many surprising results. There have been many blessings and many painful realizations. On a human level, I have experienced the loss of many friends and the public scorn of people who do not know me but judge me based on distorted reports in the news media. I have become at times a lightening rod for much anger and frustration expressed by people who have been manipulated by the fear mongering of a government that profits by waging war.

I have been ridiculed and abused by members of churches I have been called to serve. People with whom I have journeyed through illness and death, weddings and baptisms, have suddenly turned on me and called me "fool" and "traitor" and sought to run me out of town. The institutional church has reacted at times in confusion and concern that my public witness for peace would tear down the fragile walls of peaceful community, expose the sleeping apathy and threaten the financial well-being of buildings supported by shallow Christianity.

On a spiritual level, however, I have gained much strength and clarity. Learning to stand alone against a tide of wrongful, angry, violent, and undiscerning public opinion has produced an inner strength and faithful resolve that exudes from the core in my soul where the Divine Creator speaks and seeks to guide. Hours spent in private prayer and meditation; days, weeks, and months spent in a dark night of the soul; Bible study and searching the writings of spiritual masters; and precious moments of heart-felt dialogue with a few close spiritual friends have resulted in a new revelation about the condition of our culture and new directions I believe the peace movement ought to explore.

In order to become effective in preventing war, people who are interested in a peaceful world must get beyond being reactive and become proactive in creating a culture and worldview that does not allow for the possibility of war. We must change the dialogue from "opposing war" to "opposing peace."

In addition to gathering the peace movement to plan the next protest to war, the peace movement must begin to deal with the change of cultural values that will eliminate the possibility of war. In addition to planning political action, the peace movement must begin to seriously address the need for a spiritual awakening that will strengthen our common humanity and change the value system of our world from domination to shared community. Peace will become normative when war is viewed as an aberration of the human spirit rather than a solution to the political problems caused by greed. I call this spiritual awakening and cultural change "preemptive peace." Preemptive peace is a spiritual awakening that precludes the nightmare of war. Preemptive peace is not a utopian ideal but rather a realization of who we actually are as human beings without our self-centeredness, greed, attachment, and dualistic thought that leads to a separation between me and thee, us and them, the human being and the Divine Spirit who created us.

In order to create a world of preemptive peace, the peace movement must address the following issues: dehumanization, fear, visioning with spiritual unity, seeming insignificance, strengthening self-discipline, and nonviolence. When peace organizations add these issues to their agenda each time they gather, the journey toward preemptive peace—a spiritual awakening that precludes the nightmare of war—will begin.

Dehumanization

Martin Buber's famous text entitled *I/Thou* suggests that the model of a relationship between people ought to be reflective of the relationship between the human being and the Divine Creator. When we begin to see and treat each other with the same respect and reverence as we display toward the Divine Spirit, then we will be at the beginning of the road to preemptive peace. Reverence for "other" and making space for his or her uniqueness is an essential prerequisite to preemptive peace.

Reverence means to make holy (not to worship but to love as ourselves), and to honor, recognizing that we are not whole until our brothers and sisters are made whole as well. In many spiritual traditions we are taught that it is not enough to pray only for ourselves, we must also pray for our neighbors and even our enemies. Mahatma Gandhi wrote, "We must either let the law of love rule us through and through or not at all. Love among us based on hatred of others breaks down under the slightest pressure."[1]

When Gandhi says "through and through," he means for every human on the planet. Love is absolute and all-inclusive or it does not exist at all. Our love must strive for the image of what the Hindus call *Sarvodaya*—the sharing community that seeks the welfare of all. We must also acknowledge that love among ourselves while disregarding the suffering of others will eventually reveal the shallowness of our soul and the weakness of our spiritual faith.

St. Paul writes,

The eye cannot say to the hand, "I have no need of you," nor again the head to the feet, "I have no need of you." On the contrary, the members of the body that seem to be weaker are indispensable, ... If one member suffers, all suffer together with it; if one member is honored, all rejoice together with it. —1 Cor. 12:21-22, 26

It is not enough to love and care for the people in our own home and community. We must also be in right relationship with our brothers and sisters all around the world. It is especially necessary for a powerful nation like the United States to have compassion for people living in other nations not as rich and powerful.

In my heart, I believe that in the winter of 2003 the United States could have changed the course of human history. As the only remaining super-power in the world capable of annihilating any opposing force, the United States could have modeled to the world a new way to resolve global conflict through international cooperation. The United States could have been the first dominant nation in history to show that acting in peace will bring peace instead of waging a violent war we have yet to actually win—proving once again that war will never bring peace. Some day soon we must learn that fighting terrorism with the terror of war is like fighting fire with gasoline. Some day soon we must learn that the head cannot say to the feet, "I have no need of you."

The I/Thou relationship that Buber refers to, the relationship of reverence for all people, must replace the I/It relationship characterized by dehumanization that reduces the humanity of people different than us to a "thing" without soul or intrinsic divine worth. The I/It relationship must be changed so that their eyes become our eyes, their heart our heart, their home our home, and their children our children.

We must address the self-oriented view of the world that teaches us that our values and our way of living is the way everybody ought to live. It is a self-oriented and dehumanizing attitude that believes that what we want must surely be what "they" want. We devalue and dehumanize other people by assuming they want to, or should want to, look like us, live like us, and become like us. It is insulting to Africans living in the United States, for instance, when Caucasians say to them, "I'll bet you'd like to be treated like a white person." In fact, most people want to be treated with love and respect for being exactly whom and what they are. It is dehumanizing when we say, "Come, live like us, we will help you become like us, and then we will all be happy together."

Another aspect of dehumanization is not taking the time or making the effort to experience the hunger of others, the suffering of others, or the humanity of others. We may see their hunger and suffering but not really enter into it by sharing it with them, listening to them, holding their hands in our hands, and cry their tears as our own. For instance, have we taken a day or two away from our table for fasting to experience in an intentional way the pangs of hunger that children all over the world live with every day? Have we sat down with homeless people on the street to listen to their stories? Or do we sometimes think they are just weak and ought to pull themselves up by the bootstraps and get a job?

Peter Wise, director of the New Jersey Trenton Area Soup Kitchen, states that one third of the people served every day at TASK are members of the working poor—meaning that they have full-time minimum-wage jobs that will not feed their family and keep a roof over their heads. They are the victims of an unjust economic system in the wealthiest region of the United States, the wealthiest nation in the world. It is dehumanizing to assume they are weak instead of taking the time to listen to what are very often stories of tragedy and undeserved economic prejudices that create their suffering, just because they are not "like us." This dehumanization is an obstacle to preemptive peace.

Fear

Carlo Carretto has written in his book *I, Francis*, "Wickedness and violence are rooted in the fear of others. If human beings go to war, . . . it is because they fear someone. Remove the fear, and . . . you shall have peace." [2] Throughout history, xenophobia (a fear and contempt of strangers and foreigners) has led powerful people and nations to dehumanize innocent people and to inflict war and suffering upon them. The Spaniards did it to the people in the West Indies, the Germans did it to the Jews, and Anglo-Americans have done it to Native Americans, African slaves, and more recently the Iraqi people.

Preemptive peace recognizes the need to overcome fear caused by the barriers of nationality, religion, gender, and economic class. Instead of a fixation on protecting ourselves from enemies we create or that are created for us by the manipulators of fear, preemptive peace focuses on the shared values of humankind and the abundance of food, water, and home-building materials that are gifts given to us by Creation to be shared among all people.

Dr. M. Scott Peck explores the cause and method of evil in his book *People of the Lie*. In it, he describes how evil continues to exist and work in the world by confusing people and hiding in places where people would not expect to find evil—places where goodness and mercy ought to be found. A primary method by which evil thrives is to remain unnamed—conversely, an essential way to root out evil is to name it. When people are deliberately manipulated by lies and deceit, there is no doubt that the source of those lies is evil itself. When people are deliberately confused by telling them that they cannot believe what they see with their eyes because what they must believe is what they hear being said, there is no doubt that the source of their confusion is evil itself.

One example of this evil is the government of the United States, which like all governments throughout history that want to wage war, manipulates fear to induce peace-loving people to behave in ways that are abhorrent to their nature. The government of the United States used the grief, anger, and fear caused by the attack on September 11, 2001, in New York and Washington D.C. to wage a war on Iraq in 2003. The government of the United States misrepresented facts when it told the world that Iraq had weapons of mass destruction, access to nuclear weapons, connections between Saddam Hussein and Osama bin Laden, and responsibility for the destruction of the World Trade Center. None of what the government said has been proven. Until we name evil for what it is—lying, deceitful, manipulative, and deliberately confusing—there is little hope of making progress in creating preemptive peace.

Another fundamental method of evil is to distribute itself in small ways in as many people as possible. Instead of being located in one particular person, evil infests itself in a whole group of people or even a whole nation of people in small ways, creating an environment in which it can inflict suffering and death on other groups and other nations. Fear of the other, xenophobia, is the most potent and effective weapon of evil. If evil can create particles of xenophobia in masses of people, then evil can create slavery, justify greed, oppress nations, and invent reasons to go to war.

Our task as people wanting to live in a world of preemptive peace is to identify and name evil by recognizing its results and then tracing it back to its source. Our other task is to resist the cunning voice of evil when it tries to divide us from our brothers and sisters by manipulating fear to create war. Racism, sexism, homophobia, heterophobia, classism, nationalism, and patriotism are all weapons of evil that can be used to generate and manipulate fear. We must identify them and avoid them so that we can begin the path toward one world, one humanity, and one peaceful Spirit to unite us all. An essential step to preemptive peace is to stop propagating fear and reacting to fear by propagating more of the same.

While the government of the United States searches for and lives in fear of WMD (Weapons of Mass Destruction), proponents of preemptive peace must begin to create and celebrate their own WMD (Wonder of Mass Deliverance). Preemptive peace seeks to redefine the language of our time from images of fear to images of love. The First Epistle of John tells us, "There is no fear in love, but perfect love casts out fear" (1 John 4:18). The Wonder of Mass Deliverance (love) can be used to put an end to the Weapons of Mass Destruction (fear).

Visioning with Spiritual Unity

There exists within each of us a yearning for the shared vision we all possess in our deepest soul—it is our collective consciousness—that vision of truth we see as we lie on our bed alone at night in the dark—the truth that all people know in their hearts. This is the vision we must learn to share with each other and make a plan to achieve it. We must not be discouraged by the cynical voices that tell us we are just daydreamers and naïve idealists.

Elise Boulding wrote an essay entitled "Envisioning the Peaceable Kingdom." In it she writes:

> There is an element in the visioning process . . . which I call spiritual daydreaming. Spiritual daydreaming is a linking of the mind and the heart and the spirit in a looking 'out there' to see what we could become . . . Strangely, in the peace movement we haven't got the foggiest notion of what we are working for when we talk about a world without war [because] we have not harnessed this quadruple set of human talents—mind, spirit, heart and fantasy—to the task of imaging

interrelationships between social elements in a world without weapons.[3]

Boulding stresses that we need to develop a cohesive plan by establishing our long-range goal and then working backwards from there in a step-by-step process. She says that we need to look forty or fifty years into the future to a world with no weapons. We need to envision the economy, governance, education, and all the social needs of people all around the world. Then we need to work backwards until we find a starting point today that is an achievable goal: we must begin to succeed in small steps.

As we work together toward the larger goal of preemptive peace, we must continue to be active in our communities in the countless number of small ways that reveal our dedication to peace, our compassion for humanity, our shared vision of a better world, and our courage to confront evil in all of its insidious forms. Some of us will be drawn toward peace rallies—organizing, participating, publicizing, and encouraging our family, friends, and neighbors to join us. Other people will write books and magazines and newspaper articles to describe what a world without weapons and war looks and feels like. Whatever happens to be our individual contribution to the growth of preemptive peace, we must each be certain that we are working together on spiritual growth as well. Preemptive peace is a spiritual awakening that will unite our individual gifts, visions, and work into a significant cultural value system that can transform the course of human history.

Christian theology suggests that faith without works is dead. Conversely, works that do not emanate from a humanist and spiritual base are destined to fail as well. Until we begin working for peace from our common belief in the power of love that lies at the core of every humanist and major spiritual tradition—until we begin to include discussions of those commonly held beliefs in our gatherings to plan peace activities—we will continue to be a reactive group of individuals unable to coalesce the necessary power to overcome the forces of evil that propagate war. If our institutional spiritual leaders continue to be more interested in preserving the institutions of their tradition than they are in uniting and strengthening people with the values that are at the core of their traditional teaching, then we must begin to grow our own spiritual leadership in the peace movement itself so that this vital aspect of our work together can unite us more fully in our purpose by drawing us together at the root of our soul. Our shared vision of preemptive peace will arise more fully and gain far more strength by engaging our collective spirituality with our collective labor.

We must not allow our doctrines and rituals as Buddhists, Muslims, Jews, Hindus, Sikhs, Baha'is, Christians, and other faith traditions to separate us from our shared vision of the loving kindness and unity of our Universal Soul. The truth at the core of all major spiritual traditions is a shared vision and yearning of love. It is this shared vision and yearning of love that attracts people to churches, synagogues, mosques, and temples. The prayers of all people, in whatever language or faith tradition, are all seeking the same vision, the same ultimate truth, the same love, the same unity, and the same peace. Preemptive peace is a spiritual awakening that precludes the nightmare of war. Spiritual leaders of the world must begin to embrace the universal truth of all spirituality—the truth of love that brings people together in the deepest places of their soul—instead of cooperating with forces that divide people. When spiritual leaders cling to dogma that separates people from their common yearning for a peaceful world, dogma that teaches the superiority of one vision of love over another, they hinder the ultimate truth of love that must replace the falsehood of violence.

There are so many gifts and graces that the Creator has given to help us envision, shape, and build a world of preemptive peace. It is the task of the evil forces in the world to divide us and thus decrease our power. By dividing us by religion, politics, sexual orientation, and a whole array of issues that are of little significance compared to death and unimaginable human suffering caused by war, evil continues to dominate the world stage and prevent goodness and peace from gaining the upper hand. It is the task of preemptive peace to unite the world with our common spirituality in our shared vision and yearning of love. To begin to change deep-seated cultural values and enable preemptive peace to unite our lives amid the forces that seek to divide and separate, we must share our spiritual truth often and openly. Whether we are participating in a peace march, sending mail to a congressional representative, painting signs calling for peace, demonstrating against oppression, or raising money to feed the hungry, we must be doing it with a spiritual heart connected to every other spiritual heart while sharing our vision of unity and our plan to end separations that lead to war. "Deep within us," Carlo Carretto writes, "every one of us, are dreams of such a world, made peaceful with love and the sweetness of humility."[4]

The Plight of Seeming Insignificance

Preemptive peace must redefine seeming insignificance. The plight of seeming insignificance is the endless need to make mountains out of molehills. While people with worldly power go about the business of making decisions that will affect the lives of millions, those millions make daily decisions that affect only those few people who have elected to participate in their life dramas.

Insignificance occurs when nobody chooses to participate in a person's drama. When that happens, the person may elect to exercise the plight of seeming insignificance by ratcheting up the volume of his or her drama until other people cannot ignore it.

Here is where discretion on the part of others is required. They must decide whether the other person's drama has enough merit to include in their own dramas or whether the other person's drama is perhaps a manifestation of dealing negatively with feelings of insignificance. In the latter case, a response of compassion would be of more benefit than participation.

The misfortune of the plight of seeming insignificance is that all of these individual dramas consume time and energy that could be shared to build a peaceful world community. This would be an alternative to the violence and greed created by people who currently control worldly power and contribute significantly to the dramas that distract us from a common greater purpose.

When all of the seemingly insignificant people are encouraged to stop making their individual mountains out of molehills and to choose not to participate in the dramas created by the current worldly power, then the destructive dramas of the currently seemingly significant will become insignificant, along with all of the people who create them.

Creating a world community is not a matter of overthrowing the seemingly powerful but of rendering them insignificant. There are two key components to accomplishing this task:

1. Refuse to fight the wars the worldly powerful currently create.
2. Stop spending money and design a system of direct bartering. We must redefine the concept of wealth as a manifestation of world wholeness rather than personal greed.

Military might and money are the primary dramas of the worldly powerful people that must be rendered insignificant. Violence and money must be replaced with peace and compassion as the central power brokers of the world. A world community must not compete with the weapons chosen by the current world order.

A World Community Council must be formed to envision, plan, and create a nonviolent and non-hostile alternative for people. People must be allowed to peacefully choose between supporting a world vision based on sharing abundance and compassion or continuing to participate in the worldly dramas we all hate and fear, dramas that seem to render our intrinsic vision and desire for a peaceful world insignificant.

The truth is that the vast majority of people possess a mountain that a minority of seemingly powerful people in the world has reduced to a molehill by making us believe we must participate in their drama. We do not have to participate in their drama, but it will require time, strategy, and commitment in order to render their worldview insignificant.

The World Community Council will need to plan and organize alternatives for all social, economic, communication, and other systems that sustain the current necessities of life with two major exceptions: we must create a world without a need for the military or money.

The World Community Council will need to construct a long-range vision and then plan how to implement that vision over a long period of time. This is where commitment becomes paramount. The World Community is not going to occur in an overnight revolution. Indeed, we must not think of this as a revolution but rather as a life priority re-ordering. We do not intend to overthrow the current world governments but to render them insignificant.

The World Community Council should include experts in economics, energy, spirituality, agriculture, communication, medicine, transportation, and all other fields of social, educational, and humanitarian concerns. The World Community Council should be multi-national although not dedicated to maintaining borders but to preserving and sharing cultural uniqueness. The focus of the World Community Council should not be on power sharing but on developing methods for sharing the abundance of natural, human and divine resources.

Unlike democracy, communism, socialism, and other current forms of world governance, the World Community Council should not seek to form a political economic system. The World Community will be a system of justice and sharing based on the higher ideals often codified and expressed in humanism and all major world spiritualities. It will be a world order that reflects the human decency that is the desire of the vast majority of the currently seemingly insignificant.

A first priority of the World Community Council should be to begin a long-range educational program to encourage people all over the world to believe that the ideal vision of the world we hold in our hearts is not just a fantasy. It can be achieved, but not overnight and not with violence.

The World Community Council will offer deliverance rather than war. The plight of seeming insignificance is to render the current seemingly significant world order of violence insignificant by creating an alternative reality of compassion and peace for people to choose.

Let us be clear and prophetic for a moment. As long as the World Community Council appears insignificant to the current worldly power, there will be no problem. But when the World Community begins to affect the current political and economic order, the power of money and the military will be used to attempt to discredit and destroy the proposed new world order. This will occur in three steps:

1. The first weapon will be to label the World Community idealistic and refer to it in snide and jeering tones. This is the reason for the first priority given above—"encourage people all over the world to believe that the ideal vision of the world we hold in our hearts is not just a fantasy." If we are not convinced and committed to the efficacy of our objective, the first weapon of the current world power will succeed in its mission.

2. The second weapon will be to create fear by calling the World Community a form of communist or socialist revolution

seeking to destroy the current world order. The World Community will not seek to destroy the current world order but to render it insignificant by offering a compassionate and peaceful alternative.

3. The final weapon will be violence. The weapons of the current world power will be used to attempt to maintain their control. This is when the World Community must hold on to its principles of nonviolence. As weapons of mass destruction are used against people seeking a World Community, we must continue to trust in the wisdom of Gandhi, Dr. Martin Luther King Jr., and every visionary prophet throughout history. We must trust in the wonder of our own mass deliverance.

The violent attempt to kill the nonviolent World Community will lead to the ultimate victory of preemptive peace. Like the liberation of India, like the phoenix from the ashes, and like the resurrection of the dead, the plight of seeming insignificance will raise its shared mountain of peace out of the molehill of dreams we all possess.

Strengthening Self-Discipline

There are three areas of self-discipline that are common to humanism and every faith tradition that can be used as a starting point in the journey toward preemptive peace: meditation and prayer, fasting, and the practice of nonviolence. The doctrine of preemptive peace proposes that the peace movement begin to adopt these self disciplines and practice them in conjunction with political activism.

Meditation and Prayer

World peace begins with inner peace, and inner peace begins with meditation and prayer. Humanism and all major spiritual traditions teach the value of meditation and prayer as a beginning of inner peace. All spiritual journeys must begin by seeking an experience of the Divine Spirit, seeking a personal relationship with the Power that creates and unites all living beings and physical matter. One of the errors that people often make in meditation and prayer is that they do not take the time to listen. We need to stop talking in meditation and prayer so that we can listen. Instead of telling about and asking for all of the things we need and desire for ourselves, we ought to listen long and carefully to what the Divine Spirit desires from us.

In the stillness of prayer, the Divine Spirit will give us inner peace. The Divine Spirit will unite our heart with all people as we struggle to achieve peace while working through anger and violence trying to make others conform to our will so that we can love them more fully. If we will listen, the Divine Spirit will tell us to put our own desires on hold so that we might learn about our common love with people all over the world. In his book, *What Jesus Meant*, Erik Kolbell writes, "Peace comes when the enduring power and illimitable breadth of God's love is respected, trusted, and enacted."[5] It is love, and only love, that can transform a person, a heart, a nation, and a world into a perfect reflection of the Divine Will for unity and peace. It is love, and only love, that can prevail over the fear and anger that interferes with the unity and peace we all desire. It is love, and only love, that can transform our individual desire for power into the self-giving and self-sacrificing that will attain the vision of unity and peace for which we all work and pray.

In an interview with the Fellowship of Reconciliation in 1973, Cesar Chavez told Jim Forest, "The thing we have going for [the United Farmworkers Union] is that people are willing to sacrifice themselves. When you have that spirit . . . it becomes . . . just a matter of working on mechanics."[6] It is love, and only love, that can help us to overcome the self-serving nature that creates violence in the world. It is love, and only love, that will enable the peace movement to develop the willingness to sacrifice ourselves for the benefit of others who suffer more than we do the real costs of war. It is love, and only love, that is achievable through meditation and prayer, that will lead us to the spiritual awakening required for preemptive peace. Thus, preemptive peace depends on each person learning to love more deeply and broadly by attaining inner peace through prayer and meditation.

Fasting

Fasting is a spiritual discipline that can be an avenue to an experience of the Divine Spirit that can lead to a greater compassion for the world. A one-day fast brings an awareness of our attachment to food. A three-day fast helps us to understand our utter dependence on Spirit for strength as we grow in our spiritual body. After fourteen days of fasting, a person will begin to have an experience of the deep hunger that afflicts the majority of children in the world and thus enter into a deeper relationship with them in heart and soul. Fasting is a mystical experience. Fasting is not for the purpose of suffering but for freeing the soul of bodily interest so one can experience more deeply the spiritual body that is in communion with all that is holy and with the humanity of the world.

Fasting will bring solidarity with the hungry people in the world, the poor and hungry that far outnumber those of us who live in extreme wealth by global standards. To know the deep growling of a stomach empty for days and for weeks is to have real compassion for the eyes of a starving child we see on TV. While fasting, we come to personally know those eyes of imploring resignation hiding unspeakable knotting bodily pain—eyes that cannot, and should not have to, understand a world that seems so cruel. To fast is to come into contact with the unity of creation, which is also to approach a depth of love and compassion for the poor and the suffering, the hungry and the oppressed. To fast is to put on the Holy Spirit and walk a mile with people who have no shoes.

For those of us who are unbelievably wealthy by global standards, as we fast we can begin to see the world as a weaned child seeking to be held by its mother. Our love, charity, and compassion are the sweet milk the starving child so desperately needs. As we take from our table to provide for the bodily needs of others, we feed and nourish our own heart. In caring for the hungry and poor, we become like the self-sacrificing people Cesar Chavez was referring to and thus more peaceful in our soul.

In fasting, we can change our relationship with the world by deepening our gratitude and responsibility to all that has been given to us as a free gift. Furthermore, in that attitude of gratitude our inner peace will shine outward to change our world into one of preemptive peace.

Nonviolence

Ultimately, preemptive peace is more than a political movement: it is a spiritual awakening. Until we are able to call on the higher realms of human consciousness and our common desire to experience the Divinity within each human being, all of our political wrangling will accomplish little more than a series of wins and losses for each side. Violence does not occur in a vacuum but rather in an environment created by images of it. Violence feeds itself with itself, which is why we must dedicate ourselves to nonviolence.

In the struggle for racial equality that was led by Rev. Dr. Martin Luther King Jr., there was an acknowledgement that he was "depending on moral and spiritual forces. To put it another way," he wrote, "this is a movement of passive resistance and the great instrument is the instrument of love. . . . No matter how tragic the experiences are, no matter what sacrifices we have to make, we will not allow anybody to drag us so low as to hate them." [7] The nonviolent protests of Dr. King were in response to people in the United States driven by hatred that burned crosses on front lawns and dragged African Americans out of their homes at night for lynching. In the face of these cruel acts of hatred, the nonviolent resistance stood strong, lost lives, but ultimately awakened the compassionate heart of the United States to begin to put an end to the fear, dehumanization, and hate-mongering that makes racism possible and enables evil to create war. Racial equality, such as it nominally exists in the United States, was achieved at the cost of human beings engaged in nonviolent protest against a system built and sustained by violence.

The nonviolent protests of Dr. King demonstrated that awakening the compassionate heart that dwells within each person is a key to achieving preemptive peace. If we try to achieve peace with violence and war, all we do is create enemies who will sooner or later seek revenge. If we seek peace through nonviolence, people are going to die in acts of violence committed against them. The difference is that they will die for peace, and not for war. Ultimately the cruelty of guns used against people with only love in their heart will awaken the apathetic and dormant compassionate heart of the world.

Dr. King wrote that we must "awaken a sense of shame within the oppressor and challenge his false sense of superiority" [8] not by hating him but by loving him. "Freedom has always been an expensive thing," Dr. King continued, ". . . freedom is rarely gained without sacrifice." [9] When we speak of sacrifice, we may be talking about sacrificing our comfort, our job, our social standing, our friendships, or even our life. Attaining preemptive peace is going to require leadership—intelligent, courageous, and dedicated leadership. To paraphrase a writer named Holland:

God give us leaders!
A time like this demands strong minds, great hearts,
True faith and ready hands;
Leaders whom the lust of office does not kill;
Leaders whom the spoils of life cannot buy;
Leaders who possess opinions and a will;
Leaders who have honor; leaders who will not lie;
Leaders who can stand before a demagogue
And damn his treacherous flatteries without winking!
Tall leaders, sun-crowned, who live above the fog
In public duty and private thinking. [10]

Preemptive peace depends on each one of us becoming a leader with a strong mind, a great heart, honor, sun-crowned, and ready to sacrifice our special position in the world to make a place for everyone at the table of abundance the Divine Creator intends for all people. The journey to preemptive peace—a spiritual awakening that precludes the nightmare of war—will begin and succeed when people dedicated to political and spiritual activism are led by the truth we know in our common heart. It is the truth of peace, hope, and love taught to us by Abraham, Gandhi, Mohammed, Buddha, Jesus, the Rev. Dr. Martin Luther King Jr., Baha'u'llah, and every humanist and spiritual leader who has seen beyond the concern for self and into the beauty of wholeness with all of creation.

Preemptive peace is a spiritual awakening addressing the cruelty of dehumanization, the violence caused by fear, and the unity to be found in our shared vision and yearning of love. Preemptive peace is the peace we can attain by developing our common Spirit as we use our individual gifts to create a better world for our children—a world that precludes the nightmare of war.

Endnotes

[1] Walter Wink, ed., *Peace is the Way: Writings on Nonviolence from the Fellowship of Reconciliation* (New York: Orbis Books, 2000), 3.
[2] Carlo Carretto, *I Francis*, (New York: Orbis Books, 1982), 81.
[3] Walter Wink, *op. cit.*, 130-132.
[4] Carlo Carretto, *op. cit.*, 74.

[5] Erik Kolbell, *What Jesus Meant* (Louisville, KY, Westminster John Knox Press, 2003), 121.

[6] Walter Wink, *op. cit.*, 228.

[7] *Ibid.*, 175.

[8] *Ibid.*, 182.

[9] *Ibid.*, 184.

[10] *Ibid.*, 185.

When the Nonviolent Church Prays

Rev. Neal Christie

When Will God Hear a Child's Prayer?

Toward the end of the Indo-Pakistan war, I revisited my parent's home in Gujarat State in India. This was the early 1970s. Frequent air raids, images of missile blasts, and rapid evacuations punctuated family visits. I prayed for India to win. I was elated the day Indian newspaper headlines read "we" had won. Years later, when I was fifteen years old, my friend Zharar Begg, who happened to be Muslim and from Pakistan, described in detail the trauma of watching his uncles fire antiaircraft artillery over the border toward India. Zharar prayed for Pakistan to win the war. I realized my friend and I shared more than I had allowed myself to imagine.

The desire to pray predates the creation of any modern nation state. Whether we receive or inflict violence, we expect to pray as much as we expect our next breath. But prayer has never been a politically neutral act. Consider Abraham Lincoln's Second Inaugural Address in which he describes the prayer of both sides in the American Civil War. In doing so, he subscribes to a deterministic myth of redemptive violence to justify Union retribution, personally condemns the inherent evil of chattel slavery, but still expresses with honesty the struggle for people of faith on both sides to discern the failure of God to listen to their own prayers:

> Both read the same Bible, and pray to the same God; and each invokes His aid against the other. It may seem strange that any men should dare to ask a just God's assistance in wringing their bread from the sweat of other men's faces; but let us judge not that we be not judged. The prayers of both could not be answered; that of neither has been answered fully. The Almighty has His own purposes. 'Woe unto the world because of offences! for it must needs be that offences come; but woe to that man by whom the offence cometh!' Fondly do we hope—fervently do we pray—that this mighty scourge of war may speedily pass away. Yet, if God wills that it continue, until all the wealth piled by the bond-man's two hundred and fifty years of unrequited toil shall be sunk, and until every drop of blood drawn with the lash, shall be paid by another drawn with the sword, as was said three thousand years ago, so still it must be said, 'the judgments of the Lord, are true and righteous altogether.'[1]

Today, nations are caught in the downward spiral of war, scarred by the continuing outrage of apartheid ethnic relationships, race-to-the-bottom market economics, bifurcated landlocked identities, and ill-fitting notions of separate but unequal democracies. In nations like Israel and Palestine, the Democratic People's Republic of Korea and the Republic of Korea, India and Pakistan, Serbia, Albania and Croatia, and the region of Central Africa, whose childhood war-prayers do we believe God really answers?

In solidarity with victims or victors, can we claim we pray to the same God? For most privileged North American Christians, the answer depends on who our ally is at the moment. An even more urgent question involves the tools we provide to a generation rubbed raw by images of protracted violence, images that suggest either an absence or an inability for the holy to intervene for good. How apt are we to listen to God when the answer to our prayer confounds who we presume ourselves to be and indicts those national identities that have become our second nature?

We are all children of God. But our prayers often reflect a severe lack of maturity. It is criminal at worst and self-referential at best, for privileged North Americans to kneel in prayer for the 3,000 international innocents who died tragically in the World Trade Center and Pentagon and in the same breath acquit the escalating cause-and-effect that kills 40,000 a day by famine and disease related to regional conflicts. It is unconscionable to ignore the thousands of civilian Afghans and Iraqis who have died and who will die in a U.S. war, a war lacking international approval. President Bush signed an elective order forbidding cloning because it would lead us down a slippery moral slope, yet his claim of a moral precedent for waging preemptive war is such a contradiction that we ought to be moved to prayer as a first-strike act of faith-based defiance.

Several times a week pastoral leaders are well positioned to reframe a congregation's posture of prayer. The aim of this essay is to demonstrate how pastors and congregations can use spoken congregational or liturgical prayer as a reframing tool for conflict resolution and anti-violence training. This is imperative for nations at war. Gandhi's approach to a violent world was contemplation-in-action, starting with individual conversion, marches, boycotts, and taking violence onto oneself. However, King moved from a pragmatic/functional understanding of nonviolence to a more intrinsic one. Caesar Chavez, Dorothy Day, Desmond Tutu, and Nelson Mandela (to some extent) employed organizing techniques built on some of the ethics and practices of Gandhi and King.

While these traditions can inform the ethos of congregations, what faith communities do best is worship. Indeed, mercy ministries do a great job offering direct service. Advocacy calls for more just public policies. I argue that congregations can and should do both, but they ought to center these actions in a theology free from violence, more specifically in the process and content of their prayers.

Pastors can provide a space for dialogue about the language of prayer so that we can ask some crucial questions about how we pray in times of war. For example: Does our language name the creative, nonviolent God of peace in kataphatic metaphors such as mother, gardener, fire, midwife, steward, seed, city, womb, whisper, water, and others? Or do we choose images of God that claim to be redemptive through retributory violence? Are we employing silence as a means of active-listening for God? Or are we retreating into silence as a response to discomfort over the subject of violence framed within a prayer?

The collective intercessory or bidding prayer we use during worship is more than a convenient fetish because we consciously choose how to refer to the same persons, groups, social relations, events, and crises. Frequently, however, hate-speech masquerades as public prayer. Assaulted by jingoistic politicians who appeal to God's blessing via xenophobic, expansionistic, self-appointed clergy who interpret national desires and aspirations, we live in a culture that prays to confirm what it already believes to be true. A code word like "weapon" allows some to legitimize nuclear bombs as valid instruments of power. "Homeland Security," "Axis of Evil," "terrorist," "patriot" "enemies of freedom," "crusade," and "free market," all take on highly charged meanings in the context of public prayer.

Through our belief systems we co-create a version of reality. Our prayers can differentiate us from the rationalizing language of the "court prophets." Our apophatic prayers can negate the excesses of national hubris and impress upon us the Holy, which resides beyond our cookie-cutter images of God. In the end, how a community chooses to pray will ultimately shape who that community sees themselves to be and how it is that the God of their theology relates to their experience of war, to their so-called "enemy," and how it is that violence plays a role in the lives of humanity.

Stopping Violence in Our Hearts and Hate in Our Heads: Rescripting Story

Violence demands prayer. A distraught parishioner requests prayers for her daughter and also a more general prayer for protection of all U.S. combat troops serving in Iraq. Another mourns the death of his nephew, a humanitarian aid worker who died distributing food. A third offers up a prayer for revenge for the death of Israeli children killed by a suicide bomber. A parishioner chooses to pray quietly because she fears that her prayer for an enemy might distance her from the congregation. These are prayers *about* violence, but how do we pray without our prayers *being* violent?

Such a question leads us to further questions about the complexities and tension present in prayer at a time of war. How do we respond in sincerity with deep compassion? Do we listen and offer a silent prayer? Empathize and pray for protection? Do we bite our lips and reinforce with little or no critique unspoken assumptions about the violated and violator, the inadequacy of international entities to achieve peace, or the cause-and-effect of neo-colonial occupation? Or do we acquit along the way war-making interests, the strategies and tactics that force us to choose one life over another? In our prayers, do we raise up stories of people's selfless efforts at peace and call a congregation to accountability for violence? Unless we ask similar questions about the content of our prayers, we will find that the words and images of our prayers merely provoke and, in some cases unintentionally, aid in the continuance of violence through unchecked patriotism and a nationalistic theology about the presence and goodness of God.

It is the central claim of this chapter, dare I say of this book, that prayer ought to be nonviolent in nature. Prayer as an act of preemptive peace and as an act of nonviolent intervention refuses to condone any form of violence. It names cycles of violence for what they are. It does not answer what is God's to answer. The challenge for people of faith is to understand that escalated, protracted violence is always the result of frustrations ill-addressed, of skewed perceptions of others that lead us to see them as dehumanized, deceitful, aggressive, heartless, sexually licentious, unclean, and incapable of change. What is the image of God we infer from such requests?

Tribal factions and fractures always threaten to "essentialize" and even socialize differences. These factions demonize the violated by superimposing different values on apparently incompatible and irreconcilable differences. Scarce resources for human needs are withheld or distributed to select groups. Values resident in structural inequity are canonized through our mass culture and popular religious expression. Human needs are frustrated and violence escalates from local skirmishes, to ethnic genocide, to wars between nation states. At the height of the Vietnam/American War the Benedictine monk Thomas Merton explained it this way:

> Characteristic of the devil's theology is the exaggeration of all distinctions between right and wrong, good and evil. These distinctions become irreducible divisions. No longer is there a sense that we might perhaps all be more or less at fault, and that we all are expected to take on our own shoulders the wrongs of others by forgiveness, acceptance, patience, understanding, and love, and thus get to the truth. On the contrary, in the devil's theology the important thing is to be right and prove anybody absolutely wrong. In order to prove their rightness they have to punish and eliminate those who are wrong.[2]

With the drumbeat of war pounding we forget that the first act of sincere prayer is humility. Our foreign-policy declarations, which bisect the world into "holy" and "unholy," "clean" and "unclean," recoil at this notion because they equate humility with weakness. Therefore, our prayers follow suit. We pray simplistic prayers *against* the "terrorists" and *for* American troops without even recognizing that our dualistic creation of "us" versus "them" only perpetuates more violence. This allows "us" to question: If *they* are evil, are *we* God's allies? If we are God's allies, we must be ordained to kill in God's name, to root out evil wherever it may be found. We find ourselves both mourning and finding pleasure in this call. The demonic spiral of our violent scapegoating, retribution, and grief replaces authentic prayer.

Nonviolent prayer means we recognize how we choose to interpret a situation in prayer. This leads us to explain that which appears to us both bizarre and offensive in another's actions and those actions, and beliefs we can genuinely empathize with. We steer ourselves between collusion, decisive prophetic discernment, and judgmentalism. When this occurs the real challenge of congregational prayer is to connect narratives, images, and stories familiar to a congregation with the plight of those who violate and those who are violated—to align their perceptions with their own story, the larger story, and the story of those deemed as "other," with the hope of achieving shared meaning.

When we allow our prayers to share meaning with others, we begin to see that our hi[stories] as human beings run together and are shaped by the ways in which we choose to live out our lives in community.

The prophet Isaiah had it right when he said, "When the ways of the people please the Lord, God causes even their enemies to be at peace with them" (Isa. 11:6). We ask ourselves in prayer what ways are actually so pleasing to God that they also bring peace with our enemies. The biblical mandate is consistent: justice for and reconciliation with the widow, the migrant, the orphan, and the poor. We are compelled for our own survival to pray and work to meet human needs with systems that sustain them. The following prayer is one attempt to name alternative images of God, to empathize with the plight of the violated, to create shared meaning among communities at war, and to suggest an alternative future:

Jesus,
raining down on Babel's nationalistic pride,
a flood of tragic proportion, you span sea of Galilean miracles
and surge for a Jordan moment to surface clear.

You are the river flowing through the City of God,
but we lie capsized, living in memories of what has been,
Anxious for what may be—avoiding the here and now.

You sob out an advent reply of rant and praise—
"Scatter the proud . . . lift the lowly . . ."
for a world where girls are exposed to die,
Comfort Women spoils of war branded military commodities,
Women in Black standing vigil to Israel's preemptive jihad,
AIDS triples widows, displaces military might,
the poorest of the poor on earth live under a carrot and the stick—
a have it all global iconography of abundance and after-life
for the most compliant;
a hell on earth of fairy cutters, thermobaric bombs,
an everlasting half-life of nuclear detonation,
for the least recalcitrant.

We pray for international consultation,
which favors listening not just talking,
where bargaining is more than all take and no give,
where the strong do not do what they must
and the weak will do more than take what they can.

May those who refuse to be effaced
find in you the rippling light sheen,

muddy warmth in Bethesda's pool—
relief of suffering and Calvary joy exceeding,
calling us back to our baptismal selves.
When we hear "I thirst" . . .[3]

Nonviolent Liturgical Prayer

If prayer is, therefore, nonviolent and is most aptly found in congregational worship, it is ultimately fitting to engage the impact of prayer found in our liturgy. Liturgical prayer, spoken and written, spontaneous and scripted within a context of a world at war, is a pragmatic act of nonviolent intervention and conflict transformation. We are free to address through our intentions both the holy and the community seeking to experience the holy. We are free to return to mindfulness and sort fact from fiction. We are free from a place of humility to see humanity in those named as enemy, whenever we are in touch with the capacity for reverence, confession, petition, and appreciation. The result will be a greater ability to trust one another and even to desire trust in an enemy. The hoped-for effect of our prayer will be an alternate future.

Times of war are filled with images of destruction that point to our dualistic creation of the "enemy." Nonviolent prayer seeks to replace these images with a more liberating posture, hence providing images that help create an alternative future. Metaphors, images, and analogy function to conceptualize a violent conflict. Our responses, formed in our prayers, remind us that anything we trust more than God is bound to fail. God moves beyond perceived or expected boundaries. God resides at the boundary where violence thrives unchecked and where nonviolence springs to life. Anything that demands more from us than God is an idol. Anything we love, we become. Ideologies that captivate us, seduce us, and demand our time, our trust, our allegiance, our intimacy, move us away from seeing the cause-and-effect of harm from God's point of view.

All this is to say that when we pray in a context of protracted violence, our prayer is consistently political. We are carving out in our worship much-needed liminal space to admit our utter dependence on

God, our response to a conflict, and our common covenanted refusal to accommodate to the "Empire's" ideological desire for comfortable allegiance. This orientation has the capacity to ease that internal dialogue we have within ourselves, to slow our inclination for reactivity.

This kind of prayer is a holy alertness that moves us from violent scapegoating of our nation's most vulnerable prey, enabling us to pray in a more radical and spirit-formed way. This kind of prayer seduces us away from the allure of the public spectacle of national security to a new quality of freedom, based on faith commitments. Especially for more economically privileged congregations, prayer as a tactic for nonviolent action seeks a congregation's self-interest. It discerns their "called-out-ness" and demythologizes the status quo as canonically sanctioned. It prevents a relapse into "Empire." By means of prayer, people will not exhaust themselves collecting food for homeless refugees, so that they have no energy to question policies that exacerbate dislocation. Because prayer is a mediating activity, it is an activity that informs and reforms nonviolence. What a community chooses to pray for and the form that prayer takes speaks volumes about who that community sees themselves to be and reveals who they perceive God calls and commits them to become.

Consider an excerpt from Mark Twain's timeless *War Prayer*. Twain first describes the spoken prayer delivered by a minister sending troops off to war. Then he gives the unspoken, implied prayer, which begins as follows:

> O Lord our God, help us to tear their soldiers to bloody shreds with our shells; help us to cover their smiling fields with the pale forms of their patriot dead; help us to drown the thunder of the guns with the shrieks of their wounded, writhing in pain; . . .[4]

We are tempted to dismiss this prayer as unrecognizable today. However, when we look at the text and the kind of speech used in congregations to justify redemptive violence and war as holy, we find many similarities. Some of our progressive congregations could spend significant time exegeting this discourse and applying it to the church down the street, but they would be uncomfortable seeing themselves in it.

Consider for yourself those theological metaphors that are most similar to your own experience, for example, in personal prayer when you have discovered yourself on one side of a seemingly intractable conflict. Listen to your prayer from the perspective of the prayers we have grown accustomed to hearing in hymns and sacred texts. What referents are least familiar to your own experience? Which of these prayers have we convinced ourselves our enemies seek refuge in? Have you considered that our enemies fear and hate us in prayer? What emotions does this prayer elicit for you and what memories of past trauma or violation does it evoke? How does your own prayer influence your understanding of violent conflict? Moreover, is it imaginable for our enemies to share these emotions? Why do we avoid basing foreign policy on these points of congruence and contact? Who benefits from these decisions and in what way?

It is extremely difficult to pray for those who directly or indirectly have violated us or for those whom we have violated. No pastor could deny this. But the rhythm of this kind of nonviolent prayer causes us to recover our lost autonomy. We are no longer naïve and we no longer need to demonize to win. Either we pray for reconciliation, which includes within itself accountability on the part of those who have done harm, for healing and closure, envisioning an alternative future, or we will find our identity lying prostrate in allegiance to Empire and its bent towards war, enjoying a compliant peace and an unchallenged economic, social, political, and cultural hegemony.

When everyday conversation centers on escalating violence, congregations maneuver themselves around the most obvious forms of paternalistic prayer for victims to a more difficult prayer for those who victimize. Empathizing and identifying with, advocating and speaking up for peace on behalf of those who are caught up in the cycle of violence and those who expect only violation, is a different kind of prayer. Such a prayer names the common experiences of both the violated and those who violate. It is a method of preemptive peace action and conflict transformation that gradually makes us more transparent to ourselves, to God, to one another, and to our enemies. We are redeemed and disarmed to live on both sides of Calvary and to see there is no darkness where Christ is not already present. "Seek first the kingdom of God" (Matt. 6:33). Christians love their neighbor and pray for their enemies. We wrestle with the question: Where can we draw a line between love and prayer? If the line we draw is in fact an illusion, then all our congregational prayers must be in intention, form, and content part of a larger agenda for nonviolent peace.

Experiential Body Prayer as Nonviolent Action

Because liturgical prayer seeks an alternative future where violence and war will cease, congregations must find ways to embody such prayer. In 1748, Anglican priest and Methodist-movement-maker, John Wesley, suggested that we "Preserve peace where it is and restore peace where it is not." We theologically affirm God's prevenient grace—a grace that anticipates and prepares a response. Prayer in the context of protracted violence is an act of unusual faith because we move prayer from simplistic notions of intercession to prayers of identification with human communities that suffer at the hands of violence. Churches that treat prayer as a disciplined process for preserving and restoring peace will consider the following:

1. *Know where you stand as you pray.* How does a person's or congregational social location play a role in prayer? None of us are exempt from our social location, and we would be amiss if we did not pay attention to these factors in the way we pray. However, prayer is also a revelatory discourse in which we discover who we are up against, our inner selves, external relationships, and the holy. Congregations will do well to first cultivate mutual trust among themselves, to covenant a communication that values fairness and "safe space" for disagreement and that names their own experiences. We are formed by social experiences over which we have little or no control. Thus, our social experiences and locations are trajectories for revelatory prayer.

One way to attain "safe space" among our differing social experiences and locations in congregations is by beginning with a small group to start crafting new prayers of appreciation, consternation, cleaning, collusion, and confession. Pray for strength to demythologize the powerful and name their influence on our lives. Take note of the kind of prayers articulated over a set period of time by members of the congregation. Are there different prayers for peace and war offered by youth and adults, women and men, people of different classes and vocations? What cultural assets and strengths does a congregation offer to contribute to a world at peace?

Consider the following group exercise as a form of contemplative body prayer. It can be adapted to different contexts but is always done in an attitude of reverence. Invite the congregation to respond quietly to these or similar questions as they feel moved. Ask them to raise their hands, to stand where they are, or to move to the center of a circle. Have them notice how it feels and have them notice who stands with them and who does not. Invite them to return to their original places.

If you are a military veteran

If you have ever applied to be a Conscientious Objector

If you have participated in an act of civil disobedience against a war

If you have been physically wounded as a result of war

If you have experienced the death of a family member by an act of war

If you have been socialized to fear people of another nationality, religion, or ethnicity

If you or your ancestors were forced to come to the U.S., forced to relocate from where they lived or restricted to live in certain neighborhoods, by an act of legalized violence

If you or your family's property has ever been legally seized as a result of a police action

If you have ever been accused of not being patriotic enough, derided or threatened because you were perceived as less than patriotic

If you have felt uncomfortable in a group because you were viewed as too patriotic

If you have ever been arrested or detained because of an act of civil disobedience in opposition to an act of violence or war

If you have a personal relationship with a person who has become a refugee as a result of armed conflict

Close with silent prayer offered to honor the silence of those voices lost to acts of violence. If possible, invite the group to reflect in pairs on how it felt to stand alone or with others. Ask them if these memories bring up any specific feelings of discomfort, anger, fear, secretiveness, or even shame. Ask the group where in their bodies they felt these feelings. Ask the group to consider what effect these personal experiences have on the self-consciousness of an entire conflicted nation, region, an ethnic or racial group, or a generation devastated by war. Share in prayers of confession, confrontation, and cleansing.

2. *Meet designated enemies through dialogical prayers or appreciation.* Ask your congregation and yourself: Is it ever possible for us to pray not only for our enemies, but also *with* our enemies? If face-to-face discourse is impossible, can we imagine, explore, and possibly discover common interests, values, and needs beneath the intractable affirmations that divide us? What would it look like for congregations to subvert national agendas by seeking direct communication with persons whose prayers are at odds with their own?

Taken further, what would it be like for churches to hold a teleconference or town meeting with people of faith in Iraq, Iran, and the DPRK and to pray together? Is it possible to seek mutual points of spiritual expression with people of faith in "rogue" states, especially those nations defined by their relationship to the Bible and the Qur'an?

Once we appreciate each other's values, do we hear common threads, such as friendship, respect, sacrifice, empowerment, love, justice, family, and wisdom, and can we see the role of these values in maintaining civil society? It is easier to harm, violate, and kill that which is not like us. Prayer that "meets" our enemies cultivates within us the capacity for awe and surprise in seeing the other as human.

3. *Pray for proactive, preemptive peace.* When we imagine "peace" as such, we often lose ourselves in abstractions. When we ask a congregation to imagine metaphors, words, phrases, and analogies we associate with war, descriptions are quick and specific. Praying for preemptive peace means we concretely name and conjure imagery that creates an ethos of peace, such as: equitable distribution of food and clean water, dignified work with a living wage, tolerance of diverse religious and cultural expressions, participatory civil institutions, healthcare, nutrition, and literacy. We generate and explore options, appreciate possible avenues of advocacy with persons and organizations of influence, and protest those that refuse to admit to violence. We organize ourselves by mutual obligations and seek collaborative alliances for violence prevention.

Centering prayer can often be a useful tool in peace-building and providing an organized space to prevent violence. Centering prayer or meditation, with attention to listening to the pulse of our breath together, has the capacity to expand our finite awareness. Centering prayer as an act of peace-building admits the prevenience of sacred presence. It allows us to be witnesses to experience rather than actors, believing God can move through prayer in spite of us and that there are times to be still and wait on God for direction. Attentiveness to our intentions has the ability to free God to act in us and is prayer in itself.

Consider the centering prayer below as one way God acts in us to create an alternative future. It can be adapted for use in a congregational setting and accompanied by music as appropriate. Set the tone and mood in a circle with as little outside distraction as possible. Consider adapting lectionary scriptures or timely community stories, narrated by survivors of violence, to this process of prayer.

Thank you for coming to pray together. We are going to participate in a contemplative prayer to focus on places in our body where we center our energies. We will always begin at the center of our heart. To help you focus, please sit comfortably, bring your thumb and forefinger together on both hands, and place your hands on your lap. Close your eyes and breathe in and out through the center of your chest. This is your heart center. Always breathe in through your nose and out through your nose. See the color green in your heart center. Feel this as your place of God's gracious, unconditional love.

Breathe in the love and exhale whatever no longer serves you in a healthy way. Breathe in compassion. Exhale resentment. The heart center is the place of emotions and feelings. Let an image come to you of your heart's center as it opens. Perhaps it's bright like the sun. Let that fill you up as it emanates through your heart center. All healing begins here. Feel this healing energy flowing through you as you breathe in through the heart—right in the center of your chest.

Quiet your thoughts by focusing on the name of your spiritual connection: God, Jesus, love, grace. Breathe in compassion. Exhale jealousy, exhale any ideas you have learned that love is limited. Breathe in love and exhale grief. Bring to your heart center one image of those most vulnerable to violence: an orphaned child soldier, a displaced widow, a girl forced into prostitution. Breathe into this person the color of your heart center. Hold it there and release your breath.

Now we are going to breathe up to the throat center. So, breathe up from your heart and bring your energy up your spine into your throat center. Hold it there. Then slowly let it out through your throat center. The throat center is your place of creative expression. It is a place where we find our true voice. Breathe in your creativity and exhale any repression you have learned to hold onto. As you breathe in and out of your throat center, the color blue may come to you. Let that color enhance your experience here. Breathe in your expression and exhale any lies: lies that you have told or lies that have been told to you. Breathe in your creativity and release any shame you may be holding. It is now safe to fully express who you are as a person of peace. It is now safe to fully speak truth to the powers and principalities of this world. Say that to yourself: "It is now safe to speak truth." Bring to this center an image of a person who needs to hear truth. It could be someone caught up in the corruption of war, profiting from death. It could be an advocate who remains present with people in an area of violence. See this person as human, a person seeking truth like you.

Allow truth to flow from you. As you release repression, your creativity and ability to respond expands. Feel your throat center opening up. Let an image come to you now as your throat center opens, as your creativity flows. If there is anything or anyone that seems to be draining your energy in this throat center, let it come to you now and let yourself be clear so that you can breathe it out.

Now we are going to take another deep breath in and we are going to breathe into the throat center and come right up to the space located in the center of your forehand. Hold your breathe there and slowly let the breathe out. Inhale again through this space in the center of your forehead and open up. This is your place of clarity and vision. Exhale any illusions that have been taught to you by the empires of this world. Inhale clarity. Exhale confusion. Inhale faith. Exhale disbelief.

What needs within yourself are still unfulfilled so that their expression in an enemy is justified. What about me is hungry so that I can justify hunger in another person or what has been violated in me that I can allow someone else to be violated? Breathe into these illusions.

The color here is violet. Let yourself receive guidance. This is your place of guidance. As you breathe in and out through this center let yourself see God, see Jesus, see the peace. Breathe it in. Exhaling your judgments, inhaling guidance, exhaling closed mindedness, inhaling mindfulness. In this center, see what it would be like for you to create a place of justice and peace. Where would you be? Who would be there? What would you need?

And now I'd like you for a moment to bring your attention to the base of your spine and together we will breathe up to the top of our heads and then follow the breath out. And as you inhale, allow your body to feel relaxed and open up. Go to the base of your spine and inhale, bringing your attention right up to the top of your head. Hold it there and then slowly let the energy up and out, looking upwards. If you like, you can do that again. Bring your attention to the base of your spine.

Inhale all the way up your spine and hold it at the top of your head. Breathe in through your nose and then slowly let it out at the top of your head. Breathe in through your nose and then slowly let it out. Follow the breath out and connect with your image of the Holy. This is the place of unity. Let yourself unite. Let yourself feel the grace. Take it in. Inhale grace and release lack of faith. Fill yourself with that grace. Inhale oneness, release grandiosity. This is the place of surrender. Surrender to peace. Feel the humility. Quiet your thoughts.

Open up the crown center at the top of your head and let peace pour in. Let the energy pour in. Let it fill you up as your crown center opens. This is God's light. Take it in, receive it, and replenish yourself from it. Just bathe in the light. Bring your energy and your attention back down to your heart center. If there is any piece of your soul that taken from you by an act of violence, fear, greed, hate, or shame, bring it back in now. Place this part of you back into your body and into your heart center. Breathe in and out though your heart center and let your soul completely fill you up. This is your essence. Feel your essence from the tips of your toes, up to your spine through your feet, legs, back and out into your arms, hands, and fingers. Feel it in your chest, your neck, your throat, and your face. Every part of you is now present. Breathe it in now through your heart center. Feel that healing love and energy for peace. If there is anyone you want to send loving, healing energy to, put him or her in that circle right now. As you do so, gently speak their names aloud.

Connect with peace, with one another, with your soul through your heart center. Through Jesus feel the connection.

In a moment now I am going to count from one to five. You will come back to the room feeling relaxed and refreshed. One, the energy is flooding back into your body. Two, you are feeling refreshed and relaxed. Three, you are feeling hopeful, confident, and positive. Four, you are feeling unconditional love in your heart. Five, open your eyes, feeling refreshed and relaxed. Amen.[5]

Nonviolent Action Is Nonviolent Ritual Prayer

Finally, in the life of congregations, we participate in rituals, both historic and modern. Rituals provide us with a sense of meaning and purpose, which is why in a time of war it is even more imperative that we examine the ways in which our rituals, especially our rituals in worship, perpetuate or do not perpetuate violence. Our formal and informal rituals reinforce familiar messages in our congregations. They are a form of prayer in themselves. Rituals, however, are a double-edged sword. Rituals can contain sacred power to transform society, and they have the power to protract violence. For example, our choice and placement of flags, globes, familiar images in our tradition, and use of sacred spaces can do much more than legitimate and pre-ordain an ethic of violence; they often produce a sense of military memory that goes unchecked. Nonviolent ritual actions, on the other hand, can transform society by offering mindful and meaningful, culturally relevant connections with Mystery. Think about how we celebrate the sacrament of the Eucharist so that it does not reinforce the myth of redemptive violence. Do we focus on Christ's reconciliation of death into life? Is the ritual one of reconciliation with our nation's enemies?

What is more, are we intentional through the liturgical year, planning for periods of fasting, retreat, acts of mercy, and acts of justice? Does the style of our ritual worship in space, seating, and iconography contribute to nonviolence and promote peace? Do we incorporate nonviolent images and stories in our rites of baptism, confirmation, and memorials at times of death? Have we observed worship related to national holidays? Do we subvert images of domination with disinterred stories of resistance to violence, sacred protest, procession, and theater as forms of collective prayer? Can we go further than this to imagine enemies celebrating intimate rituals with us? If not, what rituals of prayer separate us and which, while celebrated separately, do we hold in common with an enemy? As we access alternative perceptions we work toward trust. Ritual, as prayer in motion, should serve to reintegrate and restore community to those who have experienced traumatic separation.

Archbishop Despond Tutu was able to steer a post-apartheid nation away from national amnesia or a victor's justice to an unheard-of restorative justice by means of the Truth and Reconciliation Commission. This was a form of collective prayer and ritual. Mothers of the Disappeared marched in Argentina and Women in Black march in Jerusalem. These are forms of ritual prayers of confession and cleansing for an alternative future. Christian Peacemaking Teams are present in Hebron and Baghdad, and their physical act of witness serves as contemplative prayer in action.

An ethic and practice of preemptive peace awakens us to how our community is in prayer. The greatest challenge to the church is to make our common liturgical prayer more charismatic, more contemplative, and more politically relevant than an occasional mourning of the tragic death of innocents after an unspeakable act of violence or shouting invective against the systemic causes of violation. A generation of politically progressive, spiritually motivated people will not choose to partner with a church that does not live up to what it says it works and prays for: "A new heaven and a new earth."

Our very soul—intention, voice, and will—is formed by the act of nonviolent prayer. Identity, perception, revelation, and commitment to nonviolent action are shaped by the form and content of our prayers. We pray to love our enemies because we are intrinsically related to them. We see ourselves in them. Who we see *they* are speaks volumes about who we see *ourselves* to be.

In the end, we will become what we pray for.

Endnotes

[1] Susan Jacoby, *Freethinkers* (New York: Metropolitan Books, 2004), 120.
[2] Thomas Merton, *New Seeds of Contemplation* (New York: New Directions Publishing Corporation, 1966; rev. ed. March 1, 1972).
[3] Neal Christie, *Christian Social Action Magazine* (Washington, D.C.: General Board of Church and Society, 2003).
[4] Mark Twain, *The War Prayer* (1923) (New York: Perennial, 2003).
[5] David Kertzer, *Ritual Politics and Power* (New Haven: Yale University Press 1988), 104.

Benediction

The following sermon by Jim Winkler was preached on March 5, 2004, at the Double Tree Hotel in Washington, D.C., in the opening worship service for the Ecumenical Advocacy Days. The Ecumenical Advocacy Days is a weekend event of peace activism designed to confront U.S. leaders on the injustices of our foreign policies. This sermon embraces all that a benediction is designed to be: a sending forth. It is a challenge for the Church to not remain silent but to find its voice and to create an ethos of peace.

The World in Which We Wish to Live

Jim Winkler

"I will seek the lost, and I will bring back the strayed, and I will bind up the injured, and I will strengthen the weak, but the fat and the strong I will destroy. I will feed them with justice." —Ezek. 34:16

My teenage children have never had a bad day in their lives. Sure, they've faced minor illnesses, felt down now and then, had to deal with conflicts, not always immediately received the toys and material possessions they wanted, but they haven't faced privation, hunger, war, violence, or homelessness. Parents the world over desire no less for their children. A bountiful life and future for our children represents the world in which we wish to live.

My wife, Robin, and I have made what seem to us to be significant sacrifices to provide a safe and secure childhood for our children, but we realize what we have done to make this happen is almost nothing compared to what parents face in places like Kinshasa, Jenin, and

Manila. We, in fact, have the luxury living here in "Rome" of not even caring, if we choose not to, about the problems those parents face.

The difference is that we here tonight draw together as followers of Jesus Christ and, so, we cannot be indifferent. Further, we gather in the midst of war. In fact, it seems as if we have now had more than 60 years of war, both hot and cold. This is not the world in which we wish to live. Like the Apostle Paul, we have come to Rome to claim our rights. Einstein once said, "The world is a dangerous place to live; not because of the people who are evil; but because of the people who don't do anything about it." We are here to do something about misplaced priorities.

It has been calculated that nearly thirteen trillion dollars was spent by the United States in military spending during the Cold War from 1948-1991. This great fortune has largely been squandered. You can't live in a missile silo or wear a tank. It is the equivalent of burying money in the ground. Imagine the paradise we would live in today had that money been spent to bring the world adequate food, clothing, and shelter. Everyone in the world could have adequate health care and free education. The environment could be clean. That is the world in which we wish to live.

We are here unashamedly to advocate before our government for priorities that meet human needs and care for God's creation. We engage in this ministry because we have heard the God of Moses calling us to do so. When Moses was anointed by God to be the first social-justice lobbyist in the court of Pharaoh, he did so unwillingly, but he went to the seat of power to demand freedom from slavery. When Esther went to King Ahasuerus, she did so at the risk of her own life, but she answered the call to save her people from genocide. When Jesus proclaimed his Nazareth Manifesto to seek release of the captives, to feed the hungry, to shelter the homeless, to clothe the naked, and to free the oppressed, he did so at the cost of his own life. Are we willing to make such a sacrifice?

There are those who believe the Bible commands us to obey the authorities, to follow the flag, and to kill our enemies. This is the false Gospel. The prophets took no public opinion polls and never gathered any focus groups. They obeyed the will of God.

I am honored to be here tonight with you. Many of you formerly and faithfully attended the annual Interfaith Impact briefings that came to an end some years ago. I want to thank the planning committee for the vision to organize this event. There were times when it may have looked doubtful about the success of this venture. Tonight is a great night. Six hundred are here!

We are on the right side of God's history. It has taken centuries for the Christian people to understand the full import of Christ's teachings. The denominations represented here tonight have already dramatically changed this nation. Sometimes we were slow to catch the vision and at times we have been on the cutting edge, but the churches here are the moral and spiritual backbone of the great movements of the past fifty years to ensure civil and human rights for all, to bring an end to the scourge of war, to save the environment, and to protect the rights of immigrants. There are times when we forget the United States has been radically changed for the better because of our ministry in the public arena. The forces of violence, racism, and greed are fighting what is ultimately a doomed rearguard action to shield their ill-gotten gains.

The denominations represented here have huge influence on Capitol Hill and in state legislatures, more than we may realize. But we have untapped potential and must more effectively mobilize the millions in our congregations who have a passion for Christ but have not made the connection between justice and mercy.

It is right and proper for Christians to provide a moral and ethical witness in the halls of government. We do not offer campaign contributions to candidates; we do not threaten to turn elected officials out of office if they don't vote as we want them to; we do not pray for the death or illness of Supreme Court justices. Politely and firmly, we remind our government of the moral imperatives of the Scriptures.

We are witnessing for Jesus Christ as we speak truth to power for the world in which we wish to live. We have a message of love to feed them with justice. Our message is countercultural. War and violence are not the answer.

Some of the denominations represented here have grown numerically, others have declined. Some face crises; others are under vicious, unprincipled attacks by groups represented here tonight, but all share unity in Christ and vision of a New Creation.

We have laid out an impressive international agenda for this weekend. Africa, Latin America, Asia, nuclear disarmament, economic justice. If we focus only on gaining members; on feeding the hungry, clothing the naked, and sheltering the homeless at the expense of freeing the oppressed; on charity and not justice, we turn a blind eye to Rome's imperial policies and bless the status quo. We must turn Rome on its head. The capital has been transformed into an armed camp by a government dedicated to enriching the wealthy and spying on its people. Dr. King reminded us a long time ago that a nation that year after year spends more on weapons of death than on programs of moral uplift approaches spiritual death. That is our plight unless we get to work.

One year ago this weekend, many of us were participating in one of the 6,500 prayer vigils for peace that took place across the globe to try to head off disastrous war against Iraq. Robin and I took our two beautiful teenagers to the Lincoln Memorial for the vigil in Washington. Peter, Paul, and Mary sang "Blowin' in the Wind," "If I Had a Hammer," and other great protest songs that we sang when we were teens protesting the Vietnam War. There were plenty of speakers but I can't remember who they were. We lit candles for peace at the end of the vigil, and as we walked to the car I asked Grace and Sam what they thought. They said, "That was soooooo coooool!" Two new peaceniks were born that night, dedicated to working for the world in which we wish to live.

About two years ago, I was walking through the wreckage of the Palestinian refugee camp of Jenin forty-eight hours after Israeli soldiers withdrew. Tiny children were digging through rubble and pulling out toys. Women were drinking tea in their living room as if it were an ordinary afternoon except the wall had been destroyed, exposing them to the passing world. Families were frantically clawing through the wreckage of their homes searching frantically for the bodies of loved ones. Death was in the air.

We live in the midst of war at a time when the American empire holds before us a vision of more and more war. This is not the world in which we wish to live. I pray one year from now we will gather again to celebrate a government committed to peace. The stakes before us are high; the peace of the world hangs in the balance.

We did not succeed in stopping the illegal invasion and conquest of Iraq, although we helped mobilize overwhelming world opinion against war. We grieve for the thousands of soldiers and citizens who have died and the thousands who are maimed and wounded, both physically and psychologically. The consequences of this war, based on a pack of lies, will be with us for generations to come. Gandhi reminds us, "When out of violence something good appears to result, this good is at best short-lived; while the evil that produces it is enduring." Did our efforts mean anything? Several months ago, I had lunch with Fr. Elias Chacour, the famous Galilean priest. The first thing he said was to thank me and others for standing up against the war. "You saved thousands of Christian lives in the Middle East and the Holy Land by opposing the war." "How did we do that?" I asked. "Because it proved to Muslims that not all Christians supported the war. When President Bush called for a crusade after 9/11, tensions soared and Christian lives were in danger. But we were able to show our Muslim brothers and sisters that most Christian leaders were against the war."

Right now, we assemble in the shadow, almost literally, of the greatest war machine in all of history. Since WWII, millions of Southeast Asians, Koreans, Central Americans, Latin Americans, Arabs, Pacific and Caribbean Islanders, and Africans have perished at the hands of our weapons and warriors. This American empire requires an enormous military apparatus. The U.S. maintains some 700 military installations worldwide. This cannot be the world in which we wish to live. Our tax system has become systematically more regressive in recent decades, made more so these past three years due to gigantic tax breaks for the rich. Thus, the disproportionate burden of supporting this oppressive imperial army falls financially on the poorest among us. Additionally, the poor are recruited by the military to serve in its ranks.

A few miles up the road from here sits the headquarters of our secret police. In this same postwar era, dozens of governments have been destabilized or overthrown, untold thousands have been assassinated or executed on their orders. All of this has been done in our name. Here and now let us reject this murder and violence. The world in which we wish to live must have no place for this madness.

2,000 years ago those who went before us in the faith were persecuted by Rome because they believed in the revolutionary teachings of Jesus on love, peace, justice, and forgiveness. The Roman Empire co-opted Christ's church in the service of war, violence, hatred, and fear. We understand now and reject the myths of redemptive violence, male superiority, white supremacy, and American exceptionalism. These are the demonic hunger-making, war-making, and desert-making systems that encircle the globe and threaten to destroy God's creation and deny us the world in which we wish to live.

Those here tonight can breathe new life into Ezekiel's vision. "I will seek the lost," the Lord tells us, "and I will bring back the strayed, and I will bind up the injured, and I will strengthen the weak, but the fat and the strong I will destroy. I will feed them with justice." Get with the program, God is saying, and I will care for you. If you don't, you face dire consequences. Let us choose life.

Our people desire to live holy lives. I believe they want to connect justice and mercy. My friend Cynthia Moe-Lobeda writes,

> We do not wish to buy shirts made in sweatshops, drink coffee grown on land that should feed its hungry children, or use metal products from mines that have displaced thousands of people. We are not pleased to be pumping toxins into our planetary home, destroying the life systems upon which life depends. Yet, we do. Our lives are intimately bound up in a moral-spiritual crisis of profound and unprecedented dimensions. The reigning model of economic globalization threatens earth, undermines cultural integrity and diversity, and endangers the lives of many who are poor in order that some might consume exorbitantly and a few accumulate vast wealth.

I myself am a descendant of the European tribes, now formed into nations, that have established political, military, and economic dominance over the world. I confess to my sin of privilege and my reluctance to forego the perks my race and class afford me. It goes without saying—still, it must be said again—that we do not separate ourselves from the world. If we are faithful followers of Jesus Christ, we live in love with the world, because the most famous passage of the New Testament declares that "God so loved the world that God sent God's only Son into the world."

Substituting redemption for punishment, eliminating hunger as an inherent part of our economic system, abolishing war as the supreme expression of hate, all of these and more are choices we must make. God has made it possible for us to do this. May the gifts of God shower and reign over the people of God. Let us dedicate ourselves to live boldly, with purpose, confidence, generous hearts, and passion. Together, we will work for the world in which we wish to live. May we bear witness together to God's vision for unity and God's command that justice and mercy be known throughout the earth.

Postlude

Creating an Ethos of Peace

Rev. Chad R. Abbott and Rev. Everett Mitchell

"Another world is not only possible, she's on her way. Maybe many of us won't be here to greet her, but on a quiet day, if I listen carefully, I can hear her breathing."[1] —Arundhati Roy

"Nada se puede lograr"

"Nothing Can Be Achieved"

si no hay revolución	if there is no revolution
reza el rico, reza el amo	the rich pray, the master prays
y te maltratan al peón	and they go ahead and oppress the worker

reza el rico, reza el amo	the rich pray, the master prays
y te maltratan al peón	and they go ahead and oppress
	the worker

| No, no, no basta rezar | No, no, no, it is not enough to pray |
| hacen falta muchas cosas | there are many more things needed |

| para conseguir la paz (Bis) | in order to achieve peace. |

| NO BASTA REZAR | (IT IS NOT ENOUGH |
| | TO PRAY) |

—Lyrics and music by Alí Primera[2]

The world in which we wish to live is one of peace and not war. The creation of such a world is on her way. In 1998, the World Council of Churches met in Harare, Zimbabwe, for its eighth Assembly of the Council. They provided a striking proposal, one that will forever change the face of the earth. They proposed a decade-long opposition to violence and war. The council gave a detailed look at the twentieth century and heralded it as the "single most violent century in human history."[3] While we could make arguments to the contrary, one has to admit that we left the twentieth century as some of the most violent people to ever walk the planet.

Our scope of violence in the twentieth century ranged from two world wars to massive genocide in Cambodia to the Vietnam War, the Iran-Contra affair, the Persian Gulf War, Hiroshima and Nagasaki, and the Korean War, to name only a few. This does not even include the genocide in Rwanda, where 800,000 people were killed in a matter of weeks while the world, including the U.S., remained silent. Whether the twentieth century was the most violent century in human history or not, we certainly find ourselves looking back in sadness at the way we have destroyed God's world. Of course, the violence has not stopped, and we have September 11th, the invasion of Afghanistan, the invasion and occupation of Iraq, the turmoil in Haiti and the Sudan, and the situation between Israelis and Palestinians as examples of continuing violence.

The World Council of Churches came together in 1998 in repentance, grief, and yet hope for the world in which we live. They put their minds together and developed an initiative called the "Decade to Overcome Violence." It is a movement to educate and inform people of all faith backgrounds for creating an ethos of peace. Their main objectives are to describe the logic and spirit of violence and how it destroys God's creation. The initiative, then, seeks a spiritual and political base for overcoming violence of any kind in this world so that we may experience God's kingdom "On earth as it is in heaven."

This is a challenge to people of faith and non-faith alike to become active in their communities locally, nationally, and internationally in creating a movement of peace. It is a call that will change the face of human history if we but listen, a chance for us to see all of humanity as a creation of God and as intertwined with our own lives and history. Lila Watson, an aboriginal Australian, once said, "If you have come to help me you can go home again. But if you see my struggles as part of your own survival, then perhaps we can work together."[4] As citizens of this world, we need to see one another's struggles as essential to our own survival. We need to work together or we will possibly see the twenty-first century end in complete annihilation of the earth.

The Church has the unique responsibility of having a voice and a tradition of non-violence during times of war. Where has that voice gone in our present time of need? When will we find the courage to speak words of peace and justice? When will we allow our words to become actions? There are many actions that the Church must take as humankind enters into uncharted territory in this world and in these times. We conclude this volume with several actions that aim to join with the World Council of Churches in creating an ethos of peace.

1. **Be Proactive.** We must be proactive in our communities by addressing issues of war with friends, neighbors, and those in political seats. This means that we must not be afraid of working in grassroots-level discussions and organizing around issues of war, peace, and justice. This may include writing to our local newspapers and submitting a letter to the editor or an op/ed piece in order to begin a forum for issues related to peace. This could also mean starting a dialogue with our state or local representatives. We can write, call, or visit our congressional representatives and dialogue with them about our concerns about a world bent on war.

2. Join the Peace Movement. Living out our faith in a proactive way ought to move us to visible representation in local, national, or international communities. The worldwide peace movement is made up of hundreds of organizations working in their own communities and countries to create an ethos of peace. It is a visible movement of protest demanding that violence and war not rule the day. This could mean anything from standing on the square of our county seat, to writing our congressperson, to marching on Washington with activist groups such as International Answer. Find a way to get involved in a local peace group as a way of engaging local churches with the community in which we do ministry.

3. Seek Justice at Home. In addition to dealing with many of the international war issues, we must also look at our own injustices at home. It is often the case that when injustice and oppression exist systemically at home, we carry these injustices over to our foreign policy. We must see ourselves for who we truly are at home before moving abroad. Whether it is racism, sexism, domestic abuse, child abuse, homophobia, ageism, discrimination of those with disability, or an unneeded war based upon the false pretenses of preemptive strike, let us deplore violence.

4. Dialogue in the Church. Truth is found in community. The Church, then, has a moral responsibility to speak truthfully and honestly about matters of war in her liturgical and communal life. Worship is an excellent space for symbols, sermons, music, dance, or drama engaging the creation of an ethos of peace. The suggestion that we must dialogue and engage issues of war in the Church does not necessitate agreement or uniformity. Dialogue suggests diversity and the possibility of being transformed by those we engage in conversation. Dialogue suggests vulnerability. Therefore, dialogue is a transformative process of mutual enrichment. We need to learn how to disagree gracefully and yet still stand up for justice. Learning how to hold both mercy and justice in tension is the work of community.

5. Be Creative. The Church must be creative in getting to the subconscious issues that allow for an alternative community and ethos to occur. This requires that we be introspective and self-critical about our involvement in the perpetuation of materialistic and militaristic values. Such introspection wrestles with more than just flesh and blood; it wrestles with principalities and powers in high places. Let the Church be committed to finding creative ways to deconstruct the dominant narratives of war seeking to both diminish and replace the values of love and justice given to us by God.

6. **Be Bold**. Creating an ethos of peace requires pastors, preachers, and lay leaders to be bold in their convictions of peace. The Church cannot shy away from conflict because it will upset the tempo of our local congregations. If the Church is to be prophetic and effective it must invoke a true spirit of dialogue among those of faith who claim the call of Christ. This may seem counter-productive, but such boldness places new voices into the already screaming consciousness of local congregations. Such boldness is not to assert our own ideas but to advocate for another alternative way of being in the world that is more reflective of Jesus' mission on earth.

7. **Be Prayerful**. The Bible reminds the Church that the prayers of the righteous avail much. When the Church is truly committed to seeing this vision of peace created, then the struggle for God's people around the world will not be done only with books, pen, paper, protest, or from the pulpit. Some of the most important work will be done on our knees, praying for God's hand to work in transforming the hearts of pharaohs across the globe. This may seem passive, but prayer is an act of defiance. Prayer suggests, in essence, that neither situations nor circumstances will have the last word. God has the last word, not terrorists, not George W. Bush, not Osama Bin Laden, not Saddam Hussein, and not fear. God has the last word.

This book is a challenge, a call to people throughout all of God's earth to create an alternative ethos to the ethos of war. We are called to create a new pathway, one where peace and justice pave the way to freedom. Most especially, this book is a challenge for the Church, that she may find her voice and that her voice would be one of peace. It is a challenge to join the World Council of Churches and peace activists throughout the world in this movement to overcome violence between 2001-2010, and beyond. We live in troubled times, and during this time of great turmoil, may we seek peace both in our own lives and in the world. May we challenge our legislative representatives to make foreign policies that deplore violence against other peoples. May we end the occupation of Iraq and Palestine, stand with those standing up for human rights in Colombia while the U.S. government supports its violent leaders, and decry the violent fanaticism of Al-Qaeda and its leaders. Let us join in this world movement, believing that all people who inhabit the earth are created by God and are therefore our sisters and brothers.

We are all interconnected, and if the Church continues to remain silent in the face of violence, we will only see more and more of our sisters and brothers throughout the world experience loss and pain. The nineteenth-century Native American, Chief Seattle, said it best, " . . . All things are connected like the blood that unites one family. Whatever befalls the earth befalls the sons and daughters of the earth. Men and women did not weave the web of life; they are merely strands in it. Whatever one does to the web, one does to oneself."[5] May the web that we weave be one of peace.

Endnotes

[1] This quote comes from Roy's speech at an event for the Lannan Foundation in New Mexico on September 18, 2002. This is also a direct quote from Amy Goodman's *The Exception to the Rulers.*

[2] This is a revolutionary song composed by Ali Primera. Primera was an activist in his native Venezuela who started his own movement *Movimento al Socialismo.* It was out of this revolutionary movement for a more just world that the song "No Basta Rezar" found its origin.

[3] See www.overcomingviolence.org. This is the official website for the Decade to Overcome Violence.

[4] Certainly this quote can be found in many places, but it is most certainly found in liberation movements for justice. This quote was found on the Partners In Peace website, www.piphaiti.org.

[5] See the *United Methodist Book of Worship* (Nashville: The United Methodist Publishing House, 1992), 425-426.

Contributors

Rev. Chad R. Abbott is a graduate of Greenville College and Princeton Theological Seminary. He currently serves as a pastor in the Greater New Jersey Annual Conference of the United Methodist Church.

Eric Anderson has been involved with youth ministry and education for fifteen very rewarding years and holds degrees from Rutgers and Columbia Universities.

Rev. Frederick Boyle is an ordained minister serving in the Greater New Jersey Annual Conference of the United Methodist Church. In addition to pastoring a local congregation, Frederick also travels and speaks on the issue of preemptive peace.

Darren Burris is a graduate of Georgetown College and Princeton Theological Seminary. He is currently a teacher in urban Philadelphia.

Rev. Neal Christie is Assistant General Secretary, Ministry of Education and Leadership Formation, General Board of Church and Society of The United Methodist Church, located in Washington, DC. He is an ordained Elder in the Greater NJ Annual Conference and a graduate of Yale University Divinity School and the New School for Social Research, NY.

Rev. Dr. Dave Davis is an ordained minister in the Presbyterian Church (USA) and serves as pastor of Nassau Presbyterian Church in Princeton, New Jersey. He earned his Ph.D. from Princeton Theological Seminary in the field of homiletics.

Rev. Jackson H. Day is pastor of Grace United Methodist Church, Upperco, Maryland, and consultant, Health Care Advocacy, with the United Methodist General Board of Church and Society in Washington, DC. In 1968-1969 he served as a chaplain with the First Brigade, Fourth Infantry Division, in the Central Highland of Vietnam.

Rev. Gregory Guice is an ordained minister in the Unity Church and serves a congregation in Fort Wayne, Indiana.

Christopher B. Hays is a graduate of Amherst College and Princeton Theological Seminary. He is a Ph.D. candidate in Hebrew Bible at Emory University and a candidate for ordination in the Presbyterian Church (USA).

Rev. Stacy Martin is an ordained minister in the Presbyterian Church (USA) and is a graduate of Princeton Theological Seminary. She currently serves as Director of Lutheran Social Ministries Immigration and Refugee Services in Trenton, New Jersey.

Dr. Kathleen E. McVey is the Joseph Ross Stevenson Professor of Church History at Princeton Theological Seminary.

Rev. Everett Mitchell is a graduate of Morehouse College and Princeton Theological Seminary. He currently works at the Evolutions Center with troubled teens in Madison, Wisconsin.

Rev. Robert Moore has been serving since 1981 as executive director of the Princeton-based Coalition for Peace Action, a regional affiliate of Peace Action in New Jersey, the largest peace organization in the United States. He also serves as pastor of East Brunswick Congregational Church (since 1988), and of Livingston Avenue United Church of Christ in New Brunswick (since 2001). From 1978-1981, he was National Secretary of Mobilization for Survival, a national coalition of over 250 organizations dedicated to the global abolition of nuclear weapons and a peace economy that prioritizes urgent human needs.

Ajit Prasadam is a Ph.D. candidate at Princeton Theological Seminary in the field of pastoral theology and is the General Secretary of the India Sunday School Union.

Dr. Luis N. Rivera-Pagán is the Henry Winters Luce Professor of Ecumenics and Mission at Princeton Theological Seminary. He has also taught at the University of Puerto Rico and is the author of *A Violent Evangelism*.

Jim Winkler serves as the General Secretary for the General Board of Church and Society of the United Methodist Church at the United Methodist Building in Washington, D.C.

Appendix

Questions to Help Break the Silence and Create an Ethos of Peace

The Ethos of War

What are the factors and circumstances that lead nations to be at war with one another?

How do the dynamics of *power, ideology,* and *tools* operate in your context?

Do you know the names of the current U.S. vice president, secretary of state, secretary of defense, attorney general, national security advisor, and secretary of homeland security? How do these people impact your everyday life?

Calling For Peace

How is your congregation organizing peace initiatives in your community and in connection with others in the world?

What are the peace organizations in your area and how might your congregation be involved in their work?

Scripture

What does the Third Commandment teach us about truth telling with regard to whether or not war is ever justifiable?

What was your response to the violence of September 11th and how did your response differ from those offered by other Christians? What is your response to the Iraq war?

Besides the Ten Commandments, what do other parts of scripture have to say about war?

World Peace

How should the Church respond to the military conflicts that the twentieth century has brought upon humanity?

In what ways can we, as United States Christians, counteract the damaging military actions of our government towards other nations in the world?

How do we go about connecting with others throughout the world against war and violence?

Youth and the Military

What do we as leaders say to our youth about war, and how might we, in turn, learn from the beliefs of our youth?

How can we protect poor urban youth from being vulnerable to the system of violence and recruitment of the military?

What do parents say to their kids about war?

Social Locations

How do the specific experiences and social locations of refugees, African Americans, military chaplains, or someone like Mahatma Gandhi impact your views of war?

How do these voices offer a viable understanding for creating alternative narratives amid the flurry of false narratives and assumptions of war?

The Counter Image

What are the counter images that we might portray in our context, for example, in newspapers or on television?

Has the church uncritically digested the images of war? If so, how can the church reclaim a prophetic critique of the church's inability to speak out regarding violence and war?

Sermons and Sermon Writing

What is the role of preaching and listening to sermons in the face of war?

How might sermons serve as a congregational discussion tool on issues of war?

Statement of Faith

What is your response to the multi-faceted set of beliefs in Christian history regarding war?

What does your faith tradition or denomination believe about war, and where in history do these beliefs trace their roots?

Spiritual Development

How does a spiritual awakening with God eliminate the creation of "the other" or the I/It relationship, which so essentially defines the ethos of war?

Which spiritual disciplines does your church participate in so that both inner peace and world peace are possible?

What can we learn from Acts 2:43-47 as it relates to the objective of preemptive peace, "to replace the power of military might and money with the vision of peace and compassion that dwells in the human heart?"

Prayer

How do we pray without being militaristic and assuming that God only supports the United States?

What role does prayer play in our spiritual development, especially as our spirituality engages issues of our public life?

Is prayer a public event and, if so, what is the content of prayer?

Jesus says, "Pray for those who hurt you." What are some honest challenges to Jesus' command to the church? How can the church make Jesus' command a possibility?

Sending Forth

Dream for a moment. What is the world in which you wish to live? Does it include war?

How do we create this world?

Breaking Silence

What does it mean for your church to break silence and speak out against war?

Who are your local and state representatives and how do you make contact with them?

Does your denomination have any agencies working on peace iniatives and policy? How might your church get involved?

What is peace, and how is it possible for the church to have a peace that surpasses all understanding?

How will you engage your faith differently after having read this book?

Index

Notes and Comments

Printed in the United States
20750LVS00004B/121-129